NEW BUFFALO

JOURNALS FROM A TAOS COMMUNE

NEW BUFFALO

JOURNALS FROM A TAOS COMMUNE

Arthur Kopecky

University of New Mexico Press
Albuquerque

Library of Congress Cataloging-in-Publication Data

Kopecky, Arthur, 1944–

New Buffalo : journals from a Taos commune /
Arthur Kopecky.— 1st ed.

    p. cm. — (CounterCulture series)

ISBN 0-8263-3395-8 (cloth : alk. paper)

1. Kopecky, Arthur, 1944—Diaries.

2. New Buffalo (Commune : N.M.)

3. Communes—New Mexico.

4. Counterculture—New Mexico. I. Title. II. Series.

HQ971.5.N7K66 2004

307.77'4'09789—dc22

                          2003022126

10   9   8   7   6   5   4   3   2   1

Printed and bound by Thomson Shore, Inc.

Display type set in Gothic 821 and 13

Body text set in Clearface 10.5/14

Design and composition: Robyn Mundy

Series

A volume in the CounterCulture Series

Editors: David Farber, History, University of New Mexico
Beth L. Bailey, American Studies, University of New Mexico

Also available:
Rebel Music: The Harvey Kubernik InnerViews
by Harvey Kubernik

Fig. 1. Carved door to the kiva. A primitive portal entering a most advanced way of thinking. Photo by Clarice Kopecky.

Dedication

In our stressful lives we may forget how fortunate we are. Whatever our ills, we do have great freedom to face them with. I'd like to dedicate this account to those who came before, to get us here. They did not struggle in vain and we appreciate it.

I also always have in mind the young people coming up. The complex world they face sometimes appears truly daunting. I hope we can be of some help with the ideas we had, the beginnings we made.

CONTENTS

LIST OF

ILLUSTRATIONS

FOREWORD

When Arthur Kopecky sent me his journals from New Buffalo commune during the 1970s, I began to read it out of a vague sense of responsibility. I had written a memoir of the same period and some innate sense of fairness wanted me to compare and contrast the two works. It turns out that while our intentions in writing were quite close, the executions are very different. I was operating within the parameters of "literature" and Arthur has chosen to present his journals in a relatively unedited manner. This is not a bad choice, for they retain much of the sketchy, unstructured energy which identifies journals. Its structure is "real time" events as they happened and all the details are not supplied for you. You must step up to meet the journals with your own imagination.

As I read, I was not prepared for the upwelling of emotion and memory. It's true that some people in our respective books overlapped, but what gripped me was the fearless, energetic, forward motion toward an imagined future. These people did not "play it safe" any more than I and my friends did. New Buffalo was emblematic of any number of communes where people came together by happenstance and "grew" a life together. The struggle and costs—the hard work, the endless labor and attention required to be self-sufficient, the learning of new skills, social and physical that made every day an adventure—are all here, clearly, in these pages. Urban kids came together and learned cabinetry, animal husbandry, carpentry, irrigation, weaving and a host of critical survival skills to make a life based "in place" and not predicated on exploitation. They gave of themselves joyously, and patched together ersatz religious practices and ceremonies to make life together joyous. They tried to reverse the legacy of private property and defensiveness, which they had inherited and attempted to refashion it into something more collegial and beautiful; something in which they could believe.

Reading Arthur's stories made me vulnerable again to the power of my own memories of days and weeks spent repairing and beautifying an old truck to serve another twenty years. I remember group activities where thirty and more people dug and constructed a sweat lodge that they bathed in, creating chants like Bach chorales in the overheated dark. There was such optimism and empowerment then; such a feeling that change was available to be personally manifested. It stands in stark contrast to this particularly dark and pre-war moment. And changes *were* made.

The young people in these pages, as in my own, did not succeed at everything they set out to accomplish, and yet, in aggregate, they were part of a quantum shift in the culture of the United States. Today, there is virtually nowhere where organic food is not available; where chiropractors and acupuncturists and ayurvedic or native American healers or herbal remedies are not recognized and employed; where women's rights, gay rights, the environment, and forms of worship alternative to Judaism and Christianity are not recognized and practiced. No one would mistake the America of 2003 for the America of the 1940s in which I was born.

So read this book and remember or learn of the seeds planted that continue to blossom today. Remember or learn what it felt like to be young, optimistic, empowered, and dedicated to making a better life. Join the denizens of New Buffalo commune; review their foibles, errors, comedies and successes and if nothing else, you will be amazed to see what persistent, dedicated, selfless, hard work can accomplish. You will be reminded of what is still necessary to do and the only manner in which I can conceive of it being done.

Peter Coyote
Mill Valley

MAP

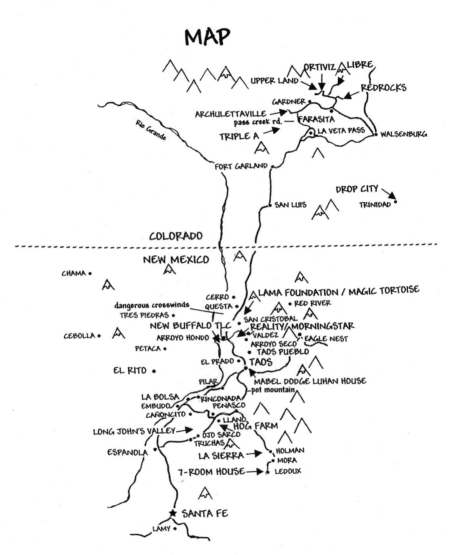

*Fig. 2. The New Buffalo pueblo in the
Sangre de Cristo Mountains. From the
personal collection of the author.*

ACKNOWLEDGMENTS

First, I must thank my wife Sandra né Johnson Kopecky. Every time we moved she made sure to pack the boot boxes with the hand-written journals, and when settled she saved them from the mice a time or two. After we finally got computerized, she spent hundreds of hours typing, deciphering, and then helping immensely with the editing. In some sense her name should be on the cover also.

I had also better acknowledge Pepe (Dan Rochon). I leaped over a very wide chasm into this emerging world and I didn't do it alone. Instead of peering over the heads in the crowd, with Pepe I was at once in the center of the action.

It was a great help that Iris Keltz pointed me in the direction of the University of New Mexico. Thanks to Professor David Farber who saw the potential and gently prodded us to "tighten some more." I am very happy to be working with the UNM Press, which has treated me with great respect.

Without the characters there would be no story. Some of them you will meet shortly. With too many names to mention, I do want to say: Thanks, folks, for being there. A few names in the book have been changed. Some may view things differently from me. I offer here my perspective and mine alone.

If all heroics are in war then we are destined to a terrible future. But heroics are also in people's efforts to help improve our lives. There are millions who turn from cynicism and give us hope and faith in the potential goodness of people. Thank you.

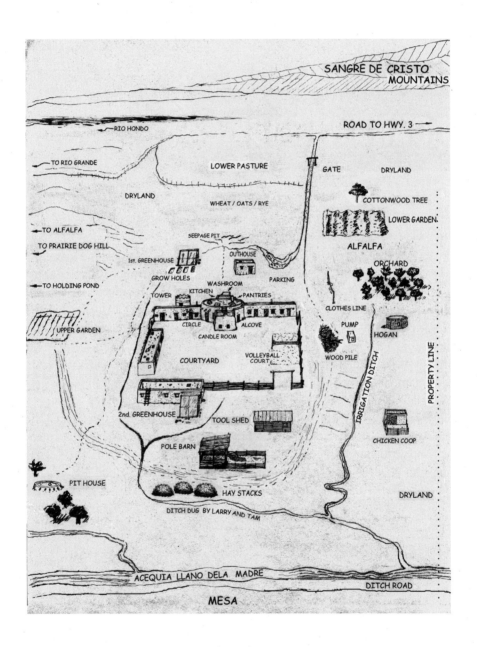

INTRODUCTION

In the late 1960s there was the horror of the Vietnam War. But there was an opposite reaction too. The "Woodstock" nation was born. Colorful school buses cruised, communes abounded, and there was a high sense of possibilities. We were so free.

In the spirit of the one-world family, friends, acquaintances, people on the road were living together. There was magic to it, and I found a group of people that became my new family, the Pride family. We "inherited" a wonderful little house in northern California, so close to the beach that we could hear the surf. It too became a commune.

Pepe, the Menominee Indian, had the spirit and the energy. I supplied the guitar and practical aspects. Carol was the blond-haired beauty. A parade of people became family for a day, or a week, or for years. To me it was a joyous phenomenon—so spontaneous—all living action and no ideology. There were so many different people. I became part of it. Subsequently I tried to figure out how to keep it going. This was modern culture being formed.

I had a degree in history from City College of New York. Seeing some history in the making, I kept a journal for twelve years. With only a backpack and a sleeping bag for possessions, I still felt rich, immersed in this sea of America's children, on potentially what could be a beautiful farm. There was a sense of purpose and a joy of living. Now, years later and finally with a computer, we have dusted off these journals and typed them up. It was like thawing out an ancient being, frozen in time and being brought back to life. Here are the journals of AnSwei (On-shway) Livingproof. They are a little

*Fig. 3. Carol, Pepe, and friends with back
doors open in the Mind Machine. From the
personal collection of the author.*

choppy, but I hope they convey the sense of the moment. So many people
had similar experiences. There are a lot of names and like a drumbeat they
help capture the spirit. Now in 2003, our spirits and beliefs are being sorely
tested. Here are some reminders and some lessons from our youth that have
a lot of good in them. And we need all the good we can get. These journals
are more than a piece of our history; they have the seed of possibilities. They
capture a small moment of time in the dawning of the Aquarian Age. You
sense that things are right with the world—that all people are one—that we
can learn to share.

At the start of one of the communes, a group took the idea of the buffalo
providing for the plains people. To this they added New to create a name. The
New Buffalo was to be a new way of providing for the people. Today we need
to think as broadly as we can to solve our dilemmas and live at peace. Herein,
among all the talk of food, is plenty of food for thought. This is a way to get
back to the garden.

The story picks up as a small band of us leave Bolinas, California in 1971. We set out with our converted Wonder Bread truck nicknamed the Mind Machine (alias the Bird truck) and one VW bus, to buy or find some land. But first to visit and help on some of these blossoming communal country farms.

JOURNAL ONE

Many have struggled so that today we can be this free, and we thank them.

June 21, 1971: Ah ha! The great Mind Machine family and psychedelic sideshow having visited many friends in Oregon is floating, flying free. Now with teepee poles on top, we sail on in this fabulous American adventure.

We spent six days pleasantly traveling to the Rainbow Farm. Visited a few days with the Pea Vine Mountain Family. Jerry, Art, Pepe, Carol, baby Kachina, Susie Creamcheese, Anny Fanny, Ray and his VW bus were with this California getaway caravan.

Rainbow Farm is the same thing as was our Bolinas commune—only more magic. Rainbow, with Garrick and Karen, is really free and open, with 50 percent turnover every week and getting up to 40 at every meal. Worked on the garden.

Enjoyed a week with Crow Farm crew in the mountains near Rogue River making a road. Spent just about every weekend at Crow Farm commune near Eugene.

We were at the Renaissance Faire for 5 days. Pepe, the clown, performed every day. Big fair—50 food booths and many teepees—fabulously crafted wares and goods. Rained 24 times. Capt. John barked for Little Egypt, who takes it almost all off, while dancing with largest snake in captivity. Capt. John, Pat, and I spent some great evenings at Devos Street Liberation House

and Ferry Street Crow Farm House. Great OM before each beautiful, somewhat poor meal. Here is the revolution and mellow, poor people but with
everything necessary.

After the Faire, Pepe—our chief—with newcomers Razberry, Ernesto,
Barbara and baby Juble, drove us to Anamika's log cabin mountain retreat after
which we journeyed to the Church of the Creative near Creswell for a gathering, and then onward to Goat Farm, near Monroe, for another happening.

It's summertime and today we're moving on to Reg and Mary's near
Portland.

June 24: Arrived at 2:30 in the afternoon. Mary very pregnant, like our redheaded Razberry. Pepe baked bread. Andre, the neighbor, brings great baskets
of fruit and vegetables.

Truck went into Portland; now we are well stocked with food. We're all
packed and ready to go. First go score some hash and then off to the hot
springs. All the way from Morocco some hash found its way to some little crib
off a little road in Oregon. And we know where it is. Too bad!

Arrived in Gold Meyer vicinity around 3 p.m. Had the teepee up in short
order—raging waters all around us. Next morning, Creamcheese and I walked
miles to the snow, up to the springs; hot water from the earth—right out of a
cave—next to a 20-foot-wide raging waterfall. Nobody around for miles; just
us two, jumping in and out of the water.

Slender Susie, full of positive energy, was our neighbor in Bolinas. When
we were packing, she said, "Can I come along?" She's very pretty with her
auburn hair and elfish smile, enhanced by one front tooth slightly overlapping
the other.

By evening it was really raining. We decide to leave in the morning.
Finally, today, we are under fairly clear skies, 100 miles north in Bellingham,
Washington, where we can see the saltwater bay. Our magic carpet, glued to
the floor of the truck, has relocated us to Bob and Viviana's. These people, a
year and a half ago, lived with us at the Bolinas commune.

Monday: Broke into the People's Store this morning with Viviana and then split
Bellingham in the rain. From the high misty mountains we have now passed
to the dry windy desert.

Washington coast was wet. High in the snowy Steven's Pass, the rain
stopped and we left the clouds behind and crossed Wenatchee and Columbia

Rivers into a land of few trees and few people. Susie found currants. Earlier we found fruit in the great orchards of pear, apple, and cherry that line the rivers. Tomorrow, Idaho.

Across the great wheat plains of Washington into the Rocky Mountains of Idaho we have traveled. Picked up a hitchhiker, the first we have seen. He served us celery and cheese hors d'oeuvres before continuing on his way to Canada. On to Montana tomorrow.

Pepe and I take turns driving. Perched behind the huge steering wheel, Pepe's dark, piercing eyes miss nothing. The still-healing scar on his naturally shiny dome gives him an Algonquin warrior look. He's very proud of his new daughter, Kachina, nestled in Carol's lap, riding next to him on the engine cover.

July 1, 1971: Clouds. Evening in Montana, some cowboys joined us for dinner. Very fine. Glad they felt so welcome. We shall pursue the sun to the east in the morning.

Thursday: Here we are in the heart of the Indian land—the old buffalo grazing ground—now the great wheat plains of Montana. Fantastic. By the collective consciousness of us all, we levitated off the highway and found a meadow by a river not far from a "cross at your own risk" bridge. Just as the sun set, we had the teepee up and the fire started. Magic.
Crossed the Rockies today and made some progress on the plains, too. Had to call in the rinky-dink, wayside, roadside engine repair, which, with a piece of wood, corrected a slight leak in the engine.

Saturday: Evening in the Dakota swampland! Hot during the day. Camped at dusk at a state campsite next to a very muddy river. Had pea soup and cabbage salad and sang the encampment to sleep.

Next day the boogie machine took us over 400 miles through the rolling plains with their beautiful ponds, ducks, and trees. The farms are quite vast; there is no open or wild land, but there is no hassle for us passing through; the road is free. Tonight, at sunset, we are camped, true gypsy fashion, next to a grove of trees. Candles light the truck. Potato soup is cooking on the campfire.

July 4, 1971: Today is our country's birthday! Many have struggled so that today we can be this free, and we thank them. It was three years ago that Pepe and I were swept up in this liberating scene. I was recently out of University and Pepe, newly arrived from Wisconsin, was staying at my pad. Pepe absorbed the music, the people, the color, and the mix of cultures at a phenomenal rate. I saw the hope of the human race in the way he adopted so many new ideas. Fate brought us together for a giant leap.

And now we have leaped to a farm near Wawina, Minnesota. Here is where Ernesto and Razberry once lived. A rutted dirt road takes us up to this settlement in the cedar swamp. Once this commune had thirty people, but now it is practically deserted. Strange. Where are the people?

Thursday: Here in Minneapolis, south from Rt. 2, through mostly marshy forest and some funky farms, we've found the people. Spent four or five nights in this funky, crowded, stagnating city. Henry and Geraldine keep a fine open house here. Fed many people each night and saw more beer and cigarettes consumed than I've ever seen. Lots of kids—upstairs and down—in the backyard. Neighbor's drunk and cursing.

Met Moe and Stan, two black brothers, at the house. They took us over to the People's Garden and for a day we did some work there. Saturday had a big barbecue in People's Park, right there in the ghetto. We set up the teepee in the park and then took it down before dark.

August 2: We arrived at our next destination, Kate's farm in Wisconsin. Hot summer day carry me away! A soft summer breeze to all our brothers and sisters throughout the world. Greetings to you from this hillside, where the Mind Machine gypsy family ever forges ahead in new knowledge and action for this Cultural Revolution!

Once there were some 550,000 American soldiers in Vietnam. Now there are some 250,000 or so. The bombing continues. Bring the troops home! In our lifetime it will happen.

Thursday night: Writing by the night fire in the teepee. Pepe and Carol returned yesterday from a great trip to Appleton, Wisconsin. I cannot tell it like Pepe—Triumphant! Saw Big Jake, Dick Shue and the Soup Band. Held hands and prayed with the whole family at each meal, as we did at Rainbow. Later had some coke at night with friends in psychedelic parts of Appleton.

Monday: Another hot, muggy, sunny day. There are so many farms just barely keeping it together, supporting one family, when many could do a fantastic trip having a good time in brotherhood with 30 or 40 people. There must be a lot of people like us in this equilibrium. Stop work—stop war. We are in a kind of limbo, and sometimes it's frustrating. There is a lot of energy—a lot of brothers and sisters building.

But the Bolinas commune is gone. Coyote gone. Wawina commune empty, Georgeville empty, People's Garden, just a little beginning. The thoughts are here—cool and together—more all the time. So much energy into war and profit. It will go the other way in our time. Now we prepare ourselves, lead our simple life, and learn to be free and live outdoors. We have worked hard and will do so again on a commune. For a while longer though, it seems our little band will keep moving.

Ernie has a fine candle shop set up: propane tank, gas burner, pots of wax, color, and wick. Plus, we have set up one of our candle wheels for tapers. A little industry is just the right step for self-support. Excellent.

Thursday morning: A storm started building and broke above us. Before long we had quite an assemblage in the teepee—plenty of room. Dinner cooking on the fire. Smoking emerald green grass—drinking home brew—fixing the teepee flaps. Someone brought in a fifth of vodka and a gallon of orange juice. A fine dinner served.

I improvised some words on the guitar. Raining out but not in—mellow and so fine—singing just put me right. About 25 people sleeping all over.

August 20: Carol off to California for a quick visit. Here am I, at the moment, alone with five naked ladies. Torg, who we met the first day we arrived at Kate's, shaved his beard and cut his hair and went off in search of a job today.

Pepe met this old Indian, Benny, who turned him on to a few things and some magic. Pepe all excited and energetic as usual.

Uh-oh! Last night, just at sunset, sheriff and local cop named Scoop drove up and ripped off Torg for sales of marijuana. They came up on the hill and called for our brother sweetly, and he comes out smiling and laughing, gets in their car and off he goes not to sleep under the stars tonight. We just looked on, and what can we do, momentarily, we soldiers of peace? Instant karma. See, one of our numbers cuts his long hair, starts to look straight and tries to find a job. Bam! He's busted.

Fig. 4. Portrait of Carol, our princess. From the personal collection of the author.

Torg will be fine. Wasn't sure what to do, so now he is a messenger of the faith among the Establishment's law enforcement people.

Thursday morning: Paula has decided to join us and will ride with the Mind Machine family for a while. We now have another member and a replenishment of funds. We also get the company of little Sierra Nanda.

The following morning dawns clear and sunny. Pepe gives the word; after six weeks or so, we are on the road—born again—Art, Pepe, Kiva, Susie Creamcheese, Paula and Sierra Nanda—a new supply of food and $200, headed for Drop City, Colorado. In Minneapolis, someone told of a gathering at Drop City, so that is our destination. First stop is at the Orphanage, an Iowa band that is renting a giant old country house.

We arrive in the evening and have a late dinner. Off early the next morning. Ride all day through cornfields and hog farms of Iowa. By evening we cross into Nebraska—very warm and windy. The moon is almost full. We camped at a rest stop and awoke in the night to thunder and great clouds.

Rose up at dawn to fresh air and overcast sky. We ride all day and gradually enter the plains. Late in the day we get to the great grasslands, which are now all cultivated. America, America. Once the home of the free Indians, now the home of so many property owners, land of the dollar and the machine—our home too. We roam it—free spirits of a different life—refugees like the Indians before us, looking for a place of peace. Unmolested we travel on the asphalt ribbons that are so many. For us in America there is freedom and peace, and through this land, on the vibration of peace and freedom, we travel. Something else, indeed, to be born of a new spirit and a part of it all.

By nightfall we are in open dry country where there are few houses and no cultivation. We have a little dinner in a Mexican café. This night is our first in the arid desert—cold and super fresh air.

Sunday we reach Trinidad and easily find Drop City. It is right in the funky suburbs; six acres owned by Drop City, Inc. Here is a collection of fantastic dome buildings, a few pigs and goats, rabbits and a teepee.

We have come to a Wake. Only about eight people are living here and are thinking of leaving. The corporation is broke, the garden burned, and the scene rather bleak looking. Fabulous place though. About 30 or 40 people gathered, to figure out what is next for this venture. After a while, we have a little council and decide to head for Paula's friends in the mountains of New Mexico.

We leave the dry plain and enter green mountains. It takes us most of the bright day to reach Taos. With help of short-haired "I'm proud to be an American" hitchhiker, we nurse the Mind Machine over the passes.

In Taos we meet a fellow who tells us of the local scene. Route 3 will take us to two communes, New Buffalo and Morningstar. He also tells us of two hot springs on the Rio Grande, so we head there.

A fine canyon and spring, this is the mighty Rio Grande of legend. Hawks soaring above—dry land bushes and stubby trees below—a new world for me. We camp by the river, cook a dinner of groats and onions and sleep well in the cold night. In the morning we awake to find ourselves, once again, at home in a new land.

Pepe's energy is incredible—his love great. He is always meeting people; his energy takes him many places. He met me and that was good. In Bolinas, he met Woody Ramsom, which brought us to the house where we did such good things. In Oregon, he met Will Chaplin and the Crow Farmers. Yesterday he met Lucy at the hot springs bath, and she has invited us to dinner at New Buffalo.

Fig. 5. Arty, 24 years old. From the personal collection of the author.

Here is a small palace of adobe and great beams, a desert courtyard, and a family of freaks just like us. There were about 20 for dinner last night. This place is really functioning. There are two horses, chickens, turkeys, a metal shop, some machinery, many things that need to be done and the most fantastic housing I have seen yet. This is my idea of a together place.

The pull of the magic is great. Here we are, after only three days, in the Southwest. I'm amazed and just like always, enchanted more than I can say. Our path is surely good.

Art's new name: Two-and-a-half years ago, when we first crossed the country in the Mind Machine, I wanted a new name. Yesterday I got one. AnSwei (On-shway) is a name I've had for a long time but never used, from Mr. Uwei at Columbia University. In addition, a last name too: Livingproof. AnSwei Livingproof—that's me—how do you do!

September 15: Today is one week since we first came to New Buffalo. Yesterday we went to pray and dance with the people at Lama Foundation, a fine community tucked into the vast Sangre de Cristo Mountains. We then saw beautiful Madeleine, a friend from New York City, who, inexplicably, is cribbing with fellow Max Finstein, a "Founder of New Buffalo." Very good to meet him, indeed.

With our arrival, a new wave of energy has come to New Buffalo. Close to 40 people to dinner. Good thing we came with a full pantry!

At New Buffalo are Chuck, Tahiti, and Larry, a quiet blond-haired man who has been here three years and is an excellent fellow. These three lead wonderful quiet prayers in the evening that start with "Heavenly Father God." Steve, who has been here the longest, says a fine prayer often at dinner that sounds about this way, " Bless all the people on the road, and bless our parents. Help us past our petty bickering to see the good we can do together." But he eats alone in his room. Ellen, who is a nice-looking girl from New York, lives in there with him. He is good at hard-vibing people.

In addition, there is Aquarius Paul who rode in on his horse a day after we arrived; he is also a core member. Naomi—beautiful and graceful—the only dedicated woman, has only been here a few weeks. Lucy, who invited us up, is going to stay, it seems.

So where is Pepe? We must make some decisions about what we do next. I rather think I know what I should do. Something is in the air.

Pepe so energized, returned from a Colorado peyote meeting. There were 60 people in a circle, in one teepee, from dusk to dawn. Several Indian men were there whose knowledge is great.

So here we are, and here we put this energy of ours. Bless our ladies who cook so fine, bless our brothers who have carried on here, and bless us all in our endeavors together.

Thursday: It is going on three weeks since we first arrived. Tahiti put up the new gate at the entrance. Larry has worked leveling the road to the pueblo with the tractor.

I have made a bed in one room, some shelves in another and straightened and cleaned the tool room. The teepee is still up; I stay there sometimes and so does Buddy, who just had his thirteenth birthday. Pepe's asleep on the stone couch in the giant circle room. Like some Stone Age monument, the center of the circle has a hearth and a pipe to catch the smoke from the open campfire. The room is dug four feet into the earth. Half way to the circular walls are four massive wood pillars that hold a crisscross of vigas and beams, which hold the roof of dirt. An earth bench wraps around the base of the wall.

Hardened earth stairs lead to three portals; a fourth door goes to a smaller room. A buffalo skull hangs on a wall. This kiva can hold over 100 people. There are skylights but no windows.

It is raining out! There is snow on the distant mountains and a little taste of winter chill. We need to gather wood. Rick, who is living here, has a panel truck and a chainsaw and sounds like he wants a tight family.

Dave, who lived here in April, has moved back and is sharing a room with Bob, who is withdrawn and silent. Ellen is working on the pit house up in the hills. In another wing, Naomi has a fine little crib. Brother Mick has set up his house in the hogan; he was a seminary student who has now made this his home. The tower attached to Paul's room is vacant.

Razberry, who stayed in Minnesota, had a baby girl, we heard. Wild how we live.

Sunday: Sun is bright and the sky is clear. Pepe and Tahiti working on the horses. Pepe was given a ten-year-old brown mare just two days ago.

Silent Bob flipped out a bit extra and was brought to Taos hospital. "Worst shape fellow" he'd ever seen, said the doctor. His father has come and taken him home—a lost soul.

Two weeks later: The moon is full, yet the sky is black and full of stars. Saturday night we had a party for Rick who turned 24. Almost 100 people here—big feed, plenty of beer, and a lot of smoke in the air. Next day, people are laid out—a big mess. By evening, super quiet and mellow. Kitchen and circle are clear. Only a small group for dinner.

Today we worked hard on the corral and barn, which is the first major project of the new, New Buffalo family. We plan to build a workshop and finish the washroom. The foundations are partly laid. We are here together, glad to have work. We are all discussing the agriculture scene. By next spring, I would certainly like to be part of an effort producing some food.

Heavenly Father God, bless our lives and prosper us and all our brothers and sisters who work for a good life for all people.

Thursday: Chuck is off to work very early every morning for $2.50 hr; he's helping build a house. Toby out cutting wood. Larry and the two Davids are getting that washroom together. Paula, Carol, and Angela working in the kitchen. One traveler working on the ditch. Bread and water for breakfast.

Donna has been laid out sick for the last six days but is getting better. It's been a relief for me; the noise and negative vibration level is down about 100 percent with her absence. Frankie, Kevin, and Buddy, her three boys, are fine.

Brother Zip came a few days ago. He is twenty years old with a teepee on his back. He worked very hard and would like to set up here. Right on! He has already been in the mountains getting some poles.

Ian, from El Paso with VW bus, left after spending a few days. He was right in there working with us, and he was glad to offer his bus for our service.

Sunday: Our second storm is upon us. A few leaks have been fixed.

Big party—all kinds of people. We are roasting the goat that was given to us a few days ago. Electric band was really good in this fine big house with lots of Anglos, Chicanos, and a few Indians from Taos Pueblo. Rick Klein was at the party. I am told he put up the original $50,000 that got Buffalo off the ground.

Some really fabulous meals coming to us from our humble kitchen. We are all eating well and so are any friends happening to be here.

Thursday: Rick and I have been running to the hot springs every morning in training for the prize fight on Saturday between Dangerous Dan (Pepe) and Pretty Boy Rick Miller. Supposed to be a Halloween party here too.

Tahiti: craftsman, metalworker, independent, constant worker. At 33, he is the firearm marshal and a granddad of New Buffalo. He was on the scene when New Buffalo was being founded. Born in Frisco, he ran away from home at 15; went sailing around the South Asian seas. In the Merchant Marines at 21, he almost died and lost the sight in one eye from a fall. He's got a short beard and a rough look with that black patch over his eye but a ready twinkle and smile. He is famous for his two workhorses. Excellent partner and friend.

Paul: Clean-shaven with light, short wavy hair, is 6' 2", strong, quiet, 31, and master builder of the barn that is going up. He and Tahiti each keep horses and tools. Very ready to work or get stoned. A loner, yet a good communal brother.

Chuck is one of the heavy brothers of the place: tall, dark, good-looking, with a bit of a beer belly. Plays the mouth harp and knows a lot of songs. A good worker, good partner and brother.

Rick Miller: Barrel chest, missing upper front teeth, is a good man with a chainsaw, hammer, or jug; he knows them all. Rick just turned 24. He got together with Laurie two days after he arrived. He's lived here before. Good worker—lots of energy—a good partner who wants to make it all happen.

Fig. 6. Tahiti, Chuck, and Paul. From the personal collection of Al Kaplan.

Larry McInteer: He is medium-sized, quiet and young with long blond hair. Sort of the father of the place now, he has been here three years. Usually just barefoot, he often leads prayer. A peyote church follower, he knows the ways of the land. Very handy and knowledgeable—good with adobe and the tractor. Larry is a very communal person.

Naomi is a beautiful, graceful brown-skinned lady. A spirit of quiet, yoga, and peace, she likes New Buffalo and keeps a simple, clean, temple of a room.

Angela—sweet young thing—stays with Chuck. Glad I'm not too much in love with her! She has black hair and a tiny nose and can melt stone with her smile. Takes care of Josephine the cow, really digs Buffalo and makes it happen. As fine a little lady as I've ever seen. She learned weaving in Guatemala.

Barn is going up.

Friday: Naomi has left. Barn is out of finances. Mind Machine brings us adobe bricks and wood.

JOURNAL TWO

In my view, the commune is part of the society. It is a revolutionary base but not in a revolution that will violently overthrow the existing government.

Fall of 1971—Sunday: Last night, Tahiti, the three Donna boys, and I returned from a wood run. Inside, the kitchen was full of people all eating pizzas. Eight more in the oven and more to be cooked. Zip, the head chef, with Paul assisting.

Absolutely clear days. Steve plowed a half-acre up front, and we got adobe bricks twice, picked up a food order and took out the garbage. Beer bought too, and then someone put an ounce of hash on the table! Made my first fire in the newly pitched teepee. Zip recast his by moonlight.

Sunday: Completely clear sky. Very quiet. Kiva is alone in the kitchen fixing dinner.

We are living in a spectacularly beautiful area of the Sangre de Cristo Mountains. Almost 14,000 feet tall, they rise to our east. Pine and cedar forests cover the slopes before the mountain peaks, and right before us are the nicely cut fields of our little valley. The wilderness to our backs stretches out endlessly. It never ceases to awe me every time I step outside. The sky is tremendous and usually a beautiful blue. And in this scene, the mudded walls of our pueblo are a compliment to the earth.

Tahiti and Paul spoke to visitor down-and-out Charlie, with the short hair from Texas, about moving on. Charlie just repaired a hole in the ground for living in.

Everyone now is on the circle cleanup schedule. The large kiva underground room, our neo-ancient temple, is where we have Circle—hold hands and pray before dinner.

We retrieved a third load of bricks for the washhouse and cedar wood and vigas.

November 30: Last night at least 50 people for dinner—more than enough food—all kinds of long-hairs, short-hairs, a few Indians and over 10 kids. Where do they come from? Where do they go? Hog Farmers came in their silver bus.

On Thanksgiving Kathie Cota had a peyote meeting put up here for New Buffalo. Terrific. From the Taos Pueblo, Frank Samora, Joe Sunhawk, and Joe Gomez honored us with their presence. In their traditional attire these elders emanate great dignity. Frank led the meeting; Bapook and Justin took care of the fire. The drum passed around and around. Many know some of the chant-like songs that have come down through the ages. Next day I was wiped out.

Last Sunday, Zip and I took over the circle room, except for about eight crashers; set up a leather and a candle craft shop. Zip repairing shoes and moccasins and making samples for Mick, who has become our salesman. We've got about $400 worth of orders for leather and candles.

Some of Steve's beer is coming out all right. Fabulous. Steve has lived here on and off for three years. He walks with a determined gait, his head bowed before him. He feeds, waters, and cleans the chickens, which is definitely important. He is really sloppy in appearance—pants always falling down. I have to yell to him "good morning" just to get him to grunt to me. When we first came here, one wall of the kitchen was not built, and he asked me to wire-screen it in to keep out the flies. He came on uptight when I didn't start immediately. A few days later, Larry adobed-in the wall as was proper. Steve has an uptight scene with each of us and has Pepe a little riled. He has it in his head that he helps keep this place going; He works with no one.

Commune living is like a crash course in living with people—how to get along. Now communes are housing and feeding people and are basically places where all people can come together.

Rick and Laura left for Oklahoma. Donna is rarely around; her children are always here and are a fine part of the family.

A new day: Cold outside. People have come here and gone. Here tonight for dinner were Cave Dave, AnSwei, Shannon, Carol, Buddy, Kevin, Frankie, Karen, new young Kathy, Tahiti, Aquarius Paul and Susie Cotcher, Paul Rotman and Catalina, Kiva, Larry, Mick, Zip, Toby, Chuck, Steve, Paula, and Sierra Nanda. That's us for now.

Washroom roof is going on. Kiva ordered the propane gas. Got $50 from Rainbow after I spent my last $4 on today's wood run.

December 9: Frosted trees in the sparkling chilled air. Susie, Paul, and Chuck going to work. Josephine the cow roaming the courtyard.

I'm in Albuquerque, on my way to New York to see my mother. Left New Buffalo deep in cold snow. I have my guitar, backpack of six years service, clean denim jacket, worn combat boots, a new beard and new earring.

"Thank you" to my brother John, who was driving somebody else's California VW bus to the East Coast—people's bus service. No heat, but John had fashioned a pair of boots out of foam and tape, and they were very good for keeping feet warm.

Monday morning: In an instant, I have transposed myself to New York City. Two rides brought me to a subway in the Bronx. Five connections later and a few wrong trains and I was standing on the street waiting for Clarice, my mom, to pick me up and take me to her apartment. She rode right by me, but I caught up to her. "You look good," she said. God, do these people drive fast! My own mother almost as bad as the guy who drove me into town!

Clarice is in good shape and an honorable-looking little lady. She works eight hours a day for a Broadway photographer in a union shop. She drives fast like all these other New York crazies, smokes cigarettes, and curses anyone on the street who doesn't get out of her way. My little mother, quite a terror; sometimes threatening to choke me. But she is now reassured that I am still a nice guy.

Clarice had a little gathering here at her place for my sister Anne and me. Anne has a little artist's studio in the village. Commune discussion really gets up a lot of energy. Most say they're sadly beyond being pioneers for anything.

Little insular families. There are the people you know and there are the other people. Once in a great while you meet somebody. LONELY in the midst of the crowd. I have already practiced the prayers that I will say when I return to New Buffalo.

Wednesday: Spent part of New Year's on the subway. Only a few days more of this so I can appreciate these moments alone.

And now, puff! I am right bam back at New Buffalo under clear skies, with hills and mountains all covered by snow. Within an hour, I was under the truck with Pepe. That night Kiva cooked a great spaghetti and meat sauce dinner, and we partied, sang, played guitars, drums, and danced wildly into the night. Heavenly Father God, all my friends here at New Buffalo, I am truly blessed and surely happy to be here.

Saturday: A glorious cold, clear day. And here are Carol and Kachina, looking very well, and Ernesto and Razberry, who traveled from Oregon to Wisconsin with the Mind Machine Family this past summer. Tall Neil Svenningson, whose father was a Navy officer, and Little Doug, in his black motorcycle jacket, are here too. Larry has moved to another scene.

The tractor is sitting down on the public road near the bridge, minus both heavy-duty 12-volt batteries and has three flat tires.

"It must be hard to write," says Ernie to me, "to capture this magic." Indeed. We sit before a fire with a big stump burning, its tentacle roots sticking out. I write by a candle's light. Ears of corn dry over our heads. We sit on pillows and rugs in our dirt house. In the dim light I can make out the buffalo skull on the wall. But it's the oneness, the love felt, which is hard to convey.

Paul and Catalina are here, a young, handsome couple. They take care of Frankie and keep an eye on Kevin, plus all the other wild animals here: the chickens, four goats, and Josephine the cow. There are five horses running free on the land. I think they rather like it that way. All the animals are loose. We're all loose; this is a very free life. We are most fortunate.

Sunday: Bright warm sun. I've been making some candles, working on the truck, and making wood runs.

Dark-skinned, beautiful Whitelight arrived from California. Her mom is from Panama; her dad worked at the canal. She's firm and lively and used to live with us in Bolinas, California.

Sunday night a prospecting cowboy, Poncho, showed up in a camper, turned us all on to some pretty good weed and card tricks. Had a good gathering in Pepe and Carol's room. We were talking about communes: Steve Gaskin's in Tennessee—1,000 acres with 400 people! The Christian commune in Oregon is an ideal sort of commune—producing—many facilities. Talked about communes in China, too.

January 17, 1972: Days are getting a little longer and warmer. Wood run is gone and wax is melting. Tahiti turning out fine belt buckles. Circle being cleaned. The kitchen buzzing with ladies figuring out what's going on. Tahiti talking about splitting as a matter of principle. Me, I talk about being right here.

Here is a society of many strong people. Among us is Buddy, a young man of 13 years. He rides the horses and helps with all the work. We like him being with us, and I'm sure it is a strong experience for him. Pepe and crew whitewashed with tierra blanca and completely cleaned the kitchen. Feeling very together. Had fabulous spaghetti feast for dinner. Drank some wine.

Tuesday: With Cave Dave, we made 196 candles. I know it is a good thing, though simple. I should be able to do a lot of things. All those years in school and five in University and I didn't learn to fix or make anything. Help my energy grow, Heavenly Father. Thank you for all these people with whom I live and work.

Friday: Last night, Eddy, whom we know from Rainbow, Oregon, showed up with two brothers and a fine young lady Leslie with a new baby; she's a perfect vision in buckskin dress. Her missing one front tooth only accents her beauty. They live near Mora with ten other people.

Pepe, after being pissed several times over people spending money on liquor, ravaged the commune, collecting money and shooting dice, so we could have four bottles of hard booze. But he's up right early in the morning, as usual, lighting the kitchen fires. This morning, we rescued the tractor and drove it up to the workshop.

Glorious Sunday: Last night Pepe and Bob, stoned on acid, slaughtered a ram that the priest Mick bought for $15 from a local rancher. They built a roasting pit in the quiet morning. Joe Cota, a very powerful man, strumming the guitar out by the woodpile; ladies gathering with their babies next to Pepe and Carol's door, patching pants in the sun.

The roast was done by noon; people cutting meat off the flank. Guitar is passing around and all are singing "Cripple Creek" ragtime stomp. A regular, fine, Sunday church meeting at New Buffalo. Cave Dave returned from a peyote meeting with two short-haired Indians in a pickup, who live at the

Taos Pueblo. End of January and it's getting back to where we have quite a lot of people coming to visit. Pepe is just so welcoming and genuinely excited to see just about anyone.

Tuesday night: Two guests in the circle room. They recently got ripped off at rifle point for some grass. Last Saturday two fellows and two girls from Morningstar were badly beaten. Stan, from Oregon, was narrowly rescued from a fight. Wild West. There is an element of Chicano men who resent the Anglos. Cowboy Bob looks a bit battered too, from a duke-out with Pepe. He's back up at Morningstar now; too much electricity and civilization down here.

The kitchen sink is repaired. For a while, we carried all the dirty water to the door and threw it out, creating a skating rink in the parking lot. Slip and slide your way to the outhouse!

There is going to be a gathering here this weekend to commemorate the New Year.

Friday: Under a clear morning sky I cleaned up the outdoor workshop—blood and gore from the butchering—old clothes flung all over. I'm happy to fill in where needed.

Saturday: Dennis Long drove Cave Dave, Frankie, and Mary to the library for Children's Story Hour that Dave has on Saturdays. Buddy and I caught a ride with them and got off at the Plateau station to set up a little candle display by the roadside.

Wednesday: Cold night out. The moon will rise late. Everyone has plenty of wood to keep warm—many separate rooms—plenty of blankets. A big stack of cut wood in the kitchen. The lushes, as Chuck calls them, gave me a dollar for antifreeze out of their own "anti-freeze" fund.

Jeff and Tom, from Morningstar, drove a truck into a ditch, dead drunk, and staggered intoBuffalo. Cave Dave took them to a fire in the pit house—booze scene—broken bottles, cans, garbage and junk vehicles in a row.

Today Tahiti gave Buffalo a donkey; we just have to pick it up. Neil made a new table for the kitchen.

Thursday: We got the donkey; picked him up in the Mind Machine. We've had goats in our converted bread truck, but never a donkey. Carol left for California. Moe and family, just arrived from Minneapolis, now have her room.

Quiet day. Tahiti sharpened the big saw. I've been cutting a lot of wood. There are 19 fires here.

Maybe 20 acres of land to the west have been plowed into fields but now are just barren earth. Out front another few acres are lifeless, from no planting and much tramping. But the pit house, up into the piñon trees, is nicely surrounded by the natural growth.

Big dance at Celso's (local highway bar) tonight with Chico Blues Band. Terrific.

February 6,1972: Here Kiva, Kathy, Catalina, Kathleen, Susie, Miriam, Razberry, Sharon, Whitelight are the ladies and Saafi, Silencio, Frankie, Malcolm, Elisa, Kevin are the kids. Art, Pepe, Buddy, Moe, Gary, Richard, Neil, Paul, Paul Rotman, Ernesto, Tahiti, Leadville Mick, Cave Dave, Dennis, Zip and Chuck, are the guys. Twenty-five adults, six kids, forty chickens, five goats, one cow, one donkey, two turkeys, and three horses. Plus Alan, John, and Lorraine are visiting from Bolinas. Also there is Charlie, who just moved his fabulous truck into the front pasture.

Second night in a row with almost 40 people in our Circle for dinner. Had a big discussion on food stamps; Paul thinks they suck. I, myself, think they help; a little connection with the government is OK.

In my view, the commune is part of the society. It is a revolutionary base, but not in a revolution that will violently overthrow the existing

Friday: Cold but clear. Aquarius Paul and Chuck cooking burrito dinner. Paul has a great force in his mind, a quality that is very different and that I like. "I won't even kill a rabbit." His conviction is deeper than any words; he does not eat meat—doesn't seem to eat much at all. Does smoke a bunch. He was in the Navy and was once a good track runner. He's an excellent carpenter, and all-round worker. Sets the style for being heavy—a tough man, next to anyone I have ever seen.

Moe, Sharon, Ernesto, Razberry, Saafi, Buddy, Elisha, Malcolm, Gary, Dennis, visitor John, and Miriam left for California.

February 15—Monday: Pepe and Tahiti returned from a most inspiring weekend in the mountains north of here with the free people of Libre, Ortiviz's, Red Rockers and Triple A in Colorado. These are four little communities that we interchange with often.

Tuesday: Went to Albuquerque in the Falcon and got 275 pounds of wax. Had some gasoline for breakfast because I had to siphon gas to get the car running. Got back just as the spaghetti dinner bell was being rung.

Heavenly Father, my brothers and sisters: In the renewed fight in South Asia, many people shall die or be maimed and wounded. Bless these all. May they somehow find some comfort in their suffering. Here we live in peace. I hope soon that all men will be able to live in peace.

Wednesday: Paul thought he was leaving and sold his horse. Money went to booze, I guess. Pepe traded his rifle, and now has taken his horse to sell to get back the rifle. Horses eat expensive food. Riders here have expensive saddles; macho trip, I guess you call it. Good animals but don't earn their keep.

Garbage cans are getting full again; too many beer cans.

Friday: Party here with the Oriental Blue Streaks electric band: Nick, Rick, and Tuck. Nick, in worse shape every time I see him, still gets it on. More than enough food for everyone. "A very good party," we all agree. Nick gets obnoxiously drunk. Chuck banged his head, but the music was good.

Saturday: Pepe shaping coins for buttons this morning. I'm melting wax for dipping. Chuck recovering with a bottle. Young Kathy taking care of the animals. Many people off to the hot springs. Tahiti working on his sculpture.

Sunday: A fine day with the sun shining, the ground thawing. A straight-looking, clean, and polished sociologist and family came from University of Missouri. They had been here a year ago. They were rather overwhelmed, especially with Pepe, with his excellent rap and flamboyant manner, handing out joints as he gets all points across. Told me as he left that the place seems to be getting better.

Madeleine is now staying here. Gentle Madeleine I once knew in New York. She is tall, with dark hair and brown eyes—perfectly beautiful. She has a quiet way of talking. We have shared some very close moments together.

Dave Gordon has moved in with us and his little girl Chamisa with him. He and Susie are sharing a room. This is Daddy Dave (Davison), one of the original organizers. Very friendly, his famous grin has one tooth missing. He is wiry, strong in the arms, has one bad leg from polio and smokes too many Lucky Strikes. It is painful for me to see him inhale.

Quite a scene at our dinners—Beggars' Banquet. Many different currents here—many people. A stranded troupe from Ledoux, with three kids, arrived. Leslie is with them, the most beautiful young woman. She is so aloof, and then she looked right at me and smiled.

Wednesday: Got a letter from Irish; he is in Alaska. This Dan Irish lived with

Fig. 7. Portrait of Dave Gordon. From the personal collection of Chamisa WeinMeister.

the Sufi, One World Family in a communal house in Marin when we were also in California. What a powerful yogi he is.

I just heard a car arrive and Tucker, a fellow from Morningstar, has arrived. I recognize his voice; he has the French accent from Quebec.

Just before dinner, eight people materialized, three without bedding. Neil is out in the circle, scrounging off the people around the fire for wine money. Bob, Tom, and Wayman, from Morningstar, are quite drunk in Paul Rotman's room—booze and tobacco city.

Friday: Dance for Max Finstein last night. Bring him back from Israel! Donna babysat the kids and made cookies. Today Dave Gordon had $134 to mail to Max.

Zip returned last night. After trading Pepe for his rifle, Zip then traded the rifle for a horse and two harnesses. He traveled down to Ojo Sarco where Chicken lives to get it. With the white 12-year-old horse with cracked feet, he made his way back to New Buffalo. Being unfamiliar with the land and the horse, it was quite a two-day journey. Zip spent one night at the Hog Farm; the rest of the time he was riding or pulling the horse.

Quiet day. No more feed for the goats, no fresh or canned food here. No kerosene, almost out of wire wick. Terrific dinner. Main course, one rooster and one guinea hen, cooked by Chef Perez.

Nixon will be back from China soon—a historic event. What I wanted for many years will now unfold, a friendlier relation with the People's Republic. Nixon got to see the aging Mao Tse Dong, one of the hugest figures in all world history.

Sunday: I had a fine day visiting Morningstar and the now defunct commune, Reality Construction Company. These are about five dry, rocky miles east from here. Incredible places—a dream world. Donna and her three sons are now moved up there.

We had an orderly meeting after supper. Decided to sell Josephine the cow for $150. Money to go for hot water installation and land tax.

Our lawyer is John Ramming who lives in Taos. Our back taxes are about $200, of which we have all but $60. We may have to remake the land deed.

Tuesday: We ordered propane gas. Washroom is being readied for hot water! Pepe has Tahiti teaching him to make belt buckles. Excellent. Susie is setting up a loom and also is baking pies to sell so we can buy kerosene. Dave brought an almost functional '57 pickup truck here today. Chamisa, Daddy Dave's little girl, got some new books. Kiva has moved up to Zip's teepee.

Wednesday: A windy, cold day. I'm making little candles. Pepe learned a lot of new tricks and is making silver buttons and balls. What a fast study he is. Chuck is cooking stuffed manicotti. Zip taking the hair off a deer hide.

Thursday: Exceptional dinner by Perez. About 40 or more for dinner, including four ladies and three guys from Ledoux. Leslie lives with the most exceptional women, and she is the jewel of them. She quietly came and stayed with me last night.

Zip is working on a saddle. Fellow Joe, who once lived here and his very delicate lady Louisa, arrived here yesterday.

March 3, 1972—Friday: Bought 200 pounds of potatoes from a fellow who came up our road. Tahiti is getting some metal work finished before he takes off on horseback. Cave Dave has the covered part of the greenhouse already for planting.

Sunday: About ten people, bringing a big salad, came up from the Hog Farm to celebrate Tahiti's birthday. Fifty people here for dinner. Ten kids sitting around the table. Some good guitar. A lid hit the table somewhat late. Very mellow.

Tuesday: Sun is hot. Tahiti finishing his munitions belt—makes his own bullets. He's a good cook too; garlic and barley for breakfast is his specialty. Art finishing some silver buttons. Louisa fooling around with the wax in the candle room.

It is night now. Here I am on the hard dirt floor of the candle room. Brother Bill Sundance just hitched in from New York, four days of travel. He's asleep on the platform bed.

Thursday: High energy today. Put two feet of dirt on the washroom roof and decided we should make a retaining wall and do all the roofs of New Buffalo. Yes. Aquarius Paul put a window in and Neil, Joe, and I went up to Reality to take apart a collapsed room. We can have the bricks for the retaining walls, a basic pueblo improvement.

Kiva baked 12 loaves of assorted shaped breads. Susie made lemon meringue pie to go with the cheese soufflé and fruit salad. Pepe bought a case of bananas, a case of grapefruit, and a case of green chiles and re-bought the Falcon, which has returned.

Friday: Eggs, fruit, cornmeal, and coffee for breakfast. Pepe meditating on top of my chimney.

We dug out the floor of the communal washroom—put the pipe under the foundation. We plan to put in cement and lay brick. After work had some football practice. Pepe took some acid and so did Alexa, a local, pleasant dream. Pepe sold the car, again, to Susie, Paul, and Davison to drive east.

Last payment on Josephine came. I was given charge of the $50. Cleaned out the seepage tank and put in the drainpipe. About 20 cars came up the road.

Saturday: Pepe and some people meditated on a Z symbol last night and wished for some women and some grass. Pepe walks out of the room, and there is this little lady with a pound of Panama Red!

It's the evening; I'm sitting in Pepe's room surrounded by many good things; the simple fine tools for making jewelry, and what is now a terrific collection of assorted coins, abalone shell pieces and turquoise. Here's a big ten-pound piece of Arizona pipestone, a beaded leather and bamboo case, six bronzed belt buckles and an empty beer bottle from the beer we bottled on Sunday. There's a silver fox skin here, too. Pepe is like a magnet for this stuff.

Sash is here with a few colorful people from Mora. Pepe flashed a few $20s and to celebrate got a bunch of six-packs and a pint of whiskey. Neil broke out a stash and a new pipe. I grabbed my guitar, and we were feeling good, singing and getting it on in the kitchen. Visitors crashing out on the periphery of the circle, right in the middle of our lives.

Sunday morning: We worked with people from Arroyo Hondo, cleaning the main irrigation ditch yesterday; about 50 men and boys were on the crew. The acequia is over three miles long. The yearly cleaning is very important.

Wood run yesterday—only two flat tires. Retainer wall on circle started. Pepe sold our teepee for $50 and is going to buy a horse. "It'll be a good one."

JOURNAL THREE

March 24, 1972—Friday: There was ditch digging this morning. We had three men on the job, including Tucker, who has made a move from Morningstar to Buffalo. He is a quiet and clean longhaired brother—very strong, very mellow and always has a ready laugh—just our spirit. He is Chuck's good friend.

Joe and Paul Rotman working in the garden. Pepe finished one necklace, worth perhaps $200. I'm making candles.

Nine guys from New Buffalo played the El Prado Dogs a game of touch football in 40-mile an hour wind. Cave Dave is going to stay at Lama Foundation for a month.

March 28: Snow fell this morning; everything is white. The wind is blowing. Our newly installed drain is clogged. Pepe took the panel truck to town; didn't want to share the ride, so about six people had to hitchhike in to do their business.

Tucker scored a heavy-duty sewing machine today for $7. He has been making antler headbands and belts. The ditch went on and we have irrigation water. Paul was out in the field all day. Cold. He also got a joint in the mail that he shared with the candle crew.

Wednesday: House is all cleaned—grill set up. A great stack of wood in the circle for the roast. A half a lamb is hanging in Neil's room for tonight's full moon party. Kiva making bread. Donna is here to help get the party started early. Judy from Vermont arrived.

Thursday morning: Clear blue sky this morning. Eggs, bacon, cheese, chiles and potatoes for breakfast. For real, I am thankful for all these good things, a dream beyond any imagining of mine.

Yesterday, just as the candles were completed, the lamb finished cooking and the Hog Farmers arrived, the New Buffalo firefighters took off for a two-hour session at the Questa High School. I just had time to kiss a few ladies hello as I split for the meeting.

Great party here—drums and many friends. Fine gypsy women dancing in the glow of the full moon, around the flickering fire. Leslie is here, as she said she would be. In her beaded buckskin dress, she could not be more perfect.

April 1, 1972: The ditch is on. Tucker and Zip working in the garden field with the water flowing. Kiva making cheesecake for Sunday. Little visiting pickup made a wood run. Pepe dug up the clogged drainage system. Now I have to explore it.

Louisa is a poised and fine young lady. Seems to be feeling very good. She has stayed with me some recent nights. Very nice.

Tuesday night: Today was Zip's birthday. Kiva cooked all day. The Chevy made a run to get sawdust and then sand. Davison reinstalled the electrical outlet in the kitchen; it's been begging to be done for at least a year. Aquarius Paul bricked about one-third of the washroom floor. Pepe bought some more cement. Then he and Chuck tried out the rubber raft in the Rio Grande.

Tucker put up his teepee today. The priest Mick took some LSD for the first time.

Thursday: Poncho arrived with his clean-looking panel truck. He gave us many pieces of rough turquoise he has been mining and showed us an old gold ring he found. He and Pepe are planning a trip.

Sunday evening: Pepe and I ran to the Black Rock hot springs. We never stopped; he was way ahead of me. Back at the commune, I started to throw the football around. Five young Spanish-speaking guys from Arroyo Hondo come up the road, so we chose them with some of the Buffalos and played a game. When we returned from the field, all kinds of people were dancing and it's look-

ing like a party. A VW bus, with eleven righteous freaks from Arizona heading north is here. Forty-eight people standing in a circle for the dinner prayer.

Now most of the crowd is off to a big dance at Ol' Martinez Hall. Oriental
Blues Streaks, with Sarah Baker, is playing and so is the Triple A Band.

Yesterday Pepe got a .38 smokeless revolver. He took it apart, fixed something, and was outside with it when Poncho came up. Poncho—not too
encouraged—so their trip is off.

Monday afternoon: In the morning I went to town with a few candles and my
wash. Met Manuel and saw his plans for a new storefront and display with fruit
and candles. Great. After that, went over to his pad and smoked a little.
Because of Manuel, I always come home with some fruit.

Thursday: Leslie left. Max, who has returned, says, "You don't meet many like
her."

Max is looking well; He is 48 years on this earth. He has a short gray beard
and is slender with a barrel chest.

One of the cleverest people here is 18-year-old Michael Glassman. He says
the fields could be planted between May 15 and May 30 with a cover crop of
alfalfa, oats, wheat, or clover. But we have no seeds now. Athletic and happy,
Michael looks like one of the Fury Freak Brothers with his head of thick, dark
curly hair. He somehow found New Buffalo in a quest from Boston. How naturally these people fit together!

I spoke to Ben Garcia, a fine man from Arroyo Hondo and a good friend
of the hip people. He is 80 years old and in excellent health. Said it looks like
even less water than last year if we don't get rain. Ben is the traditional majordomo of Arroyo Hondo.

RAID! Dawn—snow falling—quiet. I had been up to turn off the ditch,
Paul and Catalina down to milk the goat. Cars started pulling up—straight
and hip-looking plainclothesmen getting out; all kinds of heat in our parking
lot. Nine cars—over 20 men: brown uniformed, black uniformed state police
and Taos police. There are men in suits with pads and hip-looking, big narcs.
State troopers with rifles advanced on the teepees from the ditch road. Room
by room, they woke up people; must have taken them almost half an hour to
check Neil out. Everybody with different encounters. Suited men with troopers standing around showing Daddy Dave and me a copy of the warrant. Pepe
had his gun out and was putting it down when they came in his room.

Whole thing took about one-and-a-half hours. Found a few seeds here and there; a few plants in the greenhouse. "What's this?" "This is the spice shelf for cooking." "This is smoking mixture." "No, it's oregano." Girls serving coffee to some of the police, over 60 people here. "Can I feed the chickens?" Trooper says, "OK."

People gathering in the kitchen. Fellow from *Taos News*, with camera, drinking coffee with about 20 people. Art playing his guitar. Finally, in the circle, they decided to leave. No one busted—a few names taken—very mellow. Didn't even take all the plants. Neil asked the narc if they had to have them all. He said, "Just give them the big ones." Outside we watched the cars drive down the road. No one taken away—no resistance—no guns shot off. Now we're in the kitchen eating pancakes for a late breakfast on an overcast day. It's no longer snowing.

Wake up to the police—get dressed—HA! Now we'll find out who has been holding out. Alan goes and gets his hash stash. Neil gets a couple of plants. A few people come up from the camp by the river. We make a circle— say some prayers. Let's put a sign on the gate "Closed." No, we are open for business as usual.

Good dinner tonight; fine pea soup and loaves of bread baked by Carol. Ritchie and Genie here from Hog Farm. Big sing-out in the kitchen.

Saturday: I sold $30 worth of candles to the Taos Inn candle shop. Pepe making fine earrings by cutting liberty head dimes. Alan working on buttons, getting ready for the Oregon Pleasure Faire.

Tucker did an excellent watering and sweeping of the circle and kitchen. If the dirt floors are sprinkled with water before sweeping, there is very little dust.

Sunday: Long-expected Laird has arrived with heavy-duty Chevy Apache truck and some good grass. Two very straight-looking fellows drove up yesterday. "We don't mean any harm. We're not mad." One fellow, Bill, from Santa Fe— talked about dropping out—join the movement. He is a kind-looking, hard-working man.

April 17: I heard a story about Laird and The Grateful Dead. He was their first equipment manager. He grew up with Jerry Garcia.

The power wagon that levitated here Sunday is from Ian, who sometimes lives at Lama Mountain. Ian has loaned "us" the truck. Rocky drove it here. The power wagon made three runs to Carlos Trujillo's farm for manure; must be one of the most excellent farms in the Taos area.

Buffalo and the Military: Aquarius Paul served in the Navy a few years ago. Max was in the Philippines in artillery during WWII! Neil's father has a career in the American Navy; so does Zip's father. Neil, Paul, and Zip have all spent a few years in Japan—all American. Joe Novacavich, who is here from Morningstar, had a father in the American Army. Joe was somewhere in China when the communists took power in 1949. His hands are not normal, and it is sometimes a handicap to him. He was born in Frisco, I believe, and has worked there often. Tahiti knows him from the Avalon Ballroom.

History from Max: Los Alamos, New Mexico, some 50 miles away from us, is where the "A" bomb was first developed. It was from Santa Fe that Soebel and the Roseburgs supposedly relayed information that eventually reached the Soviet Union. Taos has been known to be a place for radicals of the Left.

Zip is nearly finished with a leather jacket. He lives in his teepee with Kiva. He comes down sometimes, chases his horse all over the pasture and then makes a faint attempt to beat the horse, as the sorry animal slowly carries this ranting nuisance up the hill. We are a long way from hitching up a mule to plow and cultivate the New Buffalo fields.

Four chickens killed for dinner; Chuck is going to cook them up. Chef Perez is very fastidious. He gets the kitchen all ready and before cooking he thoroughly scrubs his hands and carefully cleans his nails.

Wednesday evening: We made a wood run for cedar with the power wagon. Zip and a visitor started to dig the foundation for the new chicken house, and 50 new chicks were picked up today. They are living in Mick's room.

Philip Vargas, in a jeep, came here with voter registration forms. He is running for state senator. Max took charge of them. I got one. He came here twice today.

Tucker and I made the front page of the *Taos News*—"Commune Raid"— three paragraphs and a front-page photo, titled *Notes from the underground*.

Paul Rotman's mother is here visiting from Massachusetts. Pepe and I bought a working Maytag washing machine of impressive looking quality.

Thursday: Storm brewing and it snowed. Got $60 in food stamps. Thank you.

I hitchhiked to Ledoux, a remarkable valley, almost completely unpopulated. Lana said, "Leslie told me that if you came, AnSwei, not to let you go." 7-Room House is a good place in the mountains located in Mora County. From there, Saturday at noon, Leslie, baby Jamie, and I climbed out of the window of her room and hitched back to Buffalo. Very smooth.

Sunday: Ice cream party this afternoon with a few guests. And who is this elegant young lady who puts her arms around me? A very good thing, indeed. Leslie has quietly moved in with me.

April 24: Yesterday at the Hondo Firefighters SWFFF meeting, eight New Buffalo men showed. Morningstar was there with just about as many. Thirty-nine in all in Hondo signed up.

People worked on mudding the outside walls of the west wing. After a while, there was a lot of mud, but no clothes. I hear Zip and Kiva are going to move their teepee up to a piece of land near Questa that Zip put $100 down on.

Neil gave lawyer John Ramming, $65 for back taxes. Supposedly we owe $275 for 1972. We will see about getting that reduced. Also see about having the officers of New Buffalo be people who are living here.

Willy from the 7-Room House is here. They got raided this morning—no arrests—pretty good encounter. Willy says they went on to Rinconada. Fucked way for the government to see how we are doing.

Tuesday: Hog Farm got busted this morning; took some to jail. Diamond and a fellow Jason got busted. Now bailed out, they are here at Buffalo. Seven still in jail—total bail, $5,500. Diamond, Lobo, and lady Helene and kids, Lana, Suzan, and Steve are here from the 7-Room House.

All clouds and wind this afternoon. We have about 15 percent of the garden ready for planting; it's cultivated, fertilized and raked. A group of foreign tourists here this afternoon.

Drums, fire in the circle, kids bedding down, tambourines clanging, people calling, singing, yelling, chanting. Cymbals, bells, plenty of dinner. Hog Farm got busted. A house in Holman got busted. It's the spring clean up.

April 27: We planted lettuce, broccoli, chard, peas, carrots, beets and more. A crew of Buffalos and friends took four rafts down the Rio Grande. Mudding continued. Because of the little rain, houses can be built of the very earth, if they are maintained.

May 2: Pepe, Carol, and Kachina went up to live where Zip, Kiva, and others have their teepees, seven miles above Questa. I've got the clown outfit and a few of Pepe's shirts.

I was at the peyote meeting Monday night and Cave Dave was there. He likes living at the Lama Foundation even though he has to work harder. He

Fig. 8. AnSwei pouring candles. Photo by Clarice Kopecky.

is into revolution like me—dedicated hard work—make it shine and grow.

Local farmer O. G. Martinez was here today looking at our big tractor. We got it started easily.

The corporation is eleven guys and about seven young ladies: Louisa, Susie, Sparrow, Catalina, Leslie, Kathy and Raz. Paul, Dave Gordon, Max Finstein, Mick, Joe, Neil, AnSwei, Paul Rotman, Chuck, and Tucker are the men at Buffalo. Plus, Ian is moving here.

Two vehicles rode above us on the ditch road; people hanging off the sides, making some yells and calls. We answered. It's a visiting family passing through. They came around front and up the driveway. Fourteen young people headed north, now camped in the circle. Big party was beginning in front of the house.

I made twelve pairs of candles this morning.

Wednesday evening: Fire in the circle. Folks singing religious hymns and all sorts of music. Vegetable soup, salad, corn bread for dinner. Tucker now making some potatoes for a few of us who could eat a bit more. Around dinnertime, even with the fourteen trippers gone, our number doubled as our circle gathered for dinner prayer.

Tahiti is back from Colorado. We put up a new front gate and we intend to put up a sign! "Visitors: visiting hours—6pm to 8am. Sat and Sun. all day."

Thursday morning: Very mellow here last night. Rough hitchhiker singing some good songs. Two guests in a Pinto brought all kinds of fruit for breakfast.

Saw *Time* magazine this morning; read about the Vietnam War and McGovern for president. Says he'll cut the Pentagon by $32 billion over three years, but he'll still spend the money on something else. Diamond gave us the preamble and constitution of the IWW, based in Chicago. The workers and employers have nothing in common it starts out. I don't see it that way.

Leslie's friend Sparrow really on the job—up early getting French toast together with bread she made yesterday. Chuck finally brought his girlfriend Sandy out—young with lovely long legs.

Saturday: Today it really rained. The earth is dark brown; all the green is bright and lush. Snow on the mountains, cloaked in clouds and mist. We had our Circle outside. Lentils, brown bread, and salad for dinner. Julie, here, comes occasionally with her six kids and Chevy car. A new lady, Penelope, arrived with two boys, a baby, and a pickup truck.

Monday: Today I made candles, and Penelope's two kids gave me a helping hand. Mudding continued. Tucker has moved into Pepe's room and has fixed it so it looks terrific. Sunday, Joe started terracing and cultivating some land between the outhouse and the road; turned it into a little garden. Excellent work.

Should we put up this sign? Max, Aquarius Paul, and Davison think it is good—a little formal—whatever happens. Some people saying they definitely do live here; that is good, taking care of more business. There is a fire in the circle. Leslie is playing the guitar and singing; it sure sounds fine.

Tuesday evening: Max went to town today with the metal box containing New Buffalo "papers" to see John Ramming. "The New Buffalo copy of the deed was burned in the fire," says Max. " Neither Rick Klein who put up the bread, nor any institution seems to have a copy," reports Max. The State of New Mexico sent us a letter, stating that we owe $680 in back taxes, and that they own the land by default. "Furthermore," says Max, "they will not accept payment unless the corporation can prove ownership." Chuck asked a blessing tonight for the legislators and state leaders and asked that they be given guidance not to hassle or hinder us.

Max points out that the Gringo "stole" the land from the Indian, the Mexican, and the People through such legal bullshit. Max, however, is on the case and is consulting a lawyer at a legal aid office. So the legal structure of New Buffalo hangs in limbo. None of the officers of the Board of Directors, three people, is living at Buffalo. Robbie Gordon, Dave's brother, who is in West Virginia, is one of the officers. Some chick—Jane—is another. Someone told me she resigned. Steve is the third, I believe. He is in Boston.

The power wagon made a cedar wood run today. Chuck is now passed out after saying a really fine prayer at Circle and doing a hard day's work. Joining us were a band of gypsies associated with the 7-Room House. Diamond and Star I know by name. Leslie went off with them. She's gone. A bit of an awkward move, in an otherwise graceful love affair.

Max went to see Robert Romero who owns the Feed Bin, a big business in Taos, and is interested in buying our tractor for $1,000 on the line and $870 six months from now. They shook on it. He is supposed to be here tomorrow.

Tahiti loaded up a truck full of chests, stoves, tools, things from his room, and he split with them. Headed to Pepe and Zip's gypsy camp. I sold some candles and bought little Tony sneakers, string for wick, and band-aids. Tucker and Paul mudded again today, almost completing the main building at the Buffalo pueblo. I went running, thinking good thoughts, though feeling a bit sad this afternoon as I tried to get into cultivating and removing rocks on a piece of the garden. My favorite tool is broken. Tractor leaving seems backward. Leslie, gone.

Tonight there are about ten crashers in the circle. Ian was here real early this morning with a bag of grapefruit and contributed $150 to the treasury. This is love in action; our brother often thinks of us. Private party in Max's room.

May 11: Cool morning—below freezing last night. My birthday—28 years old. Chuck up this morning, long before the sun, getting dirt sifted for mudding. He plans to cook up a storm.

Angela and Kathleen showed up yesterday; they just returned from Guatemala. Beautiful Angela, trembling as she hugged all the people. Around 5:00 p.m. the ditch came on. We watered all the planted parts of the field and finished just as it was getting too dark to see.

Besides Angela and Kathleen, came two other beautiful young ladies. "Get out the red carpet," said Tucker, smiling, with a twinkle in his eye, as he opened the door for them. Justin, Joanne, and Larry came over, just for a short while last night. They are part of the original family.

Today Tahiti took yet another truckload of stuff away. With his lampshade and big sun sculpture tied on with his wagon parts and rugs, the truck was a real sight—art in motion.

Mick has the chickens producing over 15 eggs a day. Joe has been moving compost to his terrace garden overlooking the driveway.

Nixon is giving the Soviet Union some ultimatum and mining the waters before all the North Vietnamese ports. Imagine: We leading our peaceful life here and these people carrying on this most lost-cause war in our name. The government is not the people; not these people anyhow, nor most of our friends.

Friday: Some people had a wonderful time on my birthday. Chuck cooked an incredible feast, served about 9:00 p.m. I got a whole banana cream pie for myself and a fish from next-door neighbor Al Kaplan and Judy Macfarlane. Kiva and Zip gave me a headdress with an eagle feather.

Chuck got a little rowdy with a guy named Mike and then passed out standing in the doorway. Ended up asleep under the food counter. Lots of booze. No dope! Neil picked a fight while drunk with a fellow who is an image of Fidel Castro, only shorter, who is living at Morningstar. And Neil got righteously laid out by the fellow, who said, "I'm gonna show you the difference between a revolutionary and a punk." He is up early this morning wondering what happened.

Pepe's shop is in my care, and he has given me an assignment to cut out a few dimes for earrings. The tractor is gone, and Max has a check for $1,000.

A really big fellow and his quiet, thin lady showed up. Heavy is his name. Two flutes playing, light drumming, lots of dancing figures around the fire.

Sunday: Sun is high and the sky is clear. Tall Paul Mushen, Mei Hua, and Cam arrived from Colorado. Omar, Heavy, Sylvia, and baby Eddy are here.

Friday night we had a meeting with $1,000 lying on the ground before Max. We put about $700 aside for a new truck, $50 to Susie for the kitchen, $20 to Mick for chickens, $60 to Joe for agriculture, plus we ordered parts for the Mind Machine. Dave got $20 toward lumber for the chicken coop. It was a short, concise meeting. But now we have a farm without a tractor. Nobody knew what to plant, and it just kept getting lent out.

Today will be a pretty good day. Arty just has to remember to love and be loved.—Writer unknown.

Yesterday was Angela's birthday. Susie made cheesecakes for the birthday party. Angela is a teenager no more—twenty years old. We stayed together, she and I.

Heavy got into helping Paul and Tucker work on the tower roof. He and his lady are considering moving to the pit house. No one seems to object. At 300 pounds this Eddy is heavy. Ex Hell's Angel, he was a Marine at thirteen, fought in Vietnam.

Last night the scene finally came down with Chuck. There had been talk of it for some time. Chuck went down the road just before dinner, feeling bad.

A greeting sign is up—an expulsion of sorts—tightening up the scene a bit.

A few visitors are sleeping on the dirt floor. Mick has moved to the end room in the south wing. Yesterday I helped Angela clear out the junk, clothes, and a really shitty rug from another room.

A little heaviness here in the slight reorganization—I'm with it—Mei says she feels it is good. She is Chinese and a medical doctor, I hear. Lives with the people in Colorado near Ortiviz's.

Monday: Joe scored 100 pounds of oat seeds, 20 pounds of alfalfa seeds, bean seeds, and some fish fertilizer. Sunday we started leveling the field below the dump that Steve plowed in the fall. Last year it had about three rows of vegetables and the rest in weeds.

For the first time in my three-year experience in the commune movement, since we were at Johnson's Pastures, I am together with people who are interested in making the commune work; all accept their situation and can very well participate in a commune family.

A tall and modest visitor came after dinner. He is passing through and wanted to know if he could put in a day's labor in order to get a feel for this commune and what is happening here; I accepted his request. Davison interrupted saying he thought we were not using outside help—out by 8 a.m. I suggested the rule is good, but we still should deal with people individually and be able to accept such offers, and so it was settled. I do have a specific task leveling a field, which Charlie could help with. In addition, some people from the Fem Farm commune are visiting us.

Friday morning: Yesterday Joe, Tucker, and I went to a neighbor's house, Señor Felix Gonzales, to find out about the irrigation water. He refused, once again, to see us, sending us to Señor Medina in upper Hondo, who says he only regulates the upper side of the river. Then the ditch came on all by itself, so we proceeded to irrigate.

Joe: Every day he is up early enthusiastically working to make the land produce. He has the best picture he can get in his mind of the overall scene. We have very little knowledge.

Dave and Max are off to Colorado to try to purchase a truck for us.

JOURNAL FOUR

Joseph Cruz from the Pueblo sang
with other Indians. I went to bed
under a cedar tree on the hill
listening to their ancient songs.

May 19, 1972: The moon is half-full and extremely bright in a clear fresh sky after a dramatic day. Perhaps six people camped in the Circle, fire embers still glowing. It is very quiet.

Adam, Pam's two-year-old son, was discovered missing around 4:00 p.m. As the storm built up momentum, a search was organized, wind blowing and raining all around. All out looking, asking. Finally, just before the storm broke over us, Omar drove up with Adam. He was with Omar the entire time.

Incredible storm—rain and hail—lots of snow in the mountains. Ground is white and muddy. Dave and Max arrived with a clean 1959 Ford 1 ½-ton flatbed truck with duel rear tires. They shopped all day in Colorado and came up with just what they had in mind. It was for sale for $1,000. $650, cash on the spot, brought it to Buffalo.

Ian is doing some fine carpentry with a great assortment of tools he keeps in his room. Our brother has a lot of gray hair, is clean-shaven and is muscular with strong forearms. He cares about us a lot.

Storm was over by the time we had our dinner prayer. Courtyard pleasantly dusted with wondrous light snow—great clouds billowing and reflecting the setting sun.

Fig. 9. Ian working. Photo by Clarice Kopecky.

Pepe and the whole crew were here from his camp, all in the Mercedes. They must have enjoyed the storm in the big teepee.

After dinner, the mountains and the clouds behind them flashed a light show as the storm moved east—lightening every minute or so—some fantastic explosions. I watched them with Camille, who has returned to live here with her two-year-old son, Nico. Nico is Omar's son. They have made Tahiti's old room into a home.

Monday: Went to Juan Valdez's in Arroyo Seco and got a good load of manure with the Buffalo truck. It worked very well.

Dinner before sundown. Two young gypsy ladies came yesterday and may stay for a while. They were at the Rainbow Farm in March.

Prosperity: We are getting a little ahead. Aquarius Paul and Mick each brought in $375. We have a new 1959 truck, a lot of food, lots of good work to do, good friends, and happy kids to teach us.

Tuesday: Louisa reads my journal. She says it doesn't have any emotion. "It should be a love story." I believe it is a love story. "Of course it is," she says. Louisa and Joe are like Kiva and myself; once a couple, they remain close though with new partners.

"Joe was kind of spoiled," says Louisa. He was one of those finicky hippies who had many fetishes. He certainly is different now. Joe is twenty years old. He fired some clay with wood and cow dung he gathered.

Wednesday: Quite a few guests here, including three ladies from Michigan—one with Neil, one with Tucker (about time), and one with Ian. Also, Isabel and Aurora are still here, plus a couple visiting from Long Island in a new car. Ray, a tall Texan who lived with us in California, hitched in. He's about twenty years old and a very clean hippie.

We made two runs to Señor Valdez's spread; gave them some candles and cleaned a stall, getting a load of well-composted earth.

Louisa gives me a kiss for a candle for the kitchen.

I ran down to the river to bathe. The Hondo runs clear and cold, less than a half-mile from our wooden door. I must force myself each time to jump in it is so cold. Another half mile or so and I can jump in the Rio Grande.

A crew started taking down a wing at Reality. We gave Indio $75 for the bricks. Ian was on the crew. The parts for the Mind Machine came—$145—Paid!

Leo Vigil, who lives across the Rio Hondo from us, sent his son over with his big John Deere tractor and took the truck frame trailer we said he could have.

We now have seven goats, three adult females and four little ones. Kathleen is in charge of them.

Thursday: A big crew of men and women, packed with cheese and tuna fish sandwiches, took the big red truck up to Reality destruction project.

Booze city here in the evenings. Wine, beer, and an occasional bottle of tequila. Perhaps a dozen visitors or more last night. The place is getting up earlier as a rule despite this partying.

Friday: I am limiting my marijuana smoking—quitting beer—getting in shape. Pepe left a finished silver necklace with me for Diamond to sell. Three ladies from Michigan left. Yesterday Chris, a tall lady with a baby, arrived in a blue panel truck. She is Jasper Blowsnake's wife. Jasper died a week or two ago of a cancer in his gut. He was mentioned in the evening Circle prayer for a couple of months. Judy, another tall lady, has returned.

Sunday: Paul and Tucker started mudding the turrets on the tower. The tower is the only two-story feature of our pueblo, but it makes us a castle in the desert.

Daddy Dave and crew brought three truckloads of bricks. There are now bricks on all the roofs that need retainer walls, and a stack of bricks near the proposed chicken coop. Ray helped me a great deal cleaning the parts for the Mind Machine. Max and Madeleine spent several hours watering the garden.

Saturday night: Full moon. Wild party here started in the afternoon. Mick butchered five chickens. Jason from the Hog Farm helped do the cooking. We had cars, trucks, long-haired hippies, dark-skinned gypsies and big-chested, long-legged dancing girls getting it on in the front yard. Guitars, a banjo, three or four drums, a saxophone, a clarinet, and perhaps 80 people here. Fire in the courtyard at night. Joseph Cruz from the Pueblo came with Phil, Joe, Henry, and Benjamin, all local Indians. They sing really fine. I went to bed early in the moonlight, under a cedar tree on the hill, listening to their ancient songs.

Late that night, after 2 a.m., Angela and I went to the hot springs. Deep in the gorge by the rushing Rio Grande, life, for a little while, is perfect.

After a pancake breakfast, Wolfman, a young husky cat, is still here and that's all. He asks what he can do to help.

Monday morning: Sunday it rained—sweet rain—everything is still wet and the sky cloudy. We are blessed.

Big dance last night. Most of the commune went. Jason and Curtis from Hog Farm are still here—played guitar—Jason knows a lot of songs. Party continued when the gang got home. Cheers for Pepe, as he tossed a lid on the table!

Ray dipped a set of candles. Camille sewing, Angela weaving belts, band playing, people coming in to listen, me cutting out leather for moccasins from elk skin that Leslie gave to me. Five people asleep in the circle.

Last day of Memorial Day weekend: I'm up early, exercise, and have some breakfast with Ray who has raw peanuts, almonds, granola, walnuts, and oranges. Max is out to score corn seed. Joe ordered beans. We have two visitors, down in the garden, which is wet and fragrant. They are mixing in the rich soil we have trucked in.

Monday: This morning Ray and I delivered candles and Angela sold six belts she wove for $3 apiece. In the afternoon a storm built up and by the time we hitched back it was really raining. Our road is almost impassable. Dinner was already eaten, and Davison tells me there's a meeting, and they've been waiting on me. Uh-oh . . .

About visitors: Max is feeling a bit poorly or worried. Susie would rather just see us most of the time. Paul says, "Is this a roadhouse or is this our home?" Louisa says, very shyly, that sometimes she has a little trouble relating to so many people. Tucker says he thinks we are doing great and doesn't see a problem. Joe, Davison, and Camille feel just fine. Heavy says, "Well, we'll clear the place when it gets too many." I say we have a 6:00 p.m. to 8:00 a.m. and weekend policy. If you're upset then get those people to move on. No problem—so some tensions come—Max and Neil leave the room.

I invited a couple out that I saw in town with their packs. Knew it was going to rain so I said, "Go out to Buffalo." Also Steve Raines arrived late from Colorado with about five people.

Tonight I sleep on the circle floor. Thank you Heavenly Father for the place I have to rest. Tonight it rains. I love to listen to the rain.

People snoring in the circle—I can understand the uptightness. I could go sleep up at the open-air barn and be away from these distractions; that is the trick, I believe. We each find our place with Mother Earth and use the big houses as centers of the people's culture—for the service of the people. My thought is complex, though, for I like a tight family and quiet. Look within us to solve the problem. God bless our open house and have my brothers and sisters feel very good.

Tuesday: Clouds thick in the sky. Breakfast bell was rung for bacon and oatmeal. John visiting, who lives in the canyon by himself, about one mile away. Jug from Colorado is going to move down here with us. He is a strong, quiet man—lots of hair on his body.

Dave Gordon, Rick Klein, and Aquarius Paul went to town to see about the taxes and such. The deed is found and recorded.

Rained this morning, three days in a row! Ray and I took about eight wheelbarrow loads of gravel down the road to the worst holes, and we turned over a section of the garden. By dinnertime, Ian and Bill were helping too. Joe planting squash near the orchard.

Pepe was here this afternoon. He's got his eye on the Mind Machine. He was the one who directed it here. Rick Klein here at Circle, playing and singing some fine music in the kitchen.

Wednesday: Raz and baby Saafi are here, looking very well. She is helping down in the garden this morning with seven others. Up the road, before ham and egg breakfast, comes N.Y. Sundance with news from Oregon and Canada. He pitched in and worked all day.

Dave and Tucker worked on the chicken foundation setting up pouring forms. Also setting up to join the wings of the pueblo with walls with archways. This is classic architecture. Beautiful idea. Ian made a new mud boat.

In the afternoon, Susie discovered the ditch was on. We planted beets, beans, carrots and turned soil, spread and mixed in composted manure. Irrigated half of the garden before the water went off.

June 1, 1972: One bus here from Indiana with four long-haired brothers. Also a beautiful lady, Saffron, arrived and a hitchhiker from Pittsburgh named Keith. He just spent a few fine days at The Farm in Tennessee—500 people! Hog Farm Jason here and he has been playing tunes for about three hours. Great party. Individual cheesecakes for everyone after beans, hot sauce, and salad.

Friday: Paul, Tucker, Heavy, Ian, and Chuck poured the foundation for the chicken coop. Big salad for lunch. Bus from Indiana left. So did Saffron after doing her wash.

In the garden today we made some new designs and patterns; then we planted.

Saturday afternoon: Max and I went around Arroyo Seco looking for mulch and stopped at the Mariposa Ranch, a very big spread. We talked with Felipe Cordova. He is a fine gentleman who knows his farming and building. He has 150 acres planted in wheat and Balboa rye. He said he would give us seed. The plants are waist high now. He plants his in August. That's when we have to look forward to planting our fields.

June 4: A storm is now coming up; we can hear the frequent thunder. In the very early dawn I turned on our ditch. Before the sun rose, the water was in the garden; just what the soil really needed. Jug, Joe, and me in the field irrigating. The new terraces engineered by Jug worked excellently—big squares with a dam all around. Water completely floods the area.

Acid party here last night. I couldn't refuse. Haven't slept since yesterday. Different people levitated in through the night. Davison and I making some good music.

June 6—Election Day: Felix Gonzales came up to the house, offering to drive us down to vote. Also told us we could have the water for the afternoon before it goes to the other side of the highway. A neighbor, who is running for county commissioner on Republican ticket, brought a case of beer up to the house last night.

Dave helped me put the rear end on and bleed the brakes of the Mind Machine. Paul and Tucker took the red truck and got another load of bricks from Reality; Juggernaut went five miles up to Reality, on foot, to get the bricks ready.

I'm lying on the candle room platform. Louisa is embroidering some astrological signs on some patches for neighbor Helen, who in exchange will do her chart. She tells me to write about my emotions. "How did you feel when you were working on the irrigation?" I felt like not doing it. Nevertheless, I stayed until I could hardly see. "Write how my garden is so pretty," says Louisa. That is the terrace garden overlooking our road near the outhouse. The broccoli looks good. Also there are sunflowers, marigolds, and mint all around.

I hear an argument going down in the kitchen. Susie gets pissed at the irrigation system because it is hard to work. Joe planted cabbage and squash. Chuck cut his long hair so he can firefight.

The archway foundations were laid out and poured. These walls with arched entrances will give a spectacular look to our pueblo. Hard-working construction crew demanded a coffee and muffin break between breakfast and lunch and got it. Susie serves us so well.

Finally boosted the Mind Machine with a jump from Heavy's car. She started right up. Driving around, honking the horn, the Mind Machine is back in operation! It has lights, too. Needs a blinker and has no dashboard. So the problem was not enough juice. All the nonsense about the starter was unnecessary. Like the time we took out the fuel pump, undoing the lines and getting at some bad bolts when the problem was we were out of gas.

Camille—22 years—slim and pretty. First time I saw her was at a bar in town. I heard she had lived at Buffalo some time ago and now here she is. New

Buffalo is her home and she digs it. Cooks a lot and cleans in the kitchen "compulsively" she calls it. Also works in the garden and helped Dave tune her 1953 Ford 4-door. She doesn't like to hear any bickering. She says, "It's all right with me." Camille has a fourteen-month-old son, Nico, and he has to learn to cry less.

In the evening two fellows visiting: one baked bread and the other washed dishes. A whole truckload of people arrived to add to the eight other visitors.

Thursday: Sky overcast—the air cool. Jug has only just put on the potatoes. Joe in the garden. A case of honeydew melons in the pantry from Manuel. Susie and Paul are having another fight. "The last one," says Susie.

Friday: Big cedar wood run accomplished yesterday. Jug, Neil, and Wanda laying the corners of the chicken house. Max and I took the Mind Machine to Reality to get some lumber.

One of the archway walls was laid, and Ian worked on the wooden form for the entry. Took until 11:30 at night to vibe in the grass; only took until 10:30 p.m. the night before.

Yesterday Pepe was only down to the hot springs four times. "What, you just watch your brothers work?" says Max. "No, I don't have the time to watch them, with all the chicks around here."

Eventful day yesterday. Ron and Dick from Valdez put tires on the blue Ford and towed it away! In the evening, we loaded a truckload of iron from the trashed van near the barn, and now we have NO junks here. For the first time in several years, the junk scene is gone from behind the pueblo. Yeah!

Little, stocky Eddy—Heavy and Sylvia's boy—is about one year old. Hardly ever walks—he runs. He hardly cries—he laughs. A great kid. They use the Chevy for a crib.

Tuesday: Paul, Tucker, and crew finished putting the bricks on the new archway wall and laid down most of the bricks for the retainer wall on the western wing. Max went to town and scored the $850 that was still owed us for the tractor.

Benjamin from the Pueblo here last night, and a truckload of Hog Farmers and Davison's daughter, Syna, who is graceful, beautiful, helpful, and considerate—our angel.

Sunday Heavy, Sylvia, and I went to town, sold candles and went to see Tumack. Both he and Heavy are Hell's Angels. These ex-Marines are mellow, but don't get them excited! Heavy weighed himself in town, 267 pounds with boots. Me, 162 pounds. He is losing weight.

Heavy: Eddy is his name. Though tough, he is kind and gentle. It's been two years since he was riding a bike. Says he joined the Marines when he was thirteen—weighed 185 pounds and lied about his age. Fought in Vietnam— had some toenails pulled by a Vietnamese interrogation team, but they let him go. Sometimes he carries a little .22 six-shooter.

Davison said, " If anyone wants to live here, all they have to be is Heavy." So instant Karma and here comes Heavy and Sylvia. One night Heavy swallowed a fifth of tequila in under a minute.

Tuesday night: Pepe is here asleep on the roof. It was Pepe who directed and helped cook the superb dinner. We had eggs, rolls, sweet-and-sour pineapple sauce, rice vegetables, salad, and really hot mustard. After dinner, we had a meeting.

Only family at the meeting. Quiet. Over $900 in the treasury. No one suggested any great expense. This year we can pay to have any fields plowed that we want to plant, figure $30 a day. Aquarius Paul is treasurer.

Paul is a powerful man and a skilled worker—chief architect and master builder. Buffalo's finest tradition is in this field. As a young student, he was in school in Denmark and Switzerland. He was in an English-speaking high school in Germany.

This man has stuck with and enjoyed Buffalo, where most others who have been here in the last four years, are gone. A very modest man who makes it a conscious point not to consume a great deal. A few lamps and a clean floor he likes but not much more than that.

Wednesday: Nine visitors here, plus Doctor Richard from our family in Oregon and San Francisco. Some of our guests are speaking Spanish and some are speaking Japanese.

Jug left to resettle in Colorado. People are talking about the July Rainbow festival.

Thursday: Heavy and Sylvia moved to town with Tumack. Carol and Kachina arrived home today. They'll take over the pit house, which is a few hundred yards from the pueblo up in the trees. One guest from Mexico—no habla Inglés. I slept with Louisa under the barn roof in the wind, lightning, and rain.

Saturday evening: Kiva is here, telling us Zip got busted in Barstow, California, on a warrant from Florida—$25,000 bail!

Kiva's adventures with the police: Of course, when busted, Kiva and Zip had their coin buttons and collection of pipes, stash bags, and other assorted paraphernalia confiscated. From 1 a.m., when Zip was arrested, until 4 p.m. the next day, Kiva stayed in the police station, until they finally did return the merchandise. They put Kiva on a bus to Needles. She stayed on the bus until kicked off in some other town. She was thinking of going to the police to ask for shelter, when a squad car picked her up. In the station, the police were rather amused. One officer bought a pair of cufflinks and then they called up a motel, which put her up for the night! Now that's serving the public. She sold some coins for the bus fare to Albuquerque. She's going to try to raise as much money as possible so she can bail Zip out if his bail is reduced. Quite a gal.

Tuesday: Sun is strong—little breeze cools us off. Max is sick. Alan Ginsberg was here yesterday to see him! Max is a published poet himself. Ginsberg is a giant with great black beard. He stoops to get in through the door. His ability with words is just amazing.

Big crew out there mudding today. Paul and Tucker finished the arch with family and friends helping. Shannon, who used to live here, is visiting—clean, strong and handy. He re-enlisted and is on his way to a base in Colorado! Ian completed a screen door for the kitchen.

Big dance Wednesday night. Buffalos get in free. Davison is driver for the band, The Oriental Blue Streaks. He has their bus and equipment parked in the back by the barn. Saturday is the New Buffalo birthday party.

Thursday: Incredible acid-rock dance—gyrating bodies in motion. Sweating at the dance, side steppin' and stompin,' I took a hit of acid. Leslie appeared. "I thought you would be here." I said, "That's why I came."

Spectacular sunrise—orange-yellow—overcast day. Camille, up early, cleaning the kitchen. Leslie is on her way to Colorado. Steve is going to pick her up. Somehow, her staying with me brought them back together. Fine lady, I wish her well.

Friday: Showtime! The buffalo birthday tomorrow. Cleaning up the grounds—putting all the things away—set up an additional cook stove behind the washroom. Band's equipment is already here. Susie made a big chocolate cake in the shape of a buffalo. Camille made onion rolls and bread; Louisa, potato salad. Treasury bought watermelons and salad greens.

Jody, Margie, Stella, and a brother Tom here from Colorado with a half-

Fig. 10. Looking to the western fields through the arch. Photo by Clarice Kopecky.

ton flatbed truck. Chuck and Ian bought three turkeys to be cooked tomorrow. Beans are ready to be cooked.

New Buffalo is looking very good. Every room is occupied and well kept. The fields green, pastures lush, work areas clean and tools all put away. Twenty-nine of us all together here; a small commune; only people that we are close with—a very good sign. People should be pleased tomorrow to see the Buffalo family.

I got a letter from my mother saying she is happy that I persuaded her to come for a visit; July 24 she will arrive.

Saturday: Tucker cleaning the circle, outhouse, and raking the front yard. Davison has the band truck set up and the driveway blocked to keep cars below the house. I washed some dishes—lots of ladies cooking. There's yogurt for breakfast.

Sunday: Sky completely clear—moon almost full. Buffalo had a fantastic party; about 300 people in the Circle, singing happy birthday to New Buffalo. Bar set up in the work shed: three kegs of beer, crock of electric punch, bottles of wine. Plenty of grass passing around.

Three bands playing on the roof. People gyrating, flowing—courtyard full of dancing freaks. All the cars are parked below the big cottonwood tree in the lower pasture, just like a little festival. At dark the equipment was packed, and the drums played until dawn. Inside the circle, Wendell, on electric bass, and two excellent guitar players, got it on for many hours, creating the finest music. I was persuaded to go to bed before dawn and feel clear and fine today.

This is written in a most unfeeling manner. The party was more than just a "gyrating, flowing courtyard of dancing freaks." It was a celebration of the success of an idea. There is good family love here—sometimes it is totally diffused, but at a scene like last night, the Buffalos had so much love from each other that it grew and engulfed all the 300 people in our home. Sometimes it's so good it's unreal; sometimes it's so real. I'm a cancer; I can only feel, Arty thinks. At least he has good thoughts.—Camille

Sunday: This morning Paul and Susie bottled the beer. Place was easily cleaned up and right back to quiet. Ian brought squash bread for French toast breakfast. Many strong and beautiful people here: a few blacks, some young Chicano brothers and sisters and a few rowdy brothers from Ojo Sarco.

Monday morning: Back to work after potatoes and coffee. Max still low but walking slowly around. Joe mixing mud for Kathleen, Susie, and Angela to finish the tower and circle mudding. Construction crew at the chicken house. I'm going to the mountains.

Tuesday: I got back early this afternoon; came in the back way. Buffalo was completely still. Good journey. I left on foot using the hunter's trot; traveled for eight hours before I lay down for the night in a pine meadow on the slopes over looking Taos County. Coming back, I went south, found the Rio Hondo, and followed it into the town.

The chicken house has walls. The tower almost completely finished. I worked on one boat of mud until supper.

Davison returned from Colorado with both daughters, Syna and Chamisa. Kiva staying in the pit house with Carol. Zip still in a California jail.

Wednesday afternoon: Sun is pretty hot but cool inside to do work. Main building is finished being mudded; a slip coat of mud should seal up the cracks. This mudding we can do. Old way good way. Basically grab a handful with the straw and some sand mixed in, and slap it on the wall. Next smooth

Fig. 11. Chamisa and Syna. From the personal collection of Chamisa WeinMeister.

it out a bit. To keep the clothes clean, it's best to take them off.

Tomorrow the vigas go on the chicken coop. Beans and squash have been killed off in the night cold—not hearty enough. This morning Ray had fruit for everyone and just now brought in some ice cream and cookies.

Camille and Kathleen left for California and Oregon. Though Camille has a car, they hitchhiked! Camille is one of the "heavies" in the kitchen. She has a good, positive attitude, and now she's gone. Freako will probably be very well behaved. Omar, his dad, will take main responsibility for him.

Thursday: Morningstar brothers and sisters here earlier including Judy, an exceptional lady that is sometimes with Fidel Eddie. Someone was saying that eight Spanish guys gave them some hassle at the hot springs. Bill and Al next

Fig. 12. Children playing at the water faucet. Photo by Clarice Kopecky.

door say a dude who has been hanging out there raped a girl guest of theirs.

Louisa has four Sweet Williams blooming, purple and red. *Angela worked very hard all day making candles; Arty, as usual, slept until noon, then went and played hopscotch by the river.*—Written by Louisa.

Saturday morning: Wood: I don't even see where we're going to get wood for this winter, to say nothing of five years from now. Should we all sleep together around one fire in the winter? Get used to cold.

Nico and Chamisa are making a big noise; Kachina getting a bit into it. Mick just retrieved the mail from the post office; he gets the mail and takes care of 30 chickens for a main occupation. Joe is working in the garden that seems everyday to have less growing in it.

Saturday evening: Some classical music, Mozart, playing in the kitchen. Light dinner.

Heavy left little Eddy here for a few days; Angela is first in charge. Heavy drove away and Eddy looked at him and then turned around and started running around. Good boy.

Sunday: Clouded early today. Several groups of visitors pass quietly through. I went into the clinic. After four hours waiting, got some tetracycline for an infection—son-of-a-bitch. I first noticed it a week ago, when I crossed the hot lands to the mountains.

I was just down at the Rio Hondo for a little refresher. I hear Pepe is on his way to Oregon in Dr. Richard's Mercedes.

July 4, 1972: Joe has been a bit ill and is fasting. Still, he's out in the garden in the rain. I am very pleased to be in a storm. Odd type—lots of thunder, lightening, dark clouds and once in a while, drizzle.

The garden—blah! I guess we tried to do too much for such amateurs. Should have planted a quarter of the area we did, with the manure and soil we collected. I, myself, was too caught up in taking out rocks. Just children playing. We planted beans and corn too late. Middle of May is good, not the first week in June.

Fireworks and crackers at night. Happy birthday USA!

Wednesday: Sun in the morning—more storm and real rain in the afternoon. Icon and a lady friend arrived last night. Icon I know from our commune in Bolinas.

I did some roof repairs, so we wouldn't have a repeat of yesterday's flood. For about fifteen minutes, we had a terrific downpour. Pantry, circle, and several rooms flooded.

JOURNAL FIVE

Like a mirage, the white teepee, pitched right in the courtyard, glowed in the heart of the pueblo from its fire; the drum beat all night long.

July 5, 1972: Stars are out. "Heavenly Father, let me accomplish the tasks I set before myself." A good way, I believe. I have my health. What must I do in return? Be disciplined. In time will come joy. "Thank you for whatever that I have, this sure knowledge of what I must do." I am pleased with the setting, the people, the land, and houses. I look within myself and when I can do more, then my life will change some more again, and the communes in which I live will be at that much higher a level. "Bless my mind that I may write humorously—tell the tale well—so people can know the magic and can taste our life together."

Louisa and I went down to the river. She was cleaning and cooking, as she often does so quietly. Kiva said to her, "I see you're becoming one of the heavies in the kitchen."

Louisa and Angela are two of the foxiest young ladies one might meet anywhere. Their heads are not into the city, but help us live together in the country.

Heavy and Sylvia came today and took Eddy away, the baby who wakes up in the morning with a smile.

The circle has many guests in it: Rick, Icon, Blithe, and an Indian man named Martin, a tall thin Cheyenne. Many people pass through; only perhaps half stay any time at all. The state police were here inquiring about some runaways.

Late-night poker game at Paul's with Ian and Omar—the Egyptian Vice Lords.

Friday night: It rained again this afternoon. I finished my moccasins and did a little work with the peas in the garden. Police here again with warrants to search for two runaways from Texas. We are friendly, and they are usually courteous. Morningstar got raided but no one arrested. We have now confiscated our greenhouse plants.

Monday: Ian and Madeleine took the kids to a circus. Davison scored a stove for me.

Many people came by yesterday: Ten vehicles out front including a school bus. I played the guitar and we had a party. See if I can get something done this week.

Joe cleaned the outhouse. Louisa did some work in the greenhouse. Angela is in the kitchen cooking for us. Max typing and Ray sighting Ian's .22 rifle. Neil cut wood for the kitchen and then split.

Tuesday: Yesterday we mudded almost the entire face of the west wing. In the afternoon, Irish and a brother Roger appeared! They had been in Colorado at the Rainbow gathering. Irish is a great worker for the people from the Crow Farm family, One World Family, and the Bahá'í Tribe faith. He is a strong man, a true master of yoga. In addition, there are two long-hair fellows from Tucson and two chicks in a foreign-made station wagon. Arriving a little later is a hitchhiking young lady from Colorado; Pearl is her name. She has pitched a tent and would like to stay a bit. Excellent. Also here, a long-hair fellow from a commune near Mexico City.

Wednesday morning: And here is our wonderful Camille, back through some cosmological connection. Who brought her back? Pepe in Doctor Richard's Mercedes Benz! Pepe met Camille at the Oregon Pleasure Faire. Before returning, they visited Crow Farm. Curly, Pauly, Mike, James, and Mary Chaplain are there. They are still doing forestry work and had a pony ride at the Faire.

Pepe and I went down swimming in the Rio Grande. Pepe has such great energy; we are closer than ever. He plans to set up a silver workshop here in the candle room. Great! I am glad to hear of Crow Farm and my people in Oregon. Willy Chaplain is going to have a book published in Canada.

Rudy from Switzerland is here.

Thursday: Much happens in this world. At present, the Democratic Convention 1972 is occurring. In the city of Miami, our representative in Florida is in jail. That's Zip—$5,000 bail. Here, at the end of the day, a really fine bare-skinned, blond-haired lady helped us finish mudding the west wing.

Quite a sight, a colorful caravan headed by Bob Reynolds, a magic friend of ours from Oregon, pulled in our yard with eleven vehicles, including four school buses! They were at the incredible Rainbow gathering in the mountains. Pepe is the perfect host and master to greet these wonderful brothers and sisters. With Buffalo and the Medicine Show, we are over 50 people. There's a fire in the courtyard and lots of handsome people, music, storytelling, wine, acid, and grass. I saw a pound of hashish today, lots of fruit and hydrox cookies. Now it is very quiet, a hypnotic story being told. With Bob Reynolds is Michael, whom I know from Tuck Tucker and Hungry Hill and the Church of the Creative in Oregon. I tell Bob, "Let's get Pepe to do some new paintings on the bus."

The red truck blew something on the way to Albuquerque. With Paul driving, they limped back. If you're going to drive a lot, you're going to throw a rod once in a while. With some eleven vehicles here and perhaps twenty cars up the driveway everyday, we are lucky things work as well as they do.

Friday: Camille is terrific. *I love you!* She is often the very first up and in the kitchen. This morning she's fixing pancakes for us. By the time I was back from the river, the grinder was working to make bread, the floor clean, every counter completely clear. And here at the house is good friend Harvest Moon.

Saturday morning: Quite hot yesterday. During the night, about 3 a.m., we were called out to a forest fire. Neil, Chuck, Mick, and I went, driven by Ian. They wouldn't take me because of my long hair. The other guys got to go.

Susie scored some bread from her aunt, and with it Paul bought a pickup. Paul has been driving everyday since he got it. Now it seems he's split with the truck but without Susie.

Harvest and I went to Taos to sell candles. Harvest used to live with us in Bolinas. He's a very bright kid, full of energy, and like Pepe, he always has trade items.

Most people are at a party at Lama Mountain for Bill Gersh. Harvest came home and made 17 of his mushroom candles. A great storm came up at dinnertime; rain, lightening and thunder all around us. A young lady asleep in the candle room. I am going to look after Chamisa and Syna, since Dave is not here.

Down at the silver bridge today, three cars full of drunken Chicanos drove into the swarm of hippie vehicles and got rowdy and rather un-gentlemanly with some naked ladies. Several fights ensued. Steve, who came with Margie, was right in there and succeeded in clearing out a number of the vehicles and settling things down.

Tom from next door was over here, cursing and swearing at Buffalo; slammed out doors and was pissed at not having been woken last night and brought to the fire. Cursing and swearing, he walked into Pepe, who with a well-placed blow, instantly cooled out the situation.

Many people came after dark. Martin—tall Indian from Oklahoma— brought us some peyote. Martin Fingernail has made some tapes to record the Cheyenne language. He is one of the very few speakers left.

Joe cooked excellent cornbread muffins. Many people sitting around the table. It continues to rain and blow. I love the rain. It's cozy here, sheltered in the earth with our broad family.

Tuesday afternoon: Ray and I just returned from the mountains. Carol is working in the kitchen. Fellows got back from firefighting—made $125.

As Ray and I were leaving Sunday morning, Psychedelic John joined us. We shared our food, water, and bedding with him; he shared his hash with us. Going cross-country, he set a really good pace. We reached the peak we were headed for by noon the next day.

Zip is freed and returned. Also here is Jody, la bonita cowgirl from Texas. She wants Pepe.

Wednesday: Pepe and Martin made a traditional sweat bath this afternoon— very cleansing. Angela mudding the inside of her room.

It seems Jody has got her man. Carol is rather broken-hearted. "I hate to see them around being love birds." So perhaps they will go—not imme- diately, though.

Thursday morning: Very overcast. Ian, Tucker, Chuck, Gerard, and Mick are building the roof on the chicken house.

Neil Redwing, Michael, and I got the scene together and started bricking the rest of the washroom floor. This is to be a fairly large room with hot water, floor drain, shower, and washing machine. In the overall design of the building it is beyond the kitchen in the Northern ray of the Zia (the sun symbol) emanating from the great circle room, which is the center.

Max announces he is completely recovered. He was washing dishes today. Camille and Ray dipping 27 hangers of eight candles each.

At least six guests here at dinner for a terrific meal prepared by Camille. In addition, my mother comes Monday! I am nervous.

Friday evening: Ray, Louisa, and I sitting in the candlelight, drinking peyote tea. I gave Carol a big hug; it's not easy being in love with Pepe. She's a strong woman, but she'd rather be treated like a princess.

Ian finished an extra fine set of blocks, 40 pieces, in many shapes. He has made several window frames, doorframes, and several boxes since he has been here. This looks like his finest work.

Neil and Ray went out running around on some scam. Camille, somehow, just let her car go. I heard Neil screeching in the front yard, Ray riding shotgun. Now it seems the car must be bump started. It broke in the very busiest part of Taos. After gliding out of the 7-11, the car stalled. Arlene and two girlfriends from San Francisco were right behind. They tried to push. Right soon the police arrived, of course, and asked for a driver's license. Neil, of course, doesn't have it. They try to search the back seat, but the back doors never work. So, they tell Ray to drive and they go on their way.

Today, fellow Reggie from the Sunny Valley Tribe in Oregon and Neil Redwing were working with me on the bricking. Redwing was perfectly capable of doing his share even with only one arm. Anyhow, a story developed where Redwing once got drunk, then got into a negative situation at a bar. A woman and a .38 pistol were involved, and also a friend of Paul's, who finally carried Redwing, with Max and Neil, to his car. They put him in it and after more of the same, "Are you man enough to make me" bullshit, got him to drive away. Also involved was a raid on the police station where Redwing wanted to find solace or protection. Finding no one on duty, he stole a typewriter and left. Who can believe all this? He has now returned here, where people are feeling fine.

Four or five people from South Carolina visiting. We invited them to join us at dinner. All the Buffalo crowd, plus Pepe and Jody, Reggie, Omar, Nico, and Ian are here.

Louisa and Camille worked in the kitchen again. They are a great pleasure to be with.

And Louisa, I must say, is just something else. This lady to me is a sure turn-on. I guess I take it a bit for granted that she's around here so much, gracing this house. A very good thing in my life to be a person she really likes.

Joe is bedridden with a headache. He is very independent from the rest of us. I would not even know he is ill but that Louisa tells me. She knows him and pays attention to him and does just what a person should do, I guess, who loves someone.

Also here is a young black brother named Chicken. He plays the four-string banjo. I'd like to learn some songs from him.

July 24, 1972: *Last night, The Oriental Blue Streaks played a good set and it seemed that everyone really got it on. Arty is probably on his way here after meeting his mother at the airport. Looking forward to the surprises?*

Fifteen or so people for breakfast. Mick, Reggie, and I did a little work on the new chicken coop. Other than that, it is a very quiet and lazy day. I am thankful for the family here at New Buffalo and Mother Earth upon which we carry on. May I be humble within her womb.

Yesterday was Chamisa's birthday. Chocolate cupcakes and ice cream fit the bill. A few visitors from Fable Mountain commune in Northern California also here, staying in a teepee outside our fence line—very nice people.

Now the sun is at rest and love is all around. Well, there's no time like the present to take a toke—so if you will joint* me.

Arty and his Mom, who is very radiant, arrived before dinner. Martin just by, bringing good vibes from the medicine magic.—Writer unknown.

Tuesday—Fiesta day in Taos: Back safe and sound with Clarice. My mom, 65 years old, always liked to travel to see new places. She is staying in Louisa's room. I took Pepe's Mercedes (Dr. Richard's, actually) to go pick her up—such style—nice ride; Louisa went with me. In the morning we bought wax. It took half an hour to get the car started at the Oil Depot, but got to the airport in time. Had to push the car with mom inside and Louisa driving to get started again. Back at Buffalo with a few more pushes. After fine beans and tortilla dinner, we smoked some hash. My mother started hanging out right away with the crowd. No smoking for her, though!

Louisa and I made love last night. She is so fine. Up pretty early, feeling great. Of my mom, "She's always smiling," says Neil.

Leadville Mick and Michael went to Questa and scored 23 laying chickens and a rooster. Tahiti turned us on to them.—Mick.

*Joint is a pun on join.

Fig. 13. Clarice Kopecky.

Clarice is up early with the rest of us. She and I went visiting at Rocky's mountain log cabin where Pepe and Jody are staying. It looks like a museum. A beautiful place—very high consciousness.

Back at Buffalo, I turn mechanic. The treasury has been handed to me for my care in the amount of $163. It is almost a year-and-a-half since we left Bolinas, and now I am a commune treasurer again.

My mother sits with Susie and Carol in Paul's room and sews with them. Now she's in the kitchen with the ladies who are preparing lunch. Last night she joined us for our party. "Pass the wine," I heard her yell from behind half a dozen gyrating bodies. It is odd to hear my mother's voice among the others here at New Buffalo.

Clarice was very active with the civil rights movement. She and my Dad Joe loved to entertain friends for an evening of world politics discussion. So she has a strong spirit herself; but she doesn't like the six-seater outhouse!

Friday morning: Chuck is ill; too much drinking and tobacco. He has moved into what was Madeleine's room. Neil is still into his own thing; running around and not into any projects here. Paul considers himself out, I guess. The last thing he was into was the construction of the archway. Since Paul has stopped working on projects, his good partner Tucker has slowed down. He did clean the front yard yesterday.

Angela does weaving almost every day. She is baking today and was weeding in the garden early. She re-mudded and then painted her room, which looks excellent. She is very beautiful with her intense dark eyes.

My mother is having an excellent time. Plans to cook on Sunday. She bought ice cream last night for us all. "But I do like a hand bowl of popcorn once in awhile," says Louisa feeling better. She got dressed before Circle and her popcorn craving has returned.

I started work on the red truck yesterday—took off oil pan and valve cover. Newly appearing Jerry, our oddball brother from the California coast, worked with me.

Monday morning: *Saturday night, a medicine meeting took place on Lama Mountain. I was fortunate enough to have a place within the Lodge—Praise the Lord! I prayed for this place and the people. I feel as though I received many blessings. I pray now for a meeting here.*

Quiet today except for the usual kitchen scene—French toast. Flies! And, I don't mean 1 or 2. Seems to be a major problem and probable cause of sickness. I hope we find a solution—definitely a situation for communal action. How together are we? Arty and Michael off to Albuquerque. After a fine visit, Arty's Mom is returning home today., She really liked the people.— writer unknown

Wednesday morning. Ian and Paul Rotman putting the giant loom together in Camille's room. Reggy and Gerard mudding the chicken house roof. Max and I talked to Felipe Cordova at the Mariposa Ranch. About one week and he'll have his harvest in. We'll get our seed from him. Talked to Leo Vigil. He'll send his son over with their tractor. We must cut the weeds down on the fields we want plowed.

And on the other hand, we have Chuck sick with some disease. He passed out in the kitchen last night from drinking. Next he takes Mick's car to visit a girlfriend.

Tucker practices guitar, Neil trips off to town, Kay and Chicken are back. They also are into nothing around here. We've had several visitors, including Phyllis, who stays with Ian.

Thursday: I feel very good. Señor Vigil came over this morning. Said we could help him on a demolition job, and he would plow in return. Reggy, Gerard, and I went and finished the job for him—worked hard all day. Donald, who arrived yesterday on his Harley, gave us some help. We work because it is a commune job, and we work for the commune—great trust, faith, and spirit. Gerard, Reggy, and Ian are all strong, experienced men. This is what I like, working with these people. Brother Jim, from Colorado, has arrived.

Paul and Neil have left. Neil said a prayer for their journey and some words for New Buffalo, which has given him a good home. Many somewhat open households are hesitant to call their place a commune. Ask Neil and he'll tell you, "Yes, this is a commune." It makes me feel good now to think of him.

Our little wild chicken showed us her new generation; she hatched 9 baby chickens. Out of Sight! Our new chicken house is coming along, really right-on! Gerard and Michael staked fence posts today, and we should be able to start mudding this next week. We have enough scrap wood to build nest boxes and roosts.—Mick

Ray colored some candles, which I sold in town and made $30. Cerrafin came over this evening to see what fields we wanted to work. Wonderfully quiet here. *I like Arty Kopecky.** With Paul gone, I was given charge of the New Buffalo records and papers. Max doesn't want them. Total in treasury—$15.

Monday night: For the first time since I have known her at Webster Street in Berkeley, Carol has a place just her own. She has moved into the room once occupied by Paul and Susie. I built up Kachina's crib today so she can be contained somewhere. She can wreck the commune before anyone is up.

Got a letter from my mom. She feels that I have chosen a hard but a good life. Her mind is completely over the fear she had that I was destroying myself.

Tuesday evening: Banjo and guitar playing in the kitchen. Larry Reed, Chicken, and two visiting buses with a bunch of people are here. Chuck got drunk this afternoon in preparation for cooking, which he is now engrossed in—pork chops a la Perez. Some of us with a visiting Frenchman laid the

* Interjection by an unknown writer.

Fig. 14. Louisa, Arty, and Angela in Taos.
Photo by Clarice Kopecky.

second course on the chicken house. Cerrafin was here and we dragged the field that had bad weeds.

Pepe urges me to join him and do silver work. His business and tools are growing. He and Jody are staying here. Says he'll get the Bird truck together. It definitely should not be left lame.

Wednesday: Big storm in the mountains today. Gerard and I finished the last course of bricks, and Joe started mudding the coop. I took the axle out of the Power wagon rear wheel, replaced the gaskets and tightened it down. I hope it seals. Max says I have to work on the red truck starting Monday. I can take breaks to help mix mud for the south wing. OK.

Louisa got me to go down to the river and she washed my hair. Under the starlit night, we slept out in the bushes.

Saturday: Completely clear sky this morning, once again—no need for a fire. Paula, Sierra Nanda, and new baby arrived last evening with another couple from Minnesota. Paula was influential in levitating our Bird truck (the Mind Machine) here. She's quite an adventurer.

The neighbor's dogs attacked the goatherd last evening. One was the same dog that killed Rudy's young goat one month ago. Dogs are a big problem for the livestock all over. We've been receiving about two quarts a day from each of two goats—Camille and Kathleen in charge.

Friday: Tucker and Max both spent all their earnings at the Ol' Martinez Hall dance the other night. I learned this when we sat around the kitchen table this evening over a bottle of Tokay wine. Max and Tucker feel that if Pepe takes the Mind Machine, he should give the commune $100.

Sunday: A bus headed around the world from Santa Fe is camped nearby. They gave us about seven cases of fruit. Carol is busy now preparing pies and applesauce.

Donald and I put two truckloads of dirt and gravel on the Buffalo road. After a swim, Angela and I went up to Morningstar just in time for dinner. They have a common meal on Sundays, and I have been frequently invited. They have three fine-looking goats, lots of kids and young people. Very funky scene though, with many dogs and no water. The structures are dilapidated though still somewhat tight. Some have really fine designs.

Peach pie back at Buffalo. Some guys off to look at an engine. Mick working on the chicken coop.

Tuesday morning: I gave Angela $30 from the treasury to have the grinder and sewing machine fixed. The crankshaft of the red truck engine is scored; we need a new engine. There is one for $150.

I spoke with Leo Vigil. All along, I knew that plowing would not be enough. Here is the procedure, as I now understand it. First plow and then flatten the ground and break the clods with a tool called a "jida." Then spread the seed and go over again with the jida. Leo and son will be glad to see our operation through, but would like some more help on his demolition job. "Certainly," I said.

There is a couple, Anton and Lynn, who asked to stay. I responded that yes, there was work here they could do, and as far as I was concerned, their help would be appreciated.

Our brother Donald, who arrived a week ago, is a good man. He came in riding a Harley Davidson Superglide 1970 vintage motorcycle. He is 21, from Eugene, and is experienced in many skills and several small businesses. He knows all the Crow Farm brothers. He likes it here. Today, we took the engine out of the red truck. We pulled the engine toward the roof beams of the barn,

Fig. 15. Gerard and Ian at work on chicken house roof.
Photo by Clarice Kopecky.

pushed the truck back, and lowered the engine into a wheelbarrow.

This evening Ian and I, plus two visiting German brothers, went and bought for $125 and one super candle, a 1957 Ford engine. It came out of a ³/₄-ton pickup that was in a bad accident but did not get hurt—we hope. We have a sort of 30-day guarantee. Jackie sold it. His father checked it. Chuck, friend of El Prado Johnny, turned us on to the deal. Is this complicated or what?

Party last night. Most every one got stoned.

Thursday: Great storm clouds but only rained for about five minutes. We worked hard yesterday. Tucker joined Donald working on the engine. Ian and Gerard worked half the day putting dirt on the chicken house roof. I got some mudding going. Herman and Case from Germany, Andy from Holland, and Harold from Scotland did most of the work. Anton from France, and the little lady with him, Lynn, mudded too. Camille made pizzas for everyone.

A new day: A friend, who is in some priesthood, showed with a new model Mercedes. Perhaps six other guests here for an exquisitely fine meal: great big salad, egg foo yung, more cake and ice cream than the people could eat. Sequoia is here. Five ladies he traveled with are expected later. Sequoia is very handsome, blond, and sort of flamboyant with his deerskin jacket. All kinds of beer, wine, and grass. Very mellow.

Monday night: Don and I put another full day in on the truck, and we got it running nicely. Ian and Chuck worked on the front gate. We scored neighbor Leo's rake from O. G. Martinez and it is here ready to be worked. Michael has three friends visiting. Spanish Alexa is here.

Tuesday: Michael and friends are mudding, Chuck cutting wood, Tucker and I raked the lower field, which is ready to be plowed. Some brothers here this morning tell us about a people's school that is being organized in Arroyo Hondo. They want to exchange some labor for the use of the red truck.

Wednesday: K. C., Kay, another brother and his girl Michelle, drove up on their Harleys. All work stopped about an hour after it started; now a beer scene in the kitchen. We harvested two big stacks of weeds. They must be removed or they clog the plows.

About 40 here for dinner last night. That does bring me down a bit when so many show up right when we are going to eat. And it does affect me a bit, too, to be in such a lay-about scene. For myself, I will increase my ability and strength. It is good that I am feeling so close with Louisa.

We have another semi-wild chicken sitting on 10 eggs in the tool shed. Our first hen hatched 9 eggs and she has 7 chicks left. Pretty good percentage.—Mick

Thursday night: Yesterday was absolutely clear. Today it clouded over, and at night it rained for an hour. Very good. Yesterday we went on a wood run. Dinner was served around 4 p.m. to avoid the evening rush of visitors.

Today I drove the red truck into the mountains between here and Mora and worked with Nick and his crew of eight people from his compound in Arroyo Hondo. There he has an outstanding pottery shop, and there it is proposed the neighborhood friends start their own school. We lent a hand and did a viga run. We went to a surreal forest, over 10,000 feet up, much of which was downed by fire, I guess. Even the immense areas of felled trees had a beauty, like a giant's game of pickup sticks with immense gray tree trucks. Much of these woods have been down for at least ten years. I was in much rain today. I like it.

Fig. 16. Nick at work. Photo by Clarice Kopecky.

I went for a dip under the clouds, a million miles from the asphalt of New York.

Saturday morning: The sky is completely overcast—quiet and wet—mists rising off the mountains. I was to the river and then played with Louisa all morning. Little Kachina got us up very early.

Last night, meat loaf, potatoes and corn for dinner, with just family and a few friends. We like that. All stayed dry in our mud houses hidden in the dark rainy night. Late, a drunk Chicano drove up and ended up in Camille's room. Her yelling woke Ian, who yelled too and got rid of the character. Second time in a few days this has happened.

Next full moon is the time we came here a year ago. I am wondering these days whether I should quit at one year or go for two.

Cerrafin came today and dragged the field. We spread 200 pounds of wheat seed on the field below us, walking and throwing seed as people have done for 10,000 years. Cerrafin, in the evening, dragged the field again to bury the seed.

Ian is building doors and windows for the chicken coop.

Sunday morning: Gray sky with little sun. Ray here and Kemal, Kathleen, Sundance, Angela, Ricky, Genie, Chuck, Sandy, little Jason, Lorraine, Alan, Gerard, Max, Carol, Kachina, and Camille with Nico. Also in the Circle, me, Omar, Davison, Chamisa, Louisa, Michael, Mick and Sequoia with a fine little lady, people from Ledoux, some unknowns, and Ian. A phonograph is playing in the background.

Monday morning: I went to Lama yesterday. Ended up climbing the mountain right to the top, in the fog, drizzle, and rain picking mushrooms. Ray and I ran almost all the way from Lama to Hondo in the rain to get back. Feeling fine.

Ian took son Freddy to the DaNahazli School in Taos this morning. Plans to do it every day! He'll pick up more seed. Rained well—perfect for our fields.

Leo was here this morning to see when we would have the seed on the other field. He wants us to work on the floor of the building he is wrecking. We can have some lumber. Good. We wanted to work with Leo a little more for helping us out so well.

Dave Gordon says he is leaving this week. He has been hanging out here for nearly two months now, since he decided he was not going to live at Buffalo. Never even finished his plumbing project.

A trip to San Francisco and Oregon is proposed with Ian and van starting on Saturday. Perhaps Louisa and I will go along.

Wednesday: Rained hard yesterday. A group worked on Leo's destruction project. We got two truckloads of wood, plus Leo got a load.

Ray made two new candle wheels this morning, both work nicely. Then he and Joe went to town; they are concerned about the food and have gone shopping again.

High energy recently. Camille, Angela, and Davison left today. I miss them already.

Harvest making candles. Paul and I put a load of gravel on a bad section of our road. Mick is cooking chicken dinner.

Friday morning: Spectacular sun in partly cloudy sky. Great clouds on the mountains.

Sandy—tall and thin—and her three-year-old son Jason, moved here yesterday. Some of the ladies asked her if she wanted to live here. She is now up early, making pancakes. See, Buffalo is all right. A few girls move out and right away, Sandy moves in, cooks us good pancakes and is going shopping today with Carol.

Louisa was burned from the pressure-cooker cracking two days ago. Yesterday she was back to being fine.

Late afternoon: Joe and Harvest finishing up candles. Gerard cutting wood. Max and Carol cleaning the kitchen. Sandy cleaning the circle. $25 in the treasury. I'm leaving the journal here.

September 2, 1972: *Ian, Freddy Louisa, Arty, and Don all left for California today. I, Mick, am taking over the journal for now. Chuck, Ray, Joe, and Harvest went to Boulder to see the Grateful Dead. Tucker, Michael, and Gerard finished mudding the well house, while Kim, Paul, and I finished the chicken coop. The chickens will move in tonight!*

Sept. 3: *Party here last night. Max cooked a Chinese pork and rice dish, and Sandy cooked broccoli. We also had martinis before dinner, Tokay and music after dinner—groovy time. Saw Heavy and Sylvia who want to move back. General opinion is no. Had stuffed cabbage here for dinner, cooked by Sandy. A beautiful lady, we're lucky to have her here with us. Angela and Kathleen are back. About ten people in the circle crashed out. A lot of fun tonight. Beautiful lady Shirley and her kids are staying in Ian's room until he gets back. Then what happens?*

Sept. 4: *Great day full of energy! A group of us tore down the old chicken coop completely, and put up the retaining walls on the south wing with the bricks from the chicken coop. The old coop looks as if a missile or something hit it. Acid John is back! What with all the space cadets we have had here, we now have the uncrowned king of them all.*

Sept. 5: *Chuck, Tucker, Gerard, and Charge, a dude who wants to stay here, made a wood run. A lot of good piñon was gotten.*

Big party. Pepe here. A case of beer, five or more bottles of Tokay and a lot of grass, watermelon, and pizza in the kitchen. Kiva gave me a dashiki (for my birthday, today).

Kathleen's dog has been fighting the other dog the last three days, and Max and Tucker are unofficially telling Kathleen either the dog goes or she goes. If she goes, surely I will miss her. I really dig her.

Rather worried about Joe. He has not been relating to anyone here but Acid John. He is getting to be more of a recluse every day. I will talk to him about it soon.

Sept. 7: *Chuck's birthday! Tonight is the night of the new moon. Virgo at that. Gerard, Chuck, Michael, and Kim made a fantastic dinner of spare ribs, beans, and potato salad. Angela made some delicious sweet potato pie. A boat of mud was mixed today and Louisa's room was partially done. Max also fixed the outhouse roof. I passed the Gold Star off to Chuck. It seems Gerard has found a lady, Shirley. Good luck, bro and sis. Morningstar people down for a small get together for Chuck.*

Tom Brown, from Morningstar got drunk here last night and lost a .45 pistol he bought in Santa Fe. Chuck got a half-gallon of Tokay and he and Tom got outrageous.

9-08-72: *Ham and eggs for breakfast. Ray and Harvest are back. Joe up at Lama. When he comes back, all the Space Cadets will be united! Gerard left for California today. He and Shirley had a good fight last night; he decided it was time to travel. Good luck and God bless you wherever you go, Gerard. Kathleen and Angela got a good, pregnant goat from a lady in Costello. Max and Carol had a falling out but it seems that things are better. Groovy! Wood run planned for tomorrow. Also, a Jewish feast is planned.*

When I woke up this morning, it was raining and cold. We may have our first big frost tonight.

9-09: *Today is Rosh Hashanah, the Jewish New Year-5724. The Jews outdate us Christians by over three thousand years. We had one fantastic dinner with turkey, chopped liver, bread, and many other groovy things. Angela primarily made dinner for everyone, with all the other Jewish people helping her. Max said the prayer at Circle, and we all got stoned and OD'd on the food and the booze. Everyone a the Kaplan's, except Judy, came over and we really had mellow music. Big dance Monday night!*

9-10: *Quiet, sunshine day, very slow and lazy. Kathleen is still pissed off at the men here and left because we don't live up to her high standards of chivalry. We're not knights in armor, we're just human beings. Angela did some more weaving, while Carol cooked turkey stew from leftovers. Harvest Moon left today. Sequoia is staying in Camille's old room for a while. We have $2 in the treasury.*

9-11-72: *Big dance tonight in town. The moon is in Scorpio and the vibes at the dance were weird. The band didn't have that pizzazz. There was a fight. Tucker and Dave Gordon were roughed up and Nan, from the Rim, got a black* eye. We all came home and ate cornflakes and white sugar that Carol had stashed.

9-12-72: *Today was spent in recovering; just about everyone was hung over and moving slowly. Angela did some more of her weaving and Kathleen from Lama came down to see us. She is thinking of moving here for the winter. Quiet night.*

Toby came back! Chuck, Max, and Angela told him he could not stay longer than tonight, because he puts people into too much of a head fuck. All the mind spacers have been here for sure: Harvest Moon, Acid John, Ray, Joe, and Toby. It's really been heavy these last two weeks with these guys.

9-13-72: *I got up today, and the sun was shining. Nan and I went to the mountains in the afternoon and tripped out on the changing leaves. We had a really good time and we sealed a friendship. Max went to work on the Bethel (Holy Roller) Church in town.*

9-14-72: *We finished mudding the front of the south wing; Kim, Michael and Tucker mixed five boats of mud; when we quit, we were dead tired. Toby left to go to Morningstar. Sequoia, Angela, visiting friend Iris Keltz, and I took some of the kids to the movies tonight. Chamisa arrived yesterday and is staying with us; I hope she stays longer this time. A good kid. Max cooked a delicious tamale pie dinner tonight.*

9-15-72: *Today was a good day. The sun came up, as usual, and we mudded. Chuck and Tucker mixed the boats. Later, some of us went to the hot springs. Mick ate seven hot chile peppers. Acid John and Joe are leaving for a higher plane.*

Two drunks and a righteous dude gave $40 to the treasury today. I hope Max spends it in a good way. Two pints of whiskey and 1 case of beer was drunk this evening and Kim has the Buffalo Shuffle. The drinking hurts.

9-16-72: *Ray left Buffalo today! He was one of the space cats, but in spite of all this, he was a groovy dude. I for one will miss him. There was a wood run today with Chuck, Tucker, and Sequoia. Sequoia is a good man. He seems to fit right into the picture really well.*

Sunday: *A letter written by Ray: For the past week, I have been working in town. I feel that to continue my work it is better to leave Buffalo. I would like to say, from within my heart, that Buffalo the Family has been a great* blessing to me and I hope that I may always be close to the people here. I love you, everyone and may the Spirit guide and bless you with the answer to your prayers. Peace on the Earth, Goodwill to Men.

9-17-72: *Today was a nice, warm, sunny day and nothing was done whatsoever.*

9-18-72: *I was up at an orientation meeting of the school until the afternoon. I learned a lot from the kids. The school is a very groovy thing that I am sure will work. It is starting to rain tonight. We already have had two frosts, but we need SNOW and lots of it.*

9-19-72: *Donna is planning a party here for her son Buddy, tomorrow. It will be a big one, for sure. I am going to look for another place to live, because I can't live here with the bad vibes and low energy much longer. I don't know where I'll go.*

9-20-72: *Today was Buddy's birthday and Morningstar came over to help celebrate. It was mainly a drunken orgy—a boozing "party." I NEED a vacation for a while. Texas will look really sweet.*

9-21-72: *Dave and the band came over and Chuck took them on a wood run. The weather has changed. And, Arty, Louisa, Freddy, and Ian came back today! I'll return the journal to Arty tomorrow. It has been good recording the Buffalo family's happenings.*

Who is here at New Buffalo now? Ian and Freddy, Sequoia in Camille's room, Tucker, Arty in the candle room, Sandy and Jason, Carol and Kachina, Kim, Angela, Chuck and Max, Mick, Kathleen, Louisa, and Michael in the pit house. All family.

September 23: Absolutely clear blue sky—very pleasant weather. AnSwei back again. We were away three weeks. The commune is super. No vehicles out front. I know all the people here. Buddy and a friend rode up on two horses. The chickens are in their new house. Dirt being put on the roofs and the outhouse being mudded and re-roofed. Kitchen and circle are very clean, and there is plenty of food. One field of wheat is coming up. We have a big stack of wood. We still have a supply of candles. Kachina is running now instead of walking. Angela left to New York to earn a few bucks and then split for South America.

Louisa and I stayed together for the entire trip. We spent a little time in California, Oregon, and Washington. We did about four or five hundred miles of hitchhiking; the rest of the time we traveled with Ian and his van.

Crow Farm was quiet and functioning. They have pigs and about 20 head of cattle, plowed fields and plenty of food in the kitchen. Most of the boys—Curly Jim, Ace, Mike Torgeson, Larry, Gino, Norman Normal, and some others doing a tree-trimming job for BLM. There is talk of selling the farm, all but 50 acres. There is $15,000 or so left to be paid. Such a great effort and enterprise, it is terrible that it hasn't been paid for. What can I do? I gave them a few candles and some music. I could give my presence and labor, but I am staying at New Buffalo.

In Bolinas, my boat-building brothers are hard at work. They have a variety of band saws that run off a generator. A forge is set up for making all their hardware. From forest trees to boat, all through their skill and effort, Fisherman Dan, Michael, Hal Chase, Sherry, Bonnie, and a fellow Richard are the crew. Here is another family and work I could be part of.

The Good Earth commune is doing well in San Francisco. Tolstoi Farm in Washington doing well with 100 people, I heard. Wheeler's Ranch in Northern California, after years of incredible activity, is closed to traffic now.

Pepe is in Arizona at an Indian gathering. So where do I fit? Right here.

Saturday afternoon: Wind blowing. I know that I want to get higher. I will not always be at this consciousness. Sometimes I don't realize how pressured I am. I don't expect it to let up for years, either. Buffalo is different now; I see much has happened. Everyone is working quite cheerfully. Chuck said a grace last night giving thanks for our return.

Full moon last night. Louisa and I stayed up late and walked on the mesa. I feel good being with these people.

Sunday afternoon: We had a picnic today at Garcia Park at about 11,000 feet in the mountains. Chuck drove us all in the red flatbed truck. Mick stayed home to watch the place. Aspens and scrub oak are turning yellow. The air is exceptional. At the picnic, we elected Carol Egbert to be New Buffalo vice president and Max as secretary treasurer. We have to make an annual report to remain a legitimate corporation. Robbie Gordon remains president. Max has picked up the responsibility for the money handling and seeing the lawyer. These were falling to me before I left—more appropriate in Max's hands.

This is our family—16 people and a good size—I rather like it. Louisa whispers in my ear that she is not entirely happy, though. "What a revolution," says Max; we all agree. We like it.

Unlike most of the other people he started with, Max remains living on communes. At times lost and sometimes unsatisfied, his poetic mind sees the complexities of mankind. At times it weighs on him. As we come into winter, he feels very good. I am pleased to serve with this man, who serves the same cause as I.

Sue Reynoldson was here when we got back, a sister from the Pride family. Sue has a book with her written by a friend, Robert Houriet, *Getting Back Together*. It has a number of pages about New Buffalo three years ago—a pretty good book.

Tuesday afternoon: The sun is very strong, the sky very blue and the earth very dry. After several days of only our immediate family, many people came to Buffalo, which generated into a party. Tall blond Eric here with a British friend. They look like pioneers. Joe Cota and a lady, Anne, came over with some beer. Joe is big and strong and is studying welding. You should hear him play the ragtime piano! Of two straights, one named George Miller said a prayer at our Circle. Looks like a hardworking, tough man. Kathleen returned and Kemal came too and will stay for a while. A couple on a nicely chopped Harley, with extended front end spent the night.

Friends from near Gardner, Colorado are here. They are another little communal family and include Mei Hua, who is Chinese, Tall Paul, Bill Sundance and Jan with little Tinker. Jan was, at one time, Dave Gordon's wife. Lots of wine and beer. I should start brewing again.

Two visitors from France are here this evening.

Friday afternoon: Sunny day. I sent some visitors out and invited them to return this evening. Louisa and I up late last night. I guess I am actually being in love.

Pepe and Jody returned from trading in Arizona; Catalina was with them— such handsome people. Pepe dug some tufa for casting and buffing silver. He brought back some dried peyote and gave me a silver badger's foot for a present. I am so happy to be part of this flowing family.

Saturday afternoon: Absolutely clear sky. Jason and Mary are playing wild donkey on Freddy. Kachina is sitting in the windowsill eating one of my books, and this morning Max won the Gold Star, finally. Max has been doing all the woodcutting. He saved New Buffalo by sending in the corporate form and seeing Ramming, our lawyer, to clear up the latest bureaucratic mess.

Max also is cooking his second tamale pie in one week! This one is for the pie-baking contest tomorrow in Long John's Valley, which we all are going to. Sandy is staying home to guard the fort—milk the goat.

Sequoia made a big banana pie, and Louisa made two carrot cakes. A few of us took some acid. Dylan singing in the kitchen. While we are watching the sunset, Pepe rushes in; he'd just been held up at gunpoint for Rocky's truck! He thumbed a ride out of that spot where, for a few moments, he thought he might die at the hands of three young punks who robbed the king of the gypsies. Pepe rolled some grass and then took some acid.

Sunday: We left in the red truck with Chuck driving. After much travel in the most beautiful part of New Mexico—piñon, cedar forest, and rocky desert—we arrived at Long John's Valley. In the forests we find four or five primitive buildings, a pasture, 22 goats, a few horses, chickens and a lot of people. This settlement is situated right on a river. Razberry is living here. Friends from 7- Room House soon arrive. There are many dishes: Pecan pie, apple pies, cheesecakes, whipped cream pumpkin pie—50 pies, at least, and several hundred wild, funky folks. Great day. Scammed some gas and we were home by 10 p.m.

Louisa is so fine. We made love together.

Wednesday morning: Overcast this morning. Louisa wakes up, smiles, and tells me she loves me. Yesterday she got the Gold Star* for her work in the kitchen; Chuck presented it. A few years ago in high school, Louisa wrote a paper on how she thought communes were good. At 18, she and Joe found their way to New Buffalo and here she is now. Perfectly fine and so pretty, 5'5", about 100 pounds, we have been staying together for over a month now. She calls me "fat Art."

Thursday morning: Clouds covering the mountains and the sky above us, yet it is warm enough to go about naked. Strider, his lady Beara and daughter Diddy arrived last night. Kemal made donuts for breakfast. Tucker up early putting in the chicken house window. Tucker says he'll work on the garden next year and make it grow. Very adamant. That's my purpose here too. We will try to do two gardens next year. Max is mowing the weeds now with a scythe to compost. We'll also grow in the greenhouse.

Saturday morning: Yesterday we had some real rain. Carol cooking an excellent chicken cacciatore. Two runaways from Oklahoma, a boy and a girl about thirteen years old, here for the last two nights. We gave them Angela's room and some blankets.

Monday afternoon: *Fat Art and I went to the hot springs to relieve our bore-*

---

*At some point at New Buffalo, a gold metal star was created to be passed around as a reward and a thank you. It was already in practice before I arrived.

dom, but it did not help. Fat Art will continue this with a lot of high hippie prose, but you, dear reader, and I KNOW BETTER.—Written by Louisa.

Sunday morning the valley was covered in fog. Later there was a football game here between our local Spanish-speaking youth, Hondo Rockets and the El Prado Dogs.

Sequoia and Tucker went hunting. Ian took them up to Colorado to Kemal's pad. I am in charge of Tucker's room while he's away. There is an air of mystery about our handsome brother. He doesn't talk a lot—is completely in the present. He is the opposite of spacey. Tucker has clean sheets on his bed and a perfectly arranged room with three rugs. He is quite exceptional. Always clean-shaven with shoulder-length hair, he has a strong, quiet assurance.

Wednesday: I saw a familiar suitcase in the candle room early this morning. Don arrived hitchhiking, having had to leave his vehicle. He was so overloaded with stuff and tools that he blew the transmission. Here he is, and he and Chuck are fixing the leaking faucet. Hunting expedition back with a hindquarter.

Louisa is a little bored; misses Joe and isn't too happy with all the people here; doesn't feel like family with most. She has a cold, too. Feels she needs something? Go home or where? Whatever may be her other feelings, Louisa is really fine with me. She will feel better, I'm sure. A very bright smile she has.

JOURNAL SIX

I have been wretched and poor—clothes ragged and coat greasy—sleeping on the dirt floor. I have been and I am.

October 12, 1972: Sequoia preparing meat from the hunt. We had a great roast. Pepe, Jody, Catalina and Lee here from Lama Mountain.

Jody fits well with Pepe; always in jeans, she looks great in a cowboy hat, hanging on to the back of a motorcycle. (She looks even better hanging onto me at the dance!) Jody and Carol are so different. Carol often wears dresses. She's real country, too, caring for the goats and all, but with golden hair she's so feminine. She's the princess in the castle. But life, for better and worse, has turned out to be no fairy tale. Pepe's got a lot of women in love with him and it doesn't seem to bother him one bit.

Strider took a truckload of people to pick rosehips and apples. Kemal off to New York to a reunion with an uncle from Turkey.

Sunday evening: A panel truck, the Yellow Banana, now is ours, with all the things that need to be repaired. Don worked with Ian on it. He is setting up his crib in Angela's old room. We heard from her. She's going to study dance in N.Y.C.

Thursday morning: Because of off-and-on drizzle, there's a fire in the circle where the kids are playing. Beara is clanging music. Pancakes in the kitchen. Louisa stringing rosehips.

Fig. 17. Pepe and Kachina. Photo from the collection of Dan Rochon.

Yesterday, Pepe, Sequoia, Ian, and I took the red truck to Colorado. At the fields, just 60 miles north of us, we picked potatoes after the machine harvester had dug up the crop. We got 600 pounds, at least, in two hours for free. At the carrot packing plant, we got 700 pounds of carrots, fresh and clean, for $3. We also copped a stove that Sequoia knew about near La Veta Pass. Home after dark. We carried on the tradition of joining the harvest to the north.

Saturday morning: Sun is out, and our road is almost impassable. Last night the pueblo was full of kids. Pepe moved down here with Jody, Catalina, and the Mind Machine. He is camped in the candle room. He can't stay away from those squealy hugs from his little daughter Kachina—the wild Indian and the angel with the purest blond hair.

Many fires burning last night; it's beginning to get cold. A few rooms still don't have stoves; all have fireplaces. Stoves are considerably more efficient. We had a fire in the circle the last few nights. The flickering light casts shadows on the circular walls like spirits dancing.

Sunday night: Neil came back today. He looks good. He's been in the Northwest. His father bought him a plane ticket to come to Buffalo to celebrate his birthday.

Pepe sold a necklace for $200. He goes to bed early and is up very early. Always busy.

Yesterday we finished storing the carrots and potatoes in the root cellar. Potatoes are stacked about five deep on shelves made of chicken wire. The carrots are in a bin with sand. Fine family we have here, as we get ready to survive the winter.

Louisa has been coughing a lot the last few days. This morning she said I was very nice to her; this afternoon she told me to leave her alone—doesn't like me in her room. I'm in the candle room with Pepe, Catalina, Jody, and Sequoia, so I slept outside on the barn platform rolled up in a tarp.

Wednesday night: Chuck, Tucker, and Neil went on a wood run. "Almost no more wood out there," says Chuck.

Strider and Beara left for Colorado. He's the tallest guy and she the shortest woman. Beara is the earth woman; usually with bare feet, eating thistles and dandelions, she has smooth brown skin, black hair, and is completely uninhibited about going around naked.

Friday night: It has started to rain and is quite cold. There are at least a dozen guests. Preston, 23, says he intends to start a commune with some 35 people in Ann Arbor. Kemal is back. Paul Rotman told me how he tans sheepskins.

Sunday morning: The day dawned clear; not a trace of a cloud in the blue sky. Quite a bit of snow on the mountains. Kemal's birthday turned into a handy celebration. Susie Creamcheese, one of the very finest in our tribe, appeared. Mick and later Mama Raz joined us with baby Saafi. All are here who were here at New Buffalo this time last year.

Warm sun coming in the window and me reading a book, which tells about the Mongol people and their invasion of Russia. Quite luxurious here, under the multi-numerous covers on the candle room bed.

Jody, the sweetheart of Texas, passed out last night in Tucker's room after a wild party where I provided some of the music—whiskey and tequila, dancing, singing, shouting, drumming until late in the night.

This morning Jody brought me a sweet roll that Camille just made. Yes, Camille, Nico, and their white panel truck are here, too. You just can't feel better than this. And pretty Breeze is here with Raz. Raz is looking very healthy, her hair shinning red. Susie took a shower this morning out back. She looks good, too.

Louisa cooked us a little omelet, which we ate in the sun. She is a crank this morning because she is trying not to smoke. I don't feel so cold toward her this morning, because she came and talked to me late last night. I realize she is and was very close with Joe and I should let her work it out, whatever it is.

Sunday: Our family—milling around the pueblo. Paul firing up a sweat lodge. Pepe pounding on silver. Chuck trying to regain his senses after last nights drunk. The air is so good here. I will take off my clothes and do my exercises.

Tuesday afternoon: Snowed in, up to our assholes and still snowing heavily. The chief is sick in bed, under the American flag. The world is white. Louisa and I just cut some wood. With Susie here, the kitchen is especially together. She is fast and is making candy for Halloween.

Pepe had not been feeling well for a few days. It is analyzed; he has hepatitis—Coca-Cola piss and aching back. Pepe is clean-shaven these days but with a big mustache. He looks dark-skinned in his red long underwear. Candle room looks cheery, with all the colored candles. It is clean and swept; that is where he is staying.

Out through the candle room door, in our circle, you can see two skulls hanging; one is big and square with heavy horns, a Buffalo. On the wall also are two God's Eyes, vertically made on the same stick with feathers and some other ornaments.

Sandy's stove is finally set up and burning. Her room is very clean and looks real colorful and homey with two little rugs and Jason's quilt.

Bill Sundance is here from Colorado. Sequoia showing him how to make coin beads. Razberry and Saafi are staying with Ian. Leadville Mick is going to go back to Austin. Neil is moving into that room where Kiva and I stayed together. Now she is married to Zip and is living in town.

Sunday: Louisa just tore a page out of this book, simply because I said what is true; that she wanted me to be in love with her, which I am, no less.

We tried to start the Mind Machine so Sequoia could put together a meeting. With peyote road Jason and Jody, he decided to put the meeting on right away. Max frowned and Chuck scoffed, but they let me drive the red truck to gather the teepee and poles. The meeting finally started about 10 p.m. with perhaps 15 people. Like a mirage, the white teepee, pitched right in the courtyard, glowed in the heart of the pueblo from its fire. The drum beat all night long.

I remained up for the night, but outside the teepee, mostly in Louisa's room, where we cared for the morning corn, meat, and fruit and kept the tea hot. Louisa and Mick helped cook the breakfast the night before, and Carol made coffee cake for Sunday morning. She felt the energy, and before the sun was up, went into the meeting.

Monday: The sun is shining. Pepe is recovered! He is thinking of moving to town to do a few months of steady silver work. Chuck, our birthday cook, is planning stuffed manicotti for Sandy's birthday. She wants chocolate cake and the word is being passed around.

Jody cleaning the washroom. Ian took about 15 of us out last night for pizzas and milk shakes.

Paul Rotman is back with us, staying in the hogan. He is quiet and yet a bit rambunctious. I respect him for the work and experience he just had at Long John's Valley. He is a willing worker, skillful and looks pretty straight. He has a certain charm that many women find irresistible. *I love Arty!* Who wrote that?

November 7, 1972: Carol is sort of head of the kitchen. She has a record of who gets food stamps and when. We spend about $500 a month on food.

Ian is rumored to be leaving for another vacation and trading. And today is Election Day throughout the USA. Davison was here to take people to the polls.

Yvonne, a dark haired, dark eyed, eighteen-year-old young lady, has been staying here the last few nights. Adventuresome, these people who find us. This gal is very lively.

Sandy's birthday—Yeh!

Thursday: Paul bought seven fresh sheep hides. We cleaned two, covered them with wet brown soap and paste made of wood ash. Next, folded them in half, rolled and tied them up. Paul and I salted the others. We then made some walkways with the wood chips.

Sequoia's birthday! He is cooking barbecue chicken in the circle. Jason and Mike Duncan are over and at least a half-dozen more, all crowded in the kitchen busy with dinner.

Friday: In the early mornings the ground is frozen; the earth is white with frost. This morning, the sun shines and the ground turns to mud.

Yesterday I was at Morningstar. Their pueblo is immersed in about five inches of mud interspersed with great puddles. No attempt made to keep the common ground together.

This morning Pepe displayed his new wealth before Max on the kitchen table. He has about eighty-five stones of four kinds of turquoise, all polished and backed. Pepe has two good cases to display them in. With his craft he comes in contact with stone cutting and mining, precious stones, gold, silver, and old money of all nations. Knowledge of these things and the skill to work with them is much honored in our human culture. On the dollar are an incredible number of symbols. Magic is much related to these valued materials. With the money comes history, and with jewelry comes the designs and legends of the people. Pepe becomes knowledgeable in all these things. In addition, the trade takes him to many different parts of the country.

Max says yesterday, Chuck was disgustingly drunk. They couldn't let him handle the equipment because of his obnoxious state.

Tucker drinks, too, but I never see him drunk. He is great for a party—sings, whistles, keeps time and smiles his fabulous smile, encouraging everyone to get it on. Chuck sings too, when he is drunk, and once in a while sounds real good, but often he's a little too inebriated to make a good show.

Carol got drunk last night and had a great time at the dance. I see her often outside in the sun, knitting; that is where she is now.

Saturday: The wind is blowing and the sky is white; a storm is brewing. Paul is finishing one hide which is strung up at the barn. Ian, Pepe and others left for Oregon. Jody and Breeze went to Santa Fe to try to get in a movie. A fellow David and his woman are visiting from Massachusetts where they have a communal family. David plays mandolin and guitar.

Sunday morning: Neil predicted snow. When I awoke this morning, it was just starting, silently falling large, soft, perfect crystals. Now, two hours later, it is four inches deep. Had some guests, who arrived to this winter scene, from Rainbow Farm, Oregon.

Tahiti is here—honored guest. He has some really good songs. An Apache

Indian my age, Charley, is here at our pueblo. He says Joe Sunhawk is in the hospital in Santa Fe. Sunhawk, also called Sandoval, is a friend of New Buffalo, and it is said he is related to Geronimo. He is the most impressive American Indian I've met—strong features and noble bearing.

Louisa has finished a doll made out of a sock and all sorts of other materials. She is very clever at embroidery, crocheting, sewing, and patching things. The doll has red hair and is a re-creation of a hippie chick. I heard a story from Joe that when he and Louisa first came here, they had to ask before a council of everyone if they could stay and live at New Buffalo.

Michael Duncan, owner of the Morningstar land, is here. There is a fire in the circle. Gypsy ladies dance to a tambourine. I hear little Jason crying. Now he is quiet.

In the evening as it snowed, I ran a few miles on the mesa.

November 15: Overcast today. Chuck and I took out the garbage to the public dump. We couldn't get the truck out over a hill, so we hitched home, got all kinds of chains and bailing wire to improvise a set of chains. Max and Neil came to help, got the truck almost out but broke a brake line; the truck shot back down the hill. We then went to town and back to Buffalo and got a thing to repair a hole and make a splice. We found another hole, went to Questa and bought a new line.

As the sun set, Chuck and I put in the new line, bled the brakes, put on the new gigantic chain that Max scored and drove home. Had some rabbit that Chuck shot, lemon meringue pie that Susie baked and smoked some home-grown. Moon is out, shining lots of light these nights on the white landscape. Do we know how to have fun or what?

Friday night: Max, Carol, Chuck, Sandy, and Tucker went into Taos. In the storm, the Banana truck blew a rod. All spent the night at the band house (Mabel Dodge Luhan House). Chuck and Max have arranged to have the Banana towed back here tomorrow. Breeze has moved into the pit house and is making a cake for tonight's dinner.

Sunday morning: The skies are completely overcast and the snow still blankets the land. Ben Eagle is here with two ladies and a brother. They are cribbed with Raz in Sequoia's room. Ben has a string of horses and is a knowledgeable brother in the peyote church.

Louisa made carrot bread yesterday. She seems in her usual high spirits and even mellower; she says she is over her depression. Joe, on the fifth day of a fast, lies around and sleeps. I am swearing off tobacco and liquor. They don't do anything good for me. Not that I consume that much, but it hurts when I do.

Monday morning: Overcast again. Louisa came in to see me while I was doing exercises. She made a fire, and we made love.

Joe got some $300 from his dad and offered Louisa a plane ticket to Chi. town where her family is. So she is off, quitting New Buffalo, and me, on the spur of the moment. She was sweet. It's all over now, baby blue.

I helped Sandy fix her door. Tucker is outside cutting wood—snow coming down. I'm making candleholders. Am I bored? No. I am hardcore here; I know the scene, the free store, the shop, the wood, and the vehicles. I know the land a little, and have some idea of what to do come spring. I definitely want to do farming somewhere. Might as well be here, where a few are needed to make this commune agriculture work.

For the winter, I have my exercises and Chinese to study. I have my miniscule candle trade, and I always know of tasks around the compound to take care of. I have my running to test me against the winter. And I have a place to lay my head and friends to eat with. I will carry on with the commune. But no more Louisa. I guess I can't complain, though; I had three beautiful girls fall in love with me this year.

Sandy and Carol made beef stew for dinner. Only thirteen people at Circle, but as soon as the line formed, people started coming up the drive.

Hog Farm Jason and Lana drove up after dinner. We played guitar into the night with Neil on drums. Now, I'm going out into the sparkling moonlight to run.

Snow continues. Around midnight the full moon is so bright. With the snow clouds above, the light is so dispersed that the world seems luminescent. The snowfall is just a mist, suspended frozen in the air.

Tuesday morning: I hear Susie is going to come for Thanksgiving and bake pies. Kiva is going to come and help cook. Kids Chamisa and Syna are supposed to visit with Dave, but the snow may keep them in Colorado.

Aquarius Paul pulled up. He says he's improved his pool playing. Looks clean—a regular Marlboro-smoking, unemployed cowboy.

Susie arrived and is staying in Louisa's old room. Tucker cleaned up the kitchen, and tonight Max was in a most pessimistic frame of mind: the weight of the human world pressing on his shoulders.

At least six empty bottles of wine in the garbage. We need chicken feed. Max needs gloves. Overall, we are doing o.k.; we eat well and have wood, but our spirit and productivity are lacking a little.

Thanksgiving Day in the USA, 1972: A bright, sunny but cold day. We are snowed in and looking quite fine. All preparations are well in hand, with the kitchen especially clean and two stoves cooking. My newest song is "Rocky Raccoon".

Wade came hitchhiking in and was our only guest. We had a feast that couldn't be beat: cream cheese pies, pumpkin pies, and big loaves of bread and cranberry sauce.

Friday, Tom from next door came over with his fiddle; John Anderson came with his guitar, and Dulcimer Dan, a great musician, joined in.

Paul Rotman brought two starving horses down to our pasture from Donna's herd at Morningstar. Paul I think of as a tough man; he wants to learn and see us plowing with horses. One of the horses is quite big.

Paul is moving into Ian's room. Only one day was Louisa's room empty. Since the day after Catalina left, Paul has had Yvonne staying with him. She looks nice and she's very cheerful.

Max got 100 pounds of chicken feed, so they can live a while longer. We are going to cut down their numbers, rather than buy more food for them.

Max has been an excellent treasurer. He holds the money on him at all times and seems to keep it at about $50. Max has a very good attitude about a number of things. I can certainly work with him. I've been working well with Chuck, too.

Sunday evening: I helped some visitors get their car out of here, almost a daily task now with the mud and ice. I put some more wood chips in the mud puddles, and then put plastic in my broken window. I think of Louisa quite a lot. It certainly was pleasant living in the commune with her around.

Monday: Up early before the sun—put the battery in the truck. It was warming in the house overnight. Neil, Chuck, and I went to the forest for wood. Ten truckloads should do us for the winter. Why is our woodpile almost out when we have had the truck out every day? I'm not sure. Tomorrow we go again.

Back at the house, Kachina crying because she is stuck in the kitchen— Carol rather upset, too. Max is away in Santa Fe. I'm treasurer holding our $15.

Tuesday: Everybody went to the dance last night, except Paul and I, who took care of the kids, Jason and Kachina. Next morning we did a wood run under partly cloudy skies. Now Tucker is washing the dishes, and Chuck is cooking spaghetti dinner. And, we are plumb out of home grown, but we are doing just fine, as the temperature goes below 0°.

Thursday: Jan made us an offer. She and Kemal came down from Colorado in a Chevy; its transmission gave out. The truck is now at the band's house, and she'll give us its papers and all for a ride up to Gardner, Colorado, carrying a horse. Here's the engine for our Banana truck. So, I will go. Into the flatbed truck, a goat, some chickens, and a bit of furniture joined the horse, and we were off.

Saturday night: North to Colorado, we passed through a vast region of mountains and deforested plains. Throughout the United States, deserted farms are being "possessed" by a collection of hippies and other hardy folk. The Huerfano Valley has about eight of these settlements.

I took Jan and horse to a large house, ten miles off the paved road. There are some ten other buildings on this 400-acre farm. Bob, Silent Steve, Dale, and a fellow Peter also live at the farm in separate dwellings. Nineteen goats, one hog, three mules, a few horses, a milk cow, lots of ducks, geese, and chickens reside here too.

At this Ortiviz Farm this fall, some corn was harvested, plus onions, beets, carrots, tomatoes, and alfalfa. Just before I arrived, a hog had been slaughtered, an elk shot, and a horse accidentally strangled; that made about 1,500 pounds of the best sausage you'll ever smell on a cold Colorado morning. It was near freezing inside when I rolled out to that sizzling aroma.

Part of the farm is a pasture, about two miles from the schoolhouse; this is the upper land from which one can look out over the entire valley. Here lives a somewhat different tribe: Kemal, a great wild man, Ben Eagle and Chapita, Jade, Jim, Paul and Mei Hua. There are seven teepees set up in the snowfield; one is communal. These people all have horses, pastured higher in the mountains. I was given a pair of snowshoes so I could get around.

Kemal is a strong man. He has a small teepee to live in, one rifle and one horse. I certainly like the way he lives and believes. His black curly hair and trim black beard, frame a huge grin that reminds me of the Cheshire cat from *Alice in Wonderland.* He has arms like Charles Bronson and a very deep voice.

Ben Eagle told Chapita to serve me some meat and bread when he brought me up to his carpeted teepee. I was truly treated well by my people up there in the mountains. Great visit. After hiking the ridges for a while, I left with the truck.

Back at Buffalo at 9:00 p.m., to the palace in the snow.

Sunday: In the early light, Pepe and Ian returned; Ian almost giddy with the good time they had. Pepe is broke but has a collection of turquoise, serpentine, and some new necklaces and rings. He's full of energy, as ever. Borrows my best shirt and then asks me if there's a pair of boots around for him. Sure.

Well, with all the people working around here, all I have to do is write about their exploits. Susie did the dishes. Paul fried a rabbit for breakfast, started soup, then repaired skylights. Pepe fixing his display cabinet and has already made an abalone heart. Bill and Margy, Curtis, Jody, Shirley, and Squawfoot are here. Half the commune, the alcohol clique, is out to town.

Monday: Last night Curtis, Chicken (a drummer), and another guitar player set up their equipment and played some loud rock 'n' roll for a few onlookers and dancers.

Seeing that it was cloudy out, Sequoia, Ian, and I did a wood run. On returning, Chuck and Tucker took the truck to go get Jan's Chevy, which is now ours. The band is going to play again tonight for Margy's birthday.

Since we killed the rooster and two hens, the chickens have been laying six or eight eggs a day. Now that is much better.

Chuck has been staying with Sandy most of the time. He is tall and handsome with a trim mustache. He sure can cook Mexican food! Basically, he is a very gentle guy, but when he drinks, he just can't stop.

This morning the snow started blowing down. Inside, everyone is very cozy. The band is sleeping in their bags among their equipment.

Thursday: Overcast. I made some candles with the help of Yvonne and Mike Pots. Mike is a new and good member of this family, who used to live at Morningstar. He is very cheerful, young, and he will get into doing what needs to be done. He bought six gallons of maple syrup and sixty pounds of honey for us with money he had. He doesn't smoke, drink, or ever talk about what he'd rather be doing. Person like him can fit right in.

Max is gone to Santa Fe; I think he wants to move there with some people more his age. I am now secretary treasurer. Pepe and Ian off trading at the Santa Domingo Pueblo with the Indians.

Last night two hitchhikers headed for Denver stayed here. As a matter of fact, the chick sewed my work coat and slept in my bed. Though we did not ball, we kept warm.

Thursday night: Bill says he and Margy would like to live here for some months. He'd like the red truck to go to Colorado to pick up a couple of stoves, a loom, and other things.

The Sheik has left, a good fellow that nobody took to. May he have a good road. The poor guy had almost no teeth but was always bright and pleasant. Half his diet was oats and milk.

We got salami in the mail from Angela! Ian gave the commune $50. He's also leaving his tools.

Saturday: Wake up and the snow is blowing down out of the gray sky. Ian and Chuck getting ready to head for Florida. Chuck is taking my backpack, so he intends to return. Good solid brothers in our Buffalo family.

Tuesday: Bill, Margy, baby Piñon, and I returned to Buffalo last night. We brought a loom and yarn from Colorado, a complete weaving industry that Margy has been into for four years. She is very pretty. They were living in a teepee at the upper land.

Coming back, we rode through a blizzard, a complete white-out. For a while, I had Bill walk in front of the truck to the right so I didn't drive off the road. Peter and Dale from the farm were riding in the back! We made it home just in time for fudge, ice cream, and a lot of rosy, smiling faces around the stove. Dale and Peter thawing out nicely in the corner.

That night, Sequoia did a complete turnaround on the highway in Bill's truck and came to a stop only a few feet from the cliff. He was shaking when he got back with Ben and Chapita a little while after us.

Snowed about two inches more last night. The Mind Machine is stuck in the middle of the Buffalo road, out of gas.

My good brother Pepe is staying in the candle room with me. He is broke, but he has his tools and stones. In a year he'll trade or give away everything he has at least ten times. Pepe is renting part of a shop in a very nice house in Taos that is being opened as a craft center.

Max, this morning, moved his few things out. He is one man who made Buffalo come into being. He'll be living near Santa Fe. Good luck Max, thanks for everything. Susie too, took a few things of hers and is not living here either. She is marvelous for us when she is here.

That leaves Sandy as our only hardcore sister. She gives no complaint

Fig. 18. Sandy. Photo by Clarice Kopecky.

and is making a fancy cake for us. Also Yvonne is here, cleaning the circle and wants to take a room. And Margy has just moved in. Jody has a room here also, but her concern has little to do with the commune; she isn't here very much. But she sure is fun and good-looking! So, we'll just have to get some new ladies for the new year.

Wednesday: Fresh snow on the ground—quite cold last night. Here I am in bed. Terrible! When I returned from Colorado, I knew I should go to sleep. Instead, I stayed up late. Too much pot; that's what did me in. Instant karma. I knew what to do, but I didn't do it. Now I have a headache, which is keeping me just about motionless. I'm sorry.

Thursday: I was up at first light, getting back in motion; colored candles—cut a little kitchen wood. Paul and Yvonne went to the hot springs—said the water is very hot.

Neil saw Ramming. He had Rick Klein sign the land over to New Buffalo Corporation, again. Now the lawyer will send it in, and they should accept our tax payment. Neil and Bill brought back four bales containing over 100 of these fantastic quilts that have been made by the Ladies Lutheran Aid Organization. We are a distribution center. They certainly are beautiful and seem warm and sturdy. Oh thank you Lutheran ladies. I got a couple for my bed.

Dennis Long and Cave Dave came over. They are pleased to see Buffalo warm and lively. They tied up a drum with Sequoia and Bill for a few songs. It is traditional.

Jade, from the upper land, has been making some knives while here, using files and bone antler with the electric grinder. He, Ben, and Chapita all lived together four years ago in N.Y.C.! They were Mother Fuckers or some such and knew my brother Paul Epstein, who gave a bit of first aid training to that organization.

Saturday: Last night the battery froze dead in the truck, inside two hours.

Neil, Paul , little Jason, and I went to town, paid our $25 propane gas bill and bought 50 gallons of kerosene for the lanterns and a battery. That broke the treasury except for $1.

All the blankets we were given are already gone. "We will be given 100 more," says Neil. Neil got the Gold Star for his part in securing these blankets.

Bill working hard in what was Ian's room, which now looks like the lair of a primitive craftsman. Paul got a piece of an elk skin from some friends in Talpa that he is going to tan and make into a peyote drum skin. Another horse died at Morningstar, fallen to the ground.

December 16: *This is Neil writing here. I just heard a story of a man that went out collecting mushrooms, eating as he went. Two rays of sun came filtering through the eucalyptus trees and shone on three brilliant red mushrooms, which he gathered for the dancers at Sufi Sam's Whirling Dervishes Bazaar. When he finished he looked up and in the trees were millions of beautiful butterflies, and when he shook the trees, they all fell out. Just before they hit the ground, a gust of wind caught them, and they all flew off toward the sun and the man walked off into the midst of them.*

Tuesday morning: I just didn't have the right energy on the wood run yesterday. Back at the house, I declared myself sick and just laid down. The family had Circle in the candle room and I was served dinner in bed. On the wood run, Paul and I spent about a half-hour selecting a Christmas tree. First time I ever cut a Christmas tree.

I would seem to have a taste of hepatitis. Pepe asks me why am I worried or depressed? Maybe having been left so quickly by Louisa did affect me. So now I must get better and better than ever. Pepe shot two rabbits but left one up on the mesa for the coyotes.

Wednesday: The Christmas tree is up—looks beautiful. Jody served me breakfast in bed. And who is here? Zindor! He just walked in. Short and muscular with wild long hair, to me he is like one of the dwarfs out of Tolkien's trilogy, *Lord of the Rings*. We know him from Wisconsin—a long-time Harley rider.

Almost everyone drops in to see me. Ray came to visit. I have good friends. I'm sure I present a pitiful sight. I have been wretched and poor—clothes ragged and coat greasy—sleeping on the dirt floor. I have been and I am.

Paul sold wood and bought chicken and horse feed. Bill Gersh paid us $40 for some lumber we salvaged. Bill Sundance and Cave Dave failed to produce wood as a favor to Teles Good Morning, a famed Indian at the Taos Pueblo, so they came here to our woodpile and got some wood.

No raisins, apples, or other fruit in the house. There is rice, bulgar, a little cheese, beans, and some cabbage. Jody bought me a piece of liver, which I cooked. The kitchen and circle always remain clean. Our big beautiful tree has no ornaments, and no bowl of fruits or nuts adorn the table.

Thursday night: I certainly have a nice family. Jody is the head nurse on my case. Now I have liver, steak, fruit, and grape-nut cereal to eat and spinach for dinner. Neil comes to look in on me. Breeze came over this evening, and she spent some time with me. Paul comes in, frequently, to keep me posted on latest developments, and to find out if he has attained to a good part in the journal yet. Sundance occasionally comes in to practice a song and drink a cup of coffee. Sequoia comes to see me a few times a day.

December 22: Made it past the longest night. Today is almost like spring; I could hear the ground thawing and snow melting. This is the fifth day in a row of clear sky. The woodpile, nevertheless, goes down quickly. Bill Sundance continues to work steadily on his copper jewelry, sometimes a little frustrated. Sequoia, too, works on jewelry.

Last night, the boys tried to shoot a deer. They saw thirty, but Ray was trigger-happy and scared them off before they got a good shot.

Also last night, the tree started to get decorated with paper snowflakes, popcorn and rosehip strings, a few ornaments, and one candy cane that Jason very much wants to eat. His eyes are huge, as he gazes up in awe at that tantalizing prize. With his Dutch-cut blond hair, he has a Dennis the Menace mischievous smile, but it's hard to steal the only candy cane. We'll have to get some more.

I cleaned up a bit around the shop. The washing machine must be oiled or greased before it is used. Tucker did get it spinning, but it really whines and the wringers do not work. Jody got $147 in the mail, being on government payroll as having Cree Indian blood. She is a Wild West gal, no doubt. So, it is a familiar story; the ship comes in and the person sails out. She plans to go to Colombia! Exotic. Jody certainly is a marvelous sister. She gave me a new sweater, and it feels real good.

Margy's malamute killed six chickens last night, so he's gonna go.

Sunday: Two candles burning as the east gets light. I am feeling a definite degree improved. Lots of male guests here including Harvest Moon. Harvest gave us an excellent big candle for the circle. He has many trade items, is doing well, and is speedier and noisier than ever.

Paul, with the red truck, scored $70 worth of alfalfa at $1.25 a bale after he sold candles and made $217. So he got his feed and I got some bucks. We were given two horses by Eddie and Stony, who have charge at Morningstar. They have cut the herd from eighteen to six after some nasty deaths.

Sunday: Early morning up the driveway came a tank of a luxury sedan, a big 1951 Oldsmobile pulling a 3,000-pound trailer; Don was in it. The chainsaw he brought started immediately working on our collection of logs.

Among the people at Buffalo now are two fellows, John and Tahla. In Taos they got drunk, and a bunch of young toughs took their backpacks. So they come to us, not altogether in the glow of togetherness. Nevertheless, they are our brothers from Rainbow Farm whose originator, Garrick, just sent us a greeting. So, these are our brothers in this odd revolution, and they are feeling at home here on the Eve before Christmas.

Carol sent us a big box with popcorn and 100 candy bars! Wonderful. The kitchen is busy with potatoes, turkey, and ham being prepared. Paul and I were talking about the agriculture; where we should put gardens and a holding pond.

Paul has his white steed out and Michael Glassman, his brown. Bonito is the gelding's name—skinny, big feet, head and shoulders.

I am feeling better still.

Christmas Eve: Some are off to a peyote meeting. Pepe and Michael are cooking the immense ham and turkey in separate ovens. Big bowl of dressing made. Pumpkins for pies and makings for home-made eggnog on the table.

CHRISTMAS DAY, 1972: Marvelous blue sky and sun on the adobe walls. It's a biblical scene here in our mud and straw compound that could have existed 2000 years ago. And the love is no less genuine. Jason got a bunch of presents, and he and Sandy opened some of them in here with me. Pepe up first thing, to get back to preparing the feast. About 25 people are here. I sure am hungry.

December 26: And the feast was had after our holding hands, and then everyone crashed out. Christmas continues the next day. Some friends from Colorado Springs brought us oranges. Don gave me two big jars of peaches. Stony, from Morningstar, brought us down a venison hindquarter. Breeze made us a super fruit coffee cake.

Thursday: At dawn this morning it started snowing, and it is snowing all day. Kim, friend of Michael, returned last night! Of all the things he saw to do, he chose to return here. He doesn't usually say much. He is eighteen and a strong fellow—a good brother. With dark skin and dark hair he has a very handsome appearance. There is a certain seriousness about Kim. He has a lot of strength in reserve that augers well for our future.

Yesterday Sequoia, on foot, hunted deer all day. My mountain brother, with big chest and ready smile is now recovering, covered by a fine Mexican blanket, wearing Persian socks from Harvest.

Saturday—so they tell me: The sun is shining, but it's cold. Kim seems to have fixed the washing machine. Sandy washed some things for me and I made a wheel of candles. Pepe came home from work early today to find Kachina and Carol here from California. You couldn't get more love into his welcome. He told me to stay in bed and then went out and shot two more rabbits.

Michael says we got eight eggs today. He installed a light for the chickens to help keep them warm and wake them up. Tonight is going to be the coldest yet.

Fig. 19. Kachina, Pepe, and Carol. Photo by Clarice Kopecky.

Sunday—last day of 1972: The mountains never looked so cold. Sky gray—ground white—woodpile low. There is nothing small to cut with the bow saw. Nobody likes the big saw and the two-man saw is dull. My ax is broken.

Neil is the resident old-timer and I am, I guess, the oldest at 28 years. Sandy, Jody, Yvonne, and Margy are the ladies. Paul Rotman, Kim, Mike Pots, Michael Glassman, Neil, Sequoia, Sundance, Don and I are the men here. This now is the cold winter. Our good mountain brothers and sisters are expected over from Morningstar tonight to bring in the New Year.

Pepe is setting up an apartment and shop—going to do some moving today.

January 1, 1973: We had a quiet New Year's. I got up and played guitar for a while. No liquor! Today it is cold; the sun can hardly be made out behind the clouds. Only fire going is in the kitchen stove.

Tuesday: The ground is all covered with snow. Eggnog for breakfast—Bill's birthday—27 years old! His truck is off to town for a big shopping day.

Dusty, once of Morningstar fame, is now with us in Tucker's room, with her two beautiful kids, Corey and Morry. Morry is seven and absolutely gorgeous.

Romance on the home scene sees Paul being most affectionate with Yvonne. Paul says his wife and lover, Catalina, will be returning here soon. Pepe seems to have won back the companionship of Carol.

Paul Rotman has been a great help to me and I'm glad he is here. He has the same concern as I do, to see that the woodpile is high. Today he has taken the truck to Eagle's Nest Lumber Mill to buy mill ends. We have decided we shouldn't risk the deep snow in the forest. Through good and bad, we stick together.

Last night at our Circle were Kachina, Piñon, Jason, Corey, and Morry representing the kids of the world. They are surely a blessing to us.

Wednesday: Our no. 1 hero Paul, with Kim riding shotgun, had some trouble with the truck near Eagle's Nest and had to abandon it in someone's front yard. Don's eyes glowed with the prospect of winning the Gold Star, fixing the Red truck. Paul and Kim made it back, way after dark, in time for fabulous birthday dinner.

Today in town, Neil secured a four-page Form 1120 U.S. Corporate tax form.

What's that music I hear? It's that well known communal shuffle! Kim moved into Carol's room; Carol decided not to stay with Pepe in town, so she is back here, set up in Tucker's room; Dusty would like to stay for a spell, moved into Chuck's old room; Chuck abandoned that room in preferring Sandy's company.

Just before dark, the red truck pulls up with a load full of wood. It took Don three hours to get the new fuel pump on.

Thursday: Here comes before us a fairly young lady Mary Ellen. She has reached the end of her whatever with a smile—no skill, no craft, no money— nowhere especially to go. Can she use Buffalo as an address to get welfare? We say wait. We'll feed her and child and then after a month, if it feels she is part of the family, then she could honestly say she's living here. That's our general rule.

Saturday: Margy set up her loom in Jody's room and has been working every day. She knows how to operate it very well. Her mother tells her to put it under the bed and get a job.

Whole lotta' cooking goin' on! Sequoia has a big fire raging in the circle to barbecue chickens. Kim is making pumpkin pies and Dusty, potato salad. Carol is directing the tots; she is a very good mama.

Fig. 20. Rooms off of the courtyard at New Buffalo.

A new day: We are most fortunate. We are about twenty-two of us now at New Buffalo commune. We have a good home. And papa Art is well cared for. I have stacked my walls with bananas and grapefruits. I am honored as I sit up on my richly colored platform and greet my many friends, who take it in stride to help me out. They, too, sit here on my bed and eat bananas.

I just read about it, these last few weeks; the United States government, once again, devastated parts of North Vietnam with the most massive bombing yet. The bombs weigh 500 pounds apiece. What a terrible beating these people take from the country I live in. It is no wish of mine that they be beaten. Think; what if we dropped a similar value of refrigerators and generators and everything poor people can use? That might do more good. They never think to try that.

"We Declare Peace," that's the title of this story, and I'm sticking with it. But I support those who oppose the American aggression in Vietnam. Should we go on the warpath? Head for Washington and do a little damage? No, there's enough hate and anger. And we still love our country. So we'll live in peace and hope it spreads.

Tuesday: Wood run to Dangerous Crosswinds. Big Jim from the upper land is here—full beard, deerskin clothes, beads, fringe, knife on hip. With him is Tony—good friends of ours. Jim is quite the outdoorsman.

Wild life we lead. A few of the fellows did in $15 worth of whiskey and then, on horseback, chased two stray cows around our pasture. Then Paul, twice, started brawling in here with Sequoia and me, and Neil had to sit on him until Paul decided to go to bed. Don broke out his secret stash no. 43 to cool us out.

Wednesday: Our Buffalo family is pretty tight and back together with women and kids. Every morning, the mothers and children are in the kitchen, around sunup, when we have some sort of porridge: ground rice, grits, wheat, or oats. I don't much like oats anymore. There are eggs for the kids and, occasionally, we each have two. Margy, with a little butter and instant dry milk, makes yogurt each morning.

Margy is certainly a marvelous sister. She is quiet, slight, and pretty, and at 24 years old has an excellent craft that she is adept at. Her kid, Piñon, is now much more at home at Buffalo—not as upset. Margy is also one of the few ladies I know who is living with the father of her child. She has lived in a teepee and seems very pleased with her adobe house. We are fortunate to have these folks join our Buffalo family.

Every night for about a week, we've had at least twenty people in our Circle before dinner. We got a fellow this evening with a very lame come-on, who seems to be a narc. I gave him a blanket to help him keep warm tonight. He is going in the morning.

It snowed about three inches last night.

Friday: A bright sunny day—below 0° every night. Pepe came in last night with the people returning from the dance. He said he smoked a gram of hash, a lid of grass, dropped some acid and drank a bottle of whiskey. Wild dance. Now he says he has a headache.

A few weeks ago, Pepe finished a fine necklace. They put it on sale for $450. Next he finished another piece for $750. The one he is working on now, they'll ask $1,500. Meanwhile, he doesn't have anything to eat. But what a great artist he is becoming!

We got a seed catalogue. I hope I have it together to help produce something this coming year. I yearn often to have a teacher, but it seems we must take all the scraps of information we can, and what our helpful neighbors will tell us, and figure it out ourselves.

Paul is "pining" away at the loss of his love, Yvonne. She has cooled their relationship, and he is back alone in the hogan. He apologized for attacking me the other night when very drunk. I told him, "It is completely past." He stepped right out of character; actually, he is one of the most helpful and conscientious.

JOURNAL SEVEN

We are people living in the earth—to be stumbled upon—in the great desert.

January 13, 1973: *Arty's new book for January 1973—with love from Jody, Sandy, and Yvonne.*

A lot of people gathering here. Kemal and a young lady arrived. Kemal had said he would like to come and stay a while. With him also came Genie, Dale, Hickory, Rocky, and his little girl Kaiya. Catalina returned from three months in California. Jody and Breeze have split to make their way to Columbia. Good journey ladies.

The kitchen is somewhat dark. A lot of people talking—Jason and Corey loud as usual. Pea soup on the stove started by Carol. In the dim light, in walks Margy—gets out cookbook and is mixing up batter. She came home, found both Carol and Sandy feeling poorly, so she got conscious of the kitchen scene and made coffeecake for us. The very best, this gal. She also spent twenty minutes taking water out of the soup on seeing that there really wasn't such a crowd. Several people went to a peyote meeting.

Sunday: This morning, we find Kemal making biscuits for us. I am very pleased to have my brother Kemal moving in.

Pepe and Catalina have returned from an expedition, full of tales and smiles. Catalina is showing off the latest masterpiece, an extraordinary thunderbird and squash blossom. On each blossom is a turquoise stone set in silver. She looks absolutely stunning.

*Fig. 21. Catalina. From the personal collection of
Kathleen Woodall.*

Monday night: Chuck finally arrived. Sandy was all butterflies; he is important to her. He looks well and very clean. And who else shows up? Louisa!
Louisa came in early and curled up on my bed. I sang to her for a while and
we talked. "You don't mind Paul or Ian going on vacation, so why get mad at
me?" I am not going to follow this romance blow by blow.

Wednesday: Days warming and the ground is all wet. The circle leaks at all
the skylights; they should be raised. The idea about dirt roofs is they need to
be thick, with a little slope and a place to drain. Snow accumulations need to
be shoveled off. For now, from the candle room, I can hear the water falling.

It was a year-and-a-half ago that our caravan arrived. Carol now has made a marriage between our Pride family, and the New Buffalo original tribe by joining Max to live with him in Santa Fe. Louisa comes and Carol goes.

Last night Yvonne made cake with white frosting and sweet carrot-bread cupcakes. She is our zoo-zoo* queen. Michael is making feather earrings at the pit house. Cribbage in the kitchen. Beans on for dinner.

Thursday: I went to town and returned with a case of fruit after seeing Pepe at his workshop. He has a great collection of uncut stones. Extraordinary work is coming out of that shop. Only a year ago, Pepe had only a dapping block, punches, and a collection of coins.

Drums beating in the candle room; Sundance, Pepe, and Kemal with Catalina on tambourine. We now have sixteen people here including four kids, and feed no less than twenty people a day.

We are going to have to fill out a Corporation Tax Form to keep the New Buffalo Corporation alive. I am now secretary treasurer and starting with the new year, I am going to keep a simple record of expenses and contributions. I imagine it is very hard for many people to understand how a commune of this sort works.

Saturday morning: Today the sun is bright and the snow continues to melt. In the evening, a group of ten young people came to our home. They all are part of a private school near Dallas, Texas, and are taking a course on alternative lifestyles. As part of the course, they have a house where a different group of people live together each month.

Sunday: We got a letter from Angela and Kathleen who are cribbing together in New York City. Angela takes dance lessons; Kathleen drives a cab and says she's getting a heightened political awareness.

Monday: The sun is up in a blue sky, but it is cold. Since Chuck got back, he has done a lot of the cooking. This is his home. He's staying with Sandy. He occasionally takes her out to dinner and the movies.

Kim is preparing pizza for tomorrow. Dusty is making vegetable soup for tonight: potatoes and carrots from the root cellar.

Tucker, our jovial brother, is back with us. We have many strong brothers here now. I am proud to be with these people.

Late Monday night: Wrapped in blankets, I'm reading a book about China during the Red Guard movement of 1966, less than ten years ago. That sounds

---

*Zoo-zoos are edible treats.

rough. We certainly are fortunate to have so much in our society. Here we have great freedom, and we have love for each other restricted only by our own minds. Our path is peace. This we can hold to, steadfast. Make this communal way prosper. That is my idea.

Tuesday: I was up at dawn. The Texas people split, taking Yvonne with them. In the first sunlight, Kemal, Neil, and Paul took off for Dangerous Crosswinds. Hearty work out there lumbering. Must be 0° with the wind blowing.

Soon a second breakfast scene gets together. Catalina and I cleaned the kitchen in the interlude. Yesterday Catalina organized the pantry. So glad she is living here now. Such rosy cheeks; she can melt ice with her smile.

This evening Bill Sundance came in to talk with me. Since he has been here, he has made two squash blossom necklaces and a peyote bird pin. He says he has located a house to rent. "It is best," he says. I agree. If he is working on some goal outside this commune, (buying land and settling elsewhere), he should do it somewhere else. These are some more good people that Buffalo has given some rest to and helped on their way.

Wednesday: Sipping Coca-Cola floats last night, listening to the drum and peyote songs, we watched Don and Chuck lose $17 to Paul and Davison in a very lively cribbage match.

Thursday: Jade and two gypsy ladies, Isabel and Aurora, were our guests last night. Bill and Margy finished moving out their stuff and are no longer with us. Good luck.

Our wandering brother Ian spaced through here after traveling in Florida, the Caribbean, and New York. He is all smiles. He turned us on, gathered a few things, took a good look, kissed me and was chauffeured off by Don, headed for Frisco.

Friday: A cold morning—strong wind blowing around last night's snow. Coffee on the stove—a day for hibernation. A young lady hitchhiked up to the road, materializing in the blustering clouds of snow.

Last night Razberry and Lana came from Long John's Valley to visit. This evening Raz is making bread and Kemal, the mutton. Lots of folk in the kitchen. Baby Saafi is very mellow and happy. I love having our friends come to visit. A storm has moved in and we can see it crashing into the mountains.

I met Mr. John Ramming today, a young, prospering lawyer with a big, fat cigar. For some reason he has taken an interest in Buffalo since its incep-

Fig. 22. Louisa, Raz, and Saafi. Photo by Clarice Kopecky.

tion. He has secured a warranty deed and has Rick Klein signing over the land to New Buffalo, Inc. However, the state has not yet cashed Ramming's $685 check. When it does, it will be acknowledging "our ownership." Then we will owe Ramming $465. Ramming also helped us fill out an 1120 Corporation Tax Form.

Paul braved the -30° weather to get cream cheese for the commune. It's these gallant efforts that hold this trip together. Catalina seems to be very much in love with him.

Sunday: Yesterday Kemal complained of a pain in his back. Later in the afternoon he collapsed, and I helped him to his room. He has some torn muscles and a pinched nerve. His right foot is numb, and he is in excruciating pain.

In downtown Arroyo Hondo we have a long-haired brother who has studied massage. Paul chased him down, and he came up and worked on Kemal. Kemal's stove backed up smoke just when Jim Root arrived, and we couldn't even find Kemal. But we did find him and moved him over to Sequoia's room.

Tom Brown—notorious—is going to stay here, for a while, with Dusty.

He plans on going to Albuquerque to attend the university. Will that really happen? I hope so.

Monday: Kemal was a little better. I helped him take a shower—quite difficult for him to move around.

Joining our Buffalo family is Spotted Pony and a cheerful gal named Julia, who has *only* five kids. She has a job in Taos working for the state as a surveyor. Needs a place to stay while on the job. A welcome addition to our family, her camper and station wagon are now out back near the barn. Spotted Pony is quiet and I like him. He tends toward the outdoor life but can appreciate the adobe in this weather. He is camped in Kathleen's old room where Donna and Whitelight have also lived.

The wood run had to come back today; they found the snow drifts too deep.

Tuesday: The world is luminescent because of the snow clouds hanging over us. A wood run went toward Red River. We cut standing dead pine off the highway near the Moly Corp. Mine. It was hard work in the snow, bringing the logs to the truck up an embankment.

Sandy, Kim, and Neil all have quit smoking. I spent my last spare money on oranges and apples. Today we broke the treasury on the wood run. The last forty cents went for lemons.

Wednesday: Morry is off at school. She gets the bus in Hondo to go to a Taos public school. Kemal is off to the hospital, lying in the back seat of Don's car, in pain.

It's snowing. Several people have said a big storm with perhaps seven feet of snow is due. That would be wild. I hope my strength holds out. Julia has come home from work and brought vegetables, liver, and pork.

Paul is so wonderful that he even washed Saafi's diapers the other morning before setting out to get wood. Then to top it all off, we forgot to save him a piece of lemon meringue pie! Today in the snow, on foot, he went to town to get some fruit, vitamin C, and aspirin. What a guy!

February 1, 1973: Crystal cold snow on the ground. I took Sandy to town in the red truck to do some shopping. She spent her cash on sponges, soap, and scouring pads for the house, as is her custom.

This is the start of a new phase of existence in Vietnam. The U.S. and N. Vietnam have reached some sort of cease-fire agreement.

On the home front, we have another episode in a merry-go-round, roller-coaster Buffalo romance. Sandy says it is all over between Chuck and her again. He's out, just doesn't treat her right. And, speaking of hot and cold romance, my own true love and sweetheart is off in Albuquerque. I wonder if I will ever see her again.

Friday: The sky was absolutely clear. The universe above us sparkles down in splendor. In our pueblo tonight are many guests. From Crow Farm is Debby, whom I admired when I was last at the Farm. She tells me the FBI raided them, and Mike hit one of the agents. She is riding with a couple in a station wagon. I think Chuck might have grabbed the female half of that couple.

Kemal is back and spent a bit of the day lying naked in the sun. Neil drove the red truck and moved a ton of Tom Brown and Dusty's stuff from Morningstar over to Buffalo. I think Buffalo will get a stove out of the deal.

I was sitting in the hogan with Paul and Catalina when through the window in comes our Pepe, all decked out in fine leather and looking like a gladiator. He spent the last six days flying around putting some craft business together. He's got two grand in his pocket—quite an adventurer.

Sandy made enchiladas for our dinner. I just cut wood. Paul went to town and got medicine for Kemal and cough syrup for the coughers, all free. Now the night has closed around us, and all is quiet.

Saturday: Pepe and I worked on the Mind Machine. He has a fine silver concho belt around his waist and a pocket full of silver ornaments that he had cast. He said to me while we were working, "Everything I have is yours, you know." "I know. The whole world is ours," I said.

Six family friends shared a late meatloaf with us. Why Dusty thought it had to cook so long, I don't know. It was almost like eating in an army barracks when Dusty left; we were all guys.

Michael is going to see about gamma globulin shots for all those who haven't had hepatitis yet. Pretty bad of us to have had five cases here. Disgraceful, really, and all the ladies have deserted us. But now we know better, what to do. Kemal is feeling better.

Neil says we get sick because of the high radiation level around here. White Sands testing grounds is only a few hundred miles away where the very first A-bomb went off. And the Los Alamos Atomic Laboratories are much closer. Makes one wonder. . . . Now, here I am in bed, in my refrigerator, under the covers reading a Mickey Spillane mystery and munching some cookies that Sequoia made.

Sunday night: Buffalo has reached a somewhat low point. Sandy and Jason went to California. Nine-year-old Morry was the only female that graced our table at dinner. Chuck and Tucker are off to hear Tracy Nelson near Albuquerque.

Paul asked me why I am here. I could probably have a nice crib and girlfriend. Only twenty more years and I'll be almost fifty years old! Still, locked in here somewhere, I think, is the key to sharing wealth and hope for the future. So I stay.

Don made about $300 today selling some of his things. He's talking about going east and even to Morocco.

It was a quiet Sunday—very warm—the road started to get horribly muddy. I see how it could be drained and filled in. Lots to do to keep the place together. Four rooms and the tower not occupied.

Tuesday: Yesterday, the mud became quite incredible; our road is almost impassible. The ground is water and mud so I worked on draining the puddles. I rather like playing in the mud. The water is flowing better now.

Yesterday Paul, Tom, and I took a heavy load of mill ends from Eagles Nest Lumber Mill. Coming home I called the free clinic, and today Michael, Neil, Dusty, Tom, Morry, Corey, and Paul got gamma globulin shots. Don vacated and moved into town. He did leave a roll of plastic and a great box of hazel and walnuts. Great! Always he is helpful.

Tuesday: The last two days the water has been rushing across the land. I have to use a pick to cut the frozen ground to make channels for the water.

Chuck and Tucker are going to Florida to build houses. In addition, the tension mounts as we wonder who will be the first woman to break the spell.

Dusty is the only woman here. She's older and shorter than all of us. She is pregnant and has a jealous old man. What charming Miss will grace our noble cause and simple life? Oh, I did forget our resident surveyor, Julia. She's pretty but has a husband.

Wednesday: It was somewhat magical this morning. So strange, this great change of the land in two days—the air humid and the colors in the plants so fresh. This morning was mud city in a cloud of fog. The ground sounded like springs, and water ran in rivulets all over. Three cars traveled the road in spectacular shows of carsmanship, going every which way in the mud.

The little kids can't navigate the muck and get stuck. We do have a few dry places for them to play on. All around the base of the buildings is dry. But the rest of the ground is saturated.

Art, finally, cooked dinner for the family: chicken, rice, and vegetables. Catalina came this morning to see Paul. She broke the spell, and now Mei and Jan are here, too. Kemal is up walking, and Corey is running around all over the place. Here we sit on our mud hill, take care of our kitchen and watch the world turn.

Thursday: Into this Southwest snow fantasy come friends from New Jersey. Our kitchen is a room of trips—all kinds of people coming in. It is a heavily traveled area with a very rough dirt floor, an old corroded sink, odd collection of pots and pans, dishes and bowls, simple, dirty, wooden furniture, open cupboards and two wood-burning stoves. Spices are above the neat stack of wood. We greet a few people that we don't know every day.

Friday: It was a cold, sunny day; back to a nice zero or so degrees at night. Visiting ladies quietly cleaned the kitchen this afternoon. We put a stranger from Texas up for the night; he was collapsing from exhaustion. I'm on the floor, no fire.

Two cars bottomed-out on our road. We jacked, pushed and then towed them. We made a sign: "Don't use the road."

Saturday: I am no longer sick. This morning we are headed out on a super early morning wood run. Conditions are just right—bitter cold.

At a quiet meal this evening of pea soup and pan bread, we declared the "low ebb" had turned toward the better. Kim seems cured, and Michael is feeling better. Kemal is mobile. Spotted Pony we asked to be less of a guest or change his scene.

Sunday: We are in the clouds. A light snow is falling and sticking on the mud, turning everything white again. Today Neil organized a massive and thorough clean up: kitchen, washroom, outhouse, both pantries, and the circle. Sequoia says he is feeling very well and is making pumpkin pie.

We watched people trudge up and down the muddy road all day. Paul got together with a new girlfriend, Angie.

Monday: I went down to the river to pick watercress. "He's only one of a hundred million lost people." We have another one tonight. Chris is his name. No money and no blankets. Peculiar.

Kemal says "hello." Kim is making sauce for spaghetti. Chuck is drunk; Tom is on his way to being so. Some partners I have. Tomorrow is Corey's birthday!

Tuesday: At first light, Ian showed up to collect his things. We walked around the pueblo as the world took on shape and color and the mountains appeared.

Chuck and Tucker left for Florida, all clean, with a few things on their backs. Only about ten adults and kids here to celebrate Corey's birthday with chocolate cake and cherry pie.

Corey got a two-wheeler for his best present. He just came in making the rounds saying "good night" to the people in their rooms. Julia's five-year-old Jamie is staying here, too. He and Corey were together all day. I spent some time with them. Morry is the only one left in the kitchen. She is baking cookies for her class at school.

Friday afternoon: Leo Vigil was up here. I discussed spring planting with him. Leo helped us plant last fall and he is the only person I know with a tractor. He also has a lot of experience out here in this type of country.

Once again, the boys put together a fine meal. Only five at dinner tonight to celebrate Kim's birthday! Sequoia made the super zoo-zoo cake, which we cut into only eight pieces. Kim is all of nineteen years and Michael is still eighteen. Neil is playing his drum at the ski valley tonight.

Sunday: Sun in a blue sky. We sit in the courtyard against the wall and take in the warmth.

Yvonne has returned. Will the charm of this wonderful life fill her with energy? I hope so. She slept with me because all of her blankets got dispersed.

Friday morning: Most of us went to a dance last night. Wild people, handsome, strong, and they love to dance. Our own Yvonne was the rage, in her super short gold velvet dress.

Today tasted of spring. The sky was overcast, but warm. The road now is dry for its whole length and so is the ground between the outhouse and kitchen. The land is no longer frozen; it is now possible, with pick and shovel, to model a road out of the many ruts and holes and tracks. The plowed fields still have a foot of snow, but around the pueblo, the snow is gone, the roofs are dry.

Kim is cleaning the chicken house. Sandy cleaning the sinks and the outhouse seats. Sequoia has a little infection; I doctored—wash with soap and water—put on medicine and bandage.

Fig. 23. Michael, Peggi Sue, Sandy. Photo by Clarice Kopecky.

Saturday: This morning up early—started the kitchen fire and washed the dishes. Next with Paul, and new fellow Big Dave, went to look for wood. The country we traveled was an incredible snow-covered plain, bordered by piñon forest and mountains on the horizons. We could usually see for thirty, or even fifty miles, as we searched. We went to Tres Piedras and then south, Paul navigating. With some intense scouring, pretty much filled the truck. We didn't eat our lunch until we were driving home with the setting sun.

Sunday: I jumped out of bed this morning, when I heard chopping in the woodpile. I knew right away it was some zealous visitor. He was mauling a gnarled stump with no evident purpose or result with my newly repaired ax.

Three new guests are now cozily bedded in an adobe room. Last night, in the dark, they went up to the house of a neighbor, and thinking they were at Buffalo and being cold, they crashed in a car. A fellow then came out of the house with a shotgun to see what the invasion was. He listened to the explanation and let them have the car for the night. Very nice.

Monday: Today was very warm and sunny. Started work on the greenhouse. A few young friends are here from Morningstar. They say everyone is leaving there. Rumors have been rampant lately, that Morningstar is to be taken out of existence by request of Mr. Duncan, the owner, who has been extremely generous over the years.

In the wee morning hours, Paul and our new partner Dave returned, having found and shot a deer and a rabbit. They hunted in Angie's VW and used Dave's rifle. About time we had some venison. Sequoia also bought a half of a sheep. Lamb and venison burgers for lunch.

We have had a rush of people here and a little uneasy feeling in some of us, as to who we are living with. Three people and lady hitchhiker with a poodle split this morning, but Diane, an easy-going, authentic hippie chick, stays on. Very good.

Wednesday: Tom is off to get drunk. Larry Reed went off to get a welfare check of $100 for being crazy. Both these guys, I don't know.

Tomorrow is March 1 and we have pretty much made it through the winter. Our health now is good, and we should be getting stronger. About six of us made up an order form for seeds.

March 1, 1973: The sun is shining down upon us. The snow has melted off the wheat field revealing the lush green sprouts. The air is so fresh—exhilarating—a new season.

Diane, after cooking dinner for several nights, scrubbed the washroom floor and picked up a half pail of mud.

Kim and Michael are hitchhiking to Florida for a vacation.

Sunday evening: From California come Sandy and son Jason, returning to hugs and kisses and a dinner of elk roast, candied carrots, breads and cookies. Plenty of guests to go along with it. There's a couple who say they are refugees from Boston, headed west, and Sterno, who brought Sandy out from town. Very quiet Angie is here, too, as she often is.

No electric lights here; only candles and kerosene lanterns illuminate dim figures in this great house lit by the night. We are people living in the earth—to be stumbled upon—in the great desert. This is the picture of being close to the earth. My window is right at ground level. I am actually underground, Mr. AnSwei, who never goes to the post office.

This winter, together, we worked at surviving with disease among us and little experience in a rugged climate. I am pleased to think of the people I have been living with. And now Sandy has returned to Buffalo. As well as being with her family in California, she visited with friends at a high school commune in the Santa Cruz Mountains where some Hog Farmers are.

Monday: Today was cloudy and cold. Dave and I scoped out the retainer pond then we put the rest of the frame up for the greenhouse. It was easy with slats that Kim had cut.

Aurora and friend Isabel appeared last night at Buffalo. This morning, a lady, Holly, and Big Jim came in on the Mind Machine.

Tuesday: I feel good this evening. I ran a mile or two, up and around the mesa. Kemal is washing dishes and Sandy is making lasagna. Yvonne made a cake for Holly, who is celebrating her birthday with us. Dave made her a leather pouch for a present. Holly is tall, strong, attractive, and has a homey, sincere aura about her. She is the pioneer type. I think she will stay.

Paul is off getting this upcoming peyote meeting together. Yesterday, he found cottonwood for the meeting and got the truck stuck. Home after dark.

Saturday: Grey skies again. Things are looking up at Buffalo. Peyote meeting is coming together. We got a good truckload of manure and the kitchen is full of smiling faces. Two gals, Abby and Deborah, came up to see Kemal. He is not here so we had to entertain them. My pleasure. Abby is something else to see, voluptuous and excited, and she finds me entertaining.

To whom it may concern: Watch out for Paul and what he may tell you, ladies. One of his most used lines is, "You are everything I ever wanted for Christmas and never got."

The reply: *To whom it may concern: Yvonne is a great big flirt. She will tell you she loves you and then go off to see her sweetheart, "Pretty Boy John." It is very difficult being in love with her. Sometimes I have to find solace with some chick. But, it's never quite the same. Signed P.*

Sunday: Love blossoming at Buffalo. Sprouts are up in the ground. Big party last night. The kitchen is really busy with over thirty people around the house.

We're back to that exceptionally nice atmosphere; it's love, adventure, and community, with lots of pretty girls and handsome guys. Carol, Kachina, Pepe, and Sundance are here too, and a dozen or more mellow people from the Church.

Two of our brothers proposed a hunting trip using Abby's car. Paul advised her not to lend it, but Dave, our new brother, persisted. He's a Vietnam machine-gunner from Alabama; he is country, and he did get the manure run together yesterday. Jim, our tall quiet brother from Colorado, got involved in the scam. Tom went along. I should have interfered to help our new friend Abby. However, I was silent, and after bumming a dollar for gas, they took off "to get venison for the feast."

Jim returned in the evening; the car did not. It is over twenty-four hours since they left. Poor judgment—I feel bad that I didn't say "no," because it really sounded hair-brained, and I don't like people at the house sleazing money or vehicles from friends who come to visit us.

Back at the farm, I surveyed our whole ditch system. There are six places where the main ditch has been tapped to water the fields. This is potentially a good-sized farm. The water can reach about fifty acres. I see we have to clean the elaborate system. Here is the key to the farm, and it is dawning on me how to unlock it.

The huge teepee is up and the floor covered with sheepskins, blankets, and rugs. Tonight we go in to pray for a good spring and for this place. New Buffalo was started with a peyote meeting. The ceremony joins the spirit of the new arrivals and the Indians, and gives thanks to mother earth, father sky, and Jesus, for our life.

Tuesday: That was Sunday night. Teles Good Morning and Joe Gomez, two elder Pueblo Indians, came at dark as we were eating rice and carrots. There were at least fifty people at the house; about thirty went into the meeting.

Larry Reed looked all cleaned. He and Diane sang some very good songs. Aurora looked so regal—an Indian elegance. She sang beautifully, too. Morry and Yvonne sat next to Teles, and helped him feel good in the morning. Sundance said it was the best meeting he had attended. Richard, head of the American Church of God and a one-time Buffalo resident, poked the fire. So, Buffalo received the blessing of a number of our friends.

We found the morning absolutely clear. People stayed until noon and had a turkey feast. It was a beautiful, sunny day.

Our good man Paul escorted Abby to Eagles Nest to retrieve her car, which had been put in a garage by the police after they arrested Dave and Tom. So Paul helped close that adventure, which was the only thing taking away from the very mellow feeling that has been here.

Wednesday: We woke up to a snow-covered land and blue sky. We enclosed the greenhouse with plastic and tacked it down with roofing nails and cardboard strips. Pepe showed up for dinner. I think he's going to stay here with us.

We had a discussion about Dave and Tom. Both Sandy and Yvonne feel very uncomfortable with them. Paul objects to their sleazing booze, money, and cars off our friends. I object to Tom's loaded .38 pistol. We'll see how we resolve these things when they get back here.

The more I think about it, the more it is obvious that Buffalo needs a tractor if it is going to be a farm. To plant a field, it must be mowed, raked, plowed, harrowed, planted, and dragged. We could plant our fields if we had a tractor. No reason why this small farm shouldn't flourish. Exciting idea. No sense in having this trip take forever to get off the ground. I want to do great things. Maybe Michael and Kim will bring back some bread.

Thursday: Seeds came. Aurora, Isabel, Diane, and Yvonne got in the greenhouse this morning and prepared the soil. Looks great. I worked on the ditch, the truck, and the road.

Pepe moved in today. He is setting up shop at the pit house. He certainly has his trip together. His box must be worth about three grand in tools and silver.

Saturday: Pepe sleeps on the kitchen table next to the wall at night, and then neatly rolls up his bed roll in the morning. I've traveled over four years now with this man, my number-one teacher. We shared teepees, trucks, houses, everything. Though he's wild and rough, he is also all honesty and loves people and their cultures. I glow inside when he's around.

Yesterday I worked on the road. Holly labored all day making pizzas. Kemal worked in the sun making silver beads. Cucumbers, radishes, lettuce, spinach, and cauliflower are planted in the greenhouse.

Saturday: A year ago, I stood in Circle with eight other guys and two ladies. I said I would be blessed if I ever found myself in the reverse situation. Tonight, I came into Circle and there was just one guy and eight girls!

Kemal and I made a wooden gate for one of the places where we tap the main ditch. We walked the property and surveyed most of the ditches. I started cleaning them today. This is getting exciting.

It was just a year ago that we cleaned the main ditch. It is a completely new show this year. The ground is plenty wet, so there is no hurry. The snows are going to take much longer to melt this year. This is a good year for planting.

Sunday: We are immersed in the clouds, fog, and sprinkling rain. Chilly and damp outside. Inside, you would never know.

I ran a few miles in the afternoon. Pepe went into town and when he returned tonight, he laid five super-fine necklaces on the table. He had one made by a friend that I really thought looked excellent. Said I could have it!

I was up to Elaine Michael's place, where our friend John is the caretaker. There is a fine adobe house, an orchard, and a barnyard with chickens, ducks, and a herd of goats, geese, and even a peacock. I talked to a neighbor, O. G. Martinez, for a few minutes. He has Leo plow his fields and he doesn't know of any tractors for sale. Next I have to talk to Leo.

Monday: Lots of energy coming together here at Buffalo. I am feeling excellent. Debbie joined me cleaning the first ditch that goes to our main garden. Kemal has got a roast buried in the pit with the coals. My good brother Kemal is quite the strong man, but his leg still bothers him.

Carol and Kachina are here. Sundance, Davison, and a half-dozen of our Spanish-speaking brothers from the neighborhood were over for dinner. Two hitchhikers, Paul and Jim, are staying with Yvonne. Our friend John played the flute, which entertained the people in the courtyard in the afternoon.

JOURNAL EIGHT

We are pioneers in the commune way.

March 22, 1973: Yesterday was windy and overcast as I worked on the ditch. In the evening we had a good party with a hundred people. Everyone ate well. We had some good acoustic music—drums and guitars. Next day, only about a dozen people at dinner. The kids are all fine and making a racket.

Friday: It has been snowing off and on. Dave and I cut a big stack of wood for some of the ladies. Sandy is interested in learning to operate the candle shop, a craft we brought with us from California. Kachina is exuberantly jumping up and down outside my window.

Saturday: This morning is a flashback to winter. The frozen ground is covered with a light snow. There is an incredible noise from the wind in the trees on the hill. It is cold. But, I can see the moon above in a clear sky.

Aurora and Isabel brought Ben Eagle, Bapook, and their wives to our sumptuous feast. These ladies look like Indian princesses of some sort. Aurora is poised and severe. She has long braided hair and fine brown hands. I am honored and pleased to live in a house with such fine-looking people—a lot of style.

March 25: Neil has returned with the latest news: Nixon is in trouble over some Watergate scandal. Locally, the Morningstar eviction has come to some mellow resolution. I asked one of the young excitables up there, Tam, what was happening. "Oh, nobody's gonna kick us out, but we do have to clean it up." I went up there today after fixing our first ditch. There is excellent opportunity for farming and planting on that mesa.

Morningstar no longer has any flags. There are still at least a dozen charming houses there. I visited with Eddie, Judy, and kids for a while. Eddie is a pretty good horseman. He is also good with guns. He always dresses in army fatigues. He doesn't smoke, has some boxing experience, and is keen on people being physically capable of revolution. He is a good brother. He knows we have to get our production scene together. It will take a lot of work; there is still time to do it. This year it has been granted a new lease on life.

Price of gasoline is going up. "People are freaked out," says Neil. He is anxious to get to work because "the system" is not going to take forever to collapse. I am anxious, too, to really see us doing a good job here. Kemal talks of his being increasingly committed to New Buffalo.

Bill Sundance and family have returned. Some spirit moved them. We'll see what happens this time. The question is whether he'll put in a share equal to his ability, to make this dream right here happen. Last time, he was working night and day to fund some other vision. He has taken over Kim's bare room.

Pretty Kathy has joined us and with Dave, today, built some more of the retainer pond dam. What it needs now is a pipe and valve.

Monday night: O.k., O.k. Today wasn't just too bad. Kathy cooked enchilada pie, and there I was in the kitchen after dinner playing my guitar with Holly, Isabel, Aurora, Debbie, Diane, Dusty, and Sandy.

Took the Mind Machine to town, washed clothes and picked up Neil's drum. Ran into Ian, who turned us on to a $50 bill and said he would help us get a tractor. Good. Bill Sundance said he would put up a necklace toward a new washing machine. We may put it together yet. Meanwhile, Sequoia, Dave, Sandy, and I all turned over some soil in various places using the spade. I had to first use a pick on my little patch.

Wednesday: In the warm but cloudy afternoon, the women's liberation ditch-cleaning crew, Yvonne, Sandy, and Holly, cleaned the ditch just above the crested wheat. Dave and I installed the big wooden gate; Larry Reed started work on another gate. Kemal says he shot five prairie dogs; two of them were in tonight's stew. There is a big colony of them in the middle of our proposed fields.

Most of the house went to the dance last night. I drove the Mind Machine.

*Fig. 24. Elizabeth and Jason. From the personal
collection of the author.*

It makes incredible noise because the engine needs a new cover. As it is, the
engine is open right into the cab. The giant front windows give a panoramic
view. The Persian carpets still look good. Man, have we gotten a lot of use out
of this old Wonder Bread truck.

Friday night: Snow falls silently on our roof. Around the fire in the circle sit
three men in their blankets—one of them chants. The two are Sikhs that
Sequoia met in town and invited out to spend a night on their journey. The
third man is our own Pepe. Anything genuinely spiritual, indigenous, ignites
a flame in Pepe.

The ground outside is covered with an inch or two of snow.

Thursday: A slim and pretty friend of Sandy's, Ronnie, has moved in with her three kids. Denise, eight, and Liz, six, made some candles with me. Ronnie also has a newly born baby. Sandy met her when they lived in San Cristobal.

Friday: This morning it is snowing heavily. That last wood run was well timed. All the kids are playing in the circle. Denise, Liz, Jason, and Corey sure can make a lot of noise.

Tonight, we celebrated Yvonne's birthday. Camille came up from Albuquerque. A beautiful belly-dancing sister she is! Says she is going to move back up. Ian came to the party. Pipestone Bill and our Bill Sundance tied up a water drum in the circle and about twenty people sat around the fire, and some of our people sang peyote songs.

Saturday: I fixed up a plant-starting box with a plastic top. There are six of these sunk a foot in the ground so they give a greenhouse effect. Planted some spinach and chard. Still it is about 20° at night, somewhat cold for planting. Debbie worked on a ditch and our silversmith community was busy at their craft.

Yesterday was a wild winter scene—dark skies in the west, and strong wind out of the east. Kemal, Sequoia and I all slept in the circle. Teles Good Morning was staying in Sequoia's bed. Up early, I jump into preparation for spring planting. Sometimes I feel lonesome, sleeping alone on the cold floor.

We have many funds going now at Buffalo: washing machine, taxes, paint for the red truck, tractor and implements, and seed. What are the prospects? Between the silversmiths and Ian, there may materialize some bucks. What will the people do?

April 4. 1973: We finally had a sunny day. In the greenhouse, it got tropical. Diane, Holly, John and I planted all the remaining space with celery, lettuce, peas, peppers, broccoli, kohlrabi, and a few tomatoes. The strawberries are freaking out and growing really well.

We also turned a section of the garden and made rows. "Plant corn four inches deep now!" That is what Diane says she heard from Teles. Larry agrees.

Dave started installing the irrigation gate near the dump. The silversmiths kept up their pace. Kathy has been busily sewing. Tom hung out. I spoke with him about getting his shit together and making his next move.

Turkey cooking for a late dinner. Carol and Kachina are now staying here; back to the bosom of our family as spring becomes imminent. Catalina has returned from Mexico. To me her radiance is like a lighthouse. Paul has joined the silver workers and is making silver buttons for a down payment on a horse.

Thursday: The sun shown in a clear sky as Catalina and I cleaned the third ditch and raked an overgrown field. We installed two more of our gates. Larry set up a tent at the unpopulated end of the land. He said he would make the last box.

Our friend Ed from Rainbow Farm is here. He is part of a settlement in Mora County, at La Sierra, at about 8,500 feet. He and two other farm-working brothers have a team of horses and equipment to pull. They also have four feet of snow, so are planning to plow the snow clear and then plant. Potatoes and beans are what they are going to produce, and they already get two gallons of goat milk a day. Even with all the people here, we were able to give him a room.

Kim and Michael have returned! Kim is asleep on my floor and Michael and Pepe are out in the circle. He and Kim are always so light-hearted. I'm happy to see them.

Friday: Ed, Kim, and I cleaned the orchard ditch. Ed suggests we plant hay in the orchard. With Kemal and Catalina, the wheat field ditch was cleaned.

Every day I get a better picture of what we ought to be doing to farm this land. Michael and Kim cleared part of one field that was overgrown and has furrows. The growth we raked to the sides to let it compost.

In the middle of the day, Tom Brown and his side kick Kevin came up the road. Tom was carrying a rifle and in a nasty mood. Kevin, hardly mobile he was so drunk, was carrying a pistol on his hip. Soon after seeing them, I heard gunfire in the courtyard. Tom is talking nasty and shooting at a strange dog with Sandy and Jason not far away. I confronted him yesterday about no shooting on the land. Now I stood next to Pepe and right near Tom with the pistol in his hand, as they flung a few words.

Pepe nodded, I grabbed the gun, and Pepe gave Tom a few punches. Kevin staggered out of Dusty's room with a rifle, which Sequoia and I immediately seized. He got hit a few times. He was so drunk that he couldn't stand right. It was a hot day with probably twenty adults and kids around. Kemal took charge of the rifle; Sundance smashed the pistol. Tom retreated to Dusty's room, where he has a .38 special stashed. After a short while, Pepe, Kemal, and I come together and instantly decide to put Tom out. Kemal negotiated with Tom, and it was decided to truck his stuff up to Morningstar. I am glad the incident has finally happened, and that the family is back to only people who like one another.

Saturday: By noon the skies are all cloudy and we are getting a drizzle of rain. Carol has moved into Morry's old room. Bye Morry—hate to see her go. Dave has moved into Larry Reed's old room. Larry and Diane are into the tent, Kathy then into the end room where Dave was staying, and Neil is back into his old room. Ronnie and kids are in Tom and Dusty's old room, which was a bit of a mess.

Tuesday: A cold wind blew all day. More trays of broccoli, cabbage, and cauliflower planted and we cleaned the last field that we hope to plant.

Our good brother Strider appeared yesterday with his truck, Beara and kid. He just was two months at Rainbow Farm. Now we really are getting a good work crew together.

Wednesday: Oh, I feel good today. Though partly cloudy, the day was very warm. Strider and I finished clearing the one field, gathering the weeds by hoe. Beara and Catalina finished leveling the other field. May 1 seems to be the time to plant.

Our across-the-street neighbor came to tell us the plan is to have everyone clean their own main ditch. He was very friendly. Said he used to lease this property and grew alfalfa. That's what he now has in his fields. Our own crested wheat, after two years, is growing excellently. Our wheat field, too, is nice and green. More of the garden gets turned every day.

Neil pruned trees and we greased the truck. Pepe and crew have almost a dozen necklaces finished. Sundance is finishing one now that has 13 pieces of turquoise in it.

Michael Glassman says that the rules are: you are not supposed to gather water from the Hondo or you can lose your water rights. The ditch is our share; the rest goes to Texas. That means seedlings get water once a week. Here is where a holding pond would be very useful.

Thursday: We cleaned our main ditch yesterday. Holly cleaned out the free store, which was a total mess. Beara cleaned up the library. Kim restored the washing machine; had to go to the dump to find a belt.

April 12: The washing machine works! Another victory for our mechanical genius.

Michael and I worked really well together today. Michael was a sixteen-

Fig. 25. Eight girls showing off handmade necklaces.
From the personal collection of the author.

year-old high school dropout, our runaway from Boston. He was drawn to New Mexico and ended up at New Buffalo at this time two years ago. Good man, Michael, with his youthful exuberance.

Mr. Michael Duncan, who owns 600 acres five miles east of us, is shutting down both Reality and Morningstar. They just turned into a down-and-out encampment. For the last two nights we have seen big fires across the valley, where the last people are burning many of the burnables. We are strong here at New Buffalo, but our neighboring communes, Reality, Morningstar, and also the Female Farm are fading. It's a bit of a hard road. Some make it and some do not. Few really apply themselves.

Paul, Michael, Dave, and I went with neighbor Manuel, who is one of the three ditch commissioners, and repaired a big hole in the main ditch. It frequently washes out where a dry river crosses the ditch. It would be good to put a culvert through that one bad spot.

I can't keep track of all that goes down around here. I see several bead looms have intricate work on them. Isabel and Margy are setting up the weaving loom. The pueblo rings with the sound of hammer on anvil; Carol is pounding pennies to be made into beads. Aurora sitting cross-legged, wrapping leather around the silver chain that Pepe is holding in front of her. On the ground, on a piece of velvet, lie six more squash-blossom necklaces.

Paul created a sweat lodge for Sunday. Four times you are supposed to go in and out. After the bath, Steve and Pat Raines of Libre came by. We gave Pat our 90" loom, a nice gift to our sister community in Colorado.

It is possible we will be able to get bricks from the dying communes, Reality and Morningstar. Some of those people are here almost every day: Rebel, Phil, and Tam.

Tuesday night: We have a new and welcome addition to compliment our farming effort. John, a tall and thin twenty-year-old man, who has been handling the barnyard scene at Elaine Michael's spread, has moved here. Elaine is changing the scene there. John and goats are out.

We bought a goat today for $40, so we now have two, both milking in the renovated pen in the lower pasture. John also brought a dozen laying chickens. He handles the animals with complete assurance. He wants nothing better than to live in a farming scene.

Larry Reed ran computers for the Air Force for three years; no wonder he's so freaked out. He talks as if he likes the hip scene, but he just cannot get his energy together. He's in a constant hassle with Diane, is an incessant smoker, late sleeper, and rather "spaced-out," as we call it.

Roberta, a friend of Ronnie, is here—very quiet, a little overweight, she last was with Craig, Darrel, Bob Durant, and Dotty in Berkeley. By coincidence, these people are the old family of Carol's from four years ago, when I first met her and metamorphosed from a straight student.

Neil and Michael started the new summer outhouse out above the barn. Paul did a wood run as a gift to some Indian friends. Teles was here. He admired the flamboyant princely shirts of velvet and satin Holly has been making and wants one for himself. Holly really is terrific.

Wednesday: In the second hour of a raging, spring blizzard we are cutting pieces of beef off a 50-pound hunk of steer that Tim from the Brown house gave us. Then Señora Martinez picked up four of us to clean their ditch for $30. The sky was dark in the west as we walked home in the wind.

Anniversary: It is late at night now. The moon is almost full in a perfectly clear sky. I want to see a ditch come down to the greenhouse and vicinity so we can have grass, trees, and gardens right near the house. I would like to develop the old parking lot with trees. There is no need for a huge parking lot. "Park it here and walk up" is what our sign says at the beginning of our road.

April 20: The sun rose in a clear sky this morning. By mid-afternoon, it was snowing. Catalina was the last to come in from the fields. She was laying out rows and irrigation ditches. Her ruddy skin absolutely glows with health. Michael and I discussed the garden plan and measured the field.

Monday: Capricorn moon. Strider set up to gas the prairie dogs with car exhaust and a vacuum cleaner hose. It worked perfectly. Their village, at the north end of the wheat field, includes a good forty holes. If this works, it will be a major step in the rehabilitation of agriculture at New Buffalo.

I went up to Manuel Martinez's ranch to look at his 1939 John Deere tractor and saw what he calls a harrow, what Leo calls a "jida," and is just what we have, that Leo gave us to use. Now we need a tractor for a day.

Some people are enraptured by the peyote fast beat and the whole peyote way. Tonight they sing around the circle.

Oh yes—Mongol, who was by here less than a month ago and whose wife Naomi had her last baby in Pepe's apartment, is shot to death near Long John's Valley!

Tuesday: A new man, Sky, has moved in. He is a quiet fellow, a deep follower of the peyote road, with a lion's mane of hair and beard. Today he joined some of us amateurs working out in the garden. Sky made an irrigation pattern in the shape of a zigzag. I think the ditch is too deep, but the idea is what I needed. Straight lines are out. Larry planted one area with blue corn, four inches deep in a flat section.

Neil cleaned and reorganized the workshop. Strider gassed gophers all day and almost gassed himself. With motor running, to supply the exhaust, he fell asleep in the cab. If I hadn't noticed, he might never have woken up.

Naomi is here with twp fellows. There was a big Circle tonight at dinner. Drums playing now.

April 25: Neil keeps knocking out big jobs. He took down the old goat sheds for lumber for the new outhouse. He does a very careful job and is very concerned about not creating a mess. John continues to take care of the goats and brings us seven quarts of milk a day. Plus, he took over care of the chickens, because he is up so much earlier than Michael, who was in charge. Holly and Debbie gathered dandelion greens for dinner, and I discovered that the root of the most troublesome weed is edible!

Thursday: The ditch will go on this weekend. Must put the finishing touches on the garden in the next two days. By the first week in May, we'll get a tractor here. I'm sure I can get my friend Manuel to help.

Sundance and Sequoia are at their second meeting in two nights. They're really tripping out on the peyote way. I can't help but feel, a little, that they pray for it harder than they work for it.

Kemal returned last night with two horses. Three horses and two goats are now in the pasture.

Friday: The sun fades in a perfectly clear sky. Razberry and little Saafi are here for a short stay. She is going to move up to La Sierra. Right now she is at the Hog Farm, where there will be only three people left when she and Michael Pair leave. The Hog Farm has certainly gone through some hard times.

Strider told me today that it was Larry Reed who laid the first brick at Morningstar, that now fading institution.

Sunday: The sun is bright in the blue sky. The wind blows loudly across the desert's dry ground. At night we hear the coyotes as they patrol the hillsides.

Neil wants to plant the field across from the garden in beans and corn as he has seen done here in previous years. That will have to be plowed. Bill is preparing his teepee to be raised. Kemal's teepee is already up with Strider and family in residence.

Fine spring—good work. We are pioneers in the commune way. Now to grow in strength and knowledge and make this settlement prosper so we may enjoy and share the good things of this earth.

Monday: Sunday was pretty quiet here but a little weird; about half a dozen crazies showed up and hung around. One skinny guy, with a shaved head, could not talk, and another one sat in the circle with a blanket over his head. The third, who bows graciously, has a little dog on a leash.

Carol and Sundance had a little scene in the kitchen. He put up his teepee. It looks magnificent. I wonder if this is going to make him even more separated from the rest of us.

Monday: Michael, Kim, and I went to help on the community ditch, which we were asked to do, and got back just in time for Kachina's birthday party. Two years old! And I was there when she was born. Susie Creamcheese, Razberry, and fifty people and kids here for the party. Carol directed a play. Kachina had a good time.

Sundance came in with the news that the ditch was on. Michael, Kim, Neil, Sundance, Jesse, Diane, Sky, and Larry got tools, and we started irrigating our dry land. The sound of the water can be heard from our little knoll; the ditch is a rushing torrent. The garden looks great. The terrace worked the best and the squiggles, crosswise to the slope, look good. I can see where we could water the entire thirty acres; there is so much water.

A number of ladies here and Paul, in a combined effort, have made for me a blood-red velvet shirt with fine embroidery and silver buttons. I am so honored.

May 1. 1973: I was up before the sun today. The mountains were shrouded in clouds as I checked the ditches and watered the crested wheat field. We watered the garden and started turning over some areas for grass and alfalfa. The water is running to many places now. There are many hours of work out there to get the water to the dry areas.

Tuesday: Jade brings us this news: In the Capital, Nixon has had to fire some of his key staff, and in California, a military munitions dump blew up! This New fellow, Carl, was only recently living right near the site.

By the way, Max and Rick Klein were here. I suggested that our next move on the legal front is to withdraw from Ramming's aid. We recently got a response from Santa Fe saying they recognize our right to re-purchase the land from the State for $1,075.57.

Wednesday: This morning the water was flowing at an easy rate, five inches deep and clear. Sky got his irrigation working really well. Michael headed the planting of vegetables. I went to San Cristobal for another load of manure.

Jesse: Jesse is a tall Texan, about twenty-one years old and has lived at Morningstar for three years. He is very quiet, rough, lanky, and a bit shy. His feet have been in cowboy boots for so long, he can't wear any other kind of shoe. He knows something about mechanics and other useful stuff and has been working outside everyday. Today he got into the broken tool stash and repaired some shovels. Fixing the grinder helped considerably. Good work.

May 4: We now have put two truckloads of composted manure on one field. A whole truckload of such is a real score. Soon we'll put sweet corn in.

We had a communal meeting this morning to talk about our place and feelings—good feelings—a good group. Louisa appeared yesterday looking very nice. She stayed with me and I like her a lot.

Saturday: I have been up late many recent evenings. Still, I feel energetic and can work all day. It is getting warmer. Today it really rained and now at night, it is raining more. We turned off all the ditches. The colors are so rich. We had a rainbow right over the pueblo.

Alan showed up. He is a friend from Kansas and worked with me in the western fields. We repaired some ditches, and got water to places where it hasn't run for many years. A strong stream ran into some gopher holes. It's like connect the dots. With all the water, we should be able to clear the fields of prairie dogs—reclaim the land. We have got near a dozen big colonies, at least 500 holes. Almost by accident, we hit on the technique. Sorry, prairie dogs. Time to leave.

I went running to the Rio Grande in the rain.

Sunday: Busy place. Jesse and Sky built a table for the washroom. Then they and about five other guys took Carl's truck and brought down the famous, giant, cedar plank table from Reality, which is now oiled and in the circle room. It's a big beauty. Any rough-hewn item placed in the giant kiva takes on an aura of a relic from an ancient civilization.

New Buffalo is almost six years old. The place was given a great start, and a lot was built. Much still to be done. With Jesse here, the place has gotten a good shot of energy. Sky now seems more a part of the household and helps with some of the necessary tasks. Neil has put beets in the orchard and has the seats made for the new outhouse.

Into this mix has appeared a wonderful man, Carl Hagan. He has the spirit, is quiet, and has the pioneer look. Carl just drove up one day in a flatbed truck with beehives and equipment and is right with us every day, concerned with the growing. He came from California, like he knew exactly where he was going. God bless America.

Jim gave me $50 the other day from a jewelry sale; Kim gave me $150 from a job he held a year ago. I hold the tax fund too.

The prairie dogs must be continually hit with the water, so the new grasses can be established. They are completely rampant. "When the whole valley was poisoned for prairie dogs, Buffalo did not participate," Leo tells me. Their towns are like craters on the moon.

May 8, 1973: Our neighbor Tony Medina showed up with his rickety old tractor. He plowed and dragged the sweet corn patch and the field above the wheat. The corner of the field we planted with oats. The rest will go for beans and blue corn, as Neil wishes. Señor Medina said, "Sow the oats and then plow." He dragged the two western fields after we sowed them with our pasture mixture, brome, orchard, timothy, and alfalfa. He also dragged the area below the garden plot, and we planted that with oats and alfalfa. Everything but squash and beans can go in now.

Kim started watering the planted fields. It is a lot of work to water a newly seeded field that is not very flat. It is going to take days. It seems we can count on the water.

Bill Gersh was here today. He is in charge of dismantling Reality. He'll give us a day's notice and we will send Carl, truck, and a crew to get what we want in exchange for labor.

We'll be expanding our goatherd soon and there is a chicken sitting on fifteen eggs in the junk pile.

May 9: I got the ditch going early and watered the new oats and the alfalfa patch. Then we dug ditches to another prairie dog kingdom. I kept eight holes running simultaneously with water all night, closing all of the auxiliary holes that I could find. In the morning, Kim and Strider watered more prairie dog holes. We've become very familiar with the land. Michael doing the excellent job of gently watering the seeds—don't want to wash them out. It takes constant attention to spread the water. Very ambitious we are. Up early. OK, let's get to it!

May 11: It is my birthday, 29 years old. Louisa returned two days ago—nice birthday present. Kemal and Sundance brought home a deer. Make the rounds watering the fields. I get better all the time at controlling the water. Those big fields are getting wet.

Saturday: All day long as we worked, a storm built up in the west. Finally, in it came, a regular spring rain! We'd be in a sorry way if we had to depend on rain, but this certainly is excellent. We have some ten acres planted. The oats in the first western field are coming up. Some corn in our first patch is coming up too. The clover in the crested wheat is so lush now. Larry 's corn is beginning to show. "two waterings a year is all dry farming corn needs," says Larry. The plants are way ahead with roots probably six inches long. This evening is very quiet, with a peyote drum sounding from the hillside. The entire world is bathed fresh under a luminous cover of clouds. The mountains shine with fresh snow on the crests.

Most of our planting is done. Angela is visiting from N.Y. My pulse quickens to see her; she is so perfect. She is excited to see so much happening. Joe, Ceil, Strider, and Beara have returned.

JOURNAL NINE

Yesterday we stepped into a Van Gogh painting and cut the golden wheat field.

May 17, 1973: Carl is readying ten new hives for twenty pounds of bees, including the ten queens coming in the mail. I spoke with Angela about the crested wheat grass. She says it was Steve Andur who did all of that planting. It is now our outstanding agricultural achievement.

Friday: Sky is now stringing his newly created necklace, a real masterpiece with inlaid abalone and silver-cast birds of his own design. Michael and Kim watered the garden, and all the fields were watered. Oats are coming up all over where we planted them.

May 19: The main ditch is dry. Sky and Jesse spoke with Ben Garcia and Ernesto Martinez. The diversion for our Llano ditch has washed out because of the force of the water. Ernesto says he will come get us if he can use some labor. We had best look it over ourselves.

Ray, the Questa dentist, was here with his two little boys. He is impressed to see the garden. He sees it is important to make this happen.

From Santa Fe we got a re-purchase contract. $215 down and $36 a month for two years. We get a tax deed when paid in full. We can pay in full anytime. So next, we sign the contract and send in the initial money.

Buffalo romances: Carol and Michael stay together just about all the time. Neil and Holly stay together often, and she has worked a lot with Neil in the fields that he is preparing. Margy is looking rather pregnant. She and Sundance are getting along pretty well. Big Jim and Debbie have been living together in the hogan. Jim is very quiet and seems to have become an actual resident here. He came from the upper land in Colorado. At 6'2", in home-made leathers, he might have come west with Davy Crockett.

To New York has gone Angela and Louisa with her as far as Albuquerque.

Monday: With the moon in Capricorn, we planted a patch of sunflowers at the north end of the oats. With the water renewed this morning, Strider and I hit twenty holes in a line near the corn. The wheat-field gophers are also getting watered. The holes I have closed have remained closed. Poor little guys, but it's claim the land or no farm.

Carl, hired by the owner of the Lama Lumber Mill, successfully moved a big hive of honeybees from a tree to a box. Carl is very professional.

We signed the repurchase contract, recognizing New Mexico's right to tax us and in return the corporation gets title.

Mr. Ramming is very conversant on Buffalo matters. What his interest is, I'm not sure. For one, we are a valuable piece of real estate. We are also a famous organization. He has my respect for handling these matters in such a friendly manner, but I feel we should get away from him.

May 24: Jesse, John, Carl, and I went to the Llano ditch head gate. Five min-utes behind us came Commissioner Manuel and two others. That was good, because I didn't like to work at this important place without the knowledge of some older members of the community. We easily doubled the flow with their help and their tools. The diversion is in a thickly wooded valley and is simply created by cutting logs and stumps and moving them so as to force water into the channel that was first created several hundred years ago. From this precise spot, at a 3 percent fall, the ditch, over a three-mile run, brings the water to all the farms.

Quite a few people passing through, including two rough-looking fellows with no supplies and emaciated horses. Davison is here and working on the new Banana engine. He feels the same lack of center that I sort of feel. A few people are not turning our home on to much more than their company around dinnertime. We are aware that before the end of the meal these days, the house is pretty empty of something edible.

We reflect the hip community. That is who comes here. Still, a lot of them do not have too much together.

Friday: I got a line on a tractor, spoke to the owner, and will go see it Monday afternoon! I've been helping with the milking of the goats. We had to replant the chard, spinach, and beets.

Sunday: Cold day. The sun shines in a clear sky, but a cold wind blows across our land. The corn was set back but not killed. Leo's and Al's corn is still underground. A lot of ours is showing.

Someone, right in the middle of breakfast, combined the four-pound stash of salt with the five-pound stash of sugar leaving us only Tamari sauce to put on our oatmeal and rice. Thoughtfully, they left off combining the tamari with the molasses.

Blond Larry, another old-timer, has been parking his truck up here and hanging out in the kitchen, smoking as much as Larry Reed.

A bunch of us made off for the movies and ice cream. We couldn't eat enough banana splits after so many beans.

Tuesday: Shawna weeded a row of beets; trouble is, she forgot to leave the beets! She comes around about once a week. Then someone weeded out our onion sprouts! The frost killed the kohlrabi and broccoli.

Unfortunately Camille left. But for a little work in the kitchen, neither Aurora nor Isabel are involved in any communal endeavor. Larry Reed is the hanger-out perfecto. He could camp his tent in any one of a million places, but he likes the meals here, I guess.

I looked at a tractor—1950 Alice Chambers—with Jesse and Carl, for $250. A good price and in pretty good shape. Staying with us is John Carlos and Aileen, Morningstar leftovers; Goat John invited them here. They are whiling away the days waiting for a $400 check so they can go to Italy—people hanging out, waiting for their ship to come in.

Sandy is looking to move. She has welfare and has not developed any skills. She does a good job taking responsibility in the kitchen, though. Ronnie, another welfare mother, has already left. So much freedom and abundance that people are not forced to produce anything. *Skills? Typing or clerking? Are not candle making, cleaning, cooking, gardening, and taking care of child, crocheting, and sewing, skills? These are skills that I know she is adept at, more than the illustrious author, you.*—Writer unknown.

May 29: The peyotes started out in Larry McInteer's truck to get sand for the meeting. They didn't get far, for the hood blew off into the front window, smashing the glass. To Larry, I said "Karma." This is a commune. Too many private autos here. They can't all be maintained, and very few people pay attention to the communal vehicles.

Thursday: Sky is the one who is usually up first, starts the fire, and grinds the corn, wheat, or rice for cereal.

Yesterday we went up to Cerro and bought the tractor! Yeah! Jesse and I drove on the side of the highway, about ten miles to get home. One of the two small front tires is missing. Regardless of all the bumps, I could not have felt much better. It needs some work. By fall planting, we should be ready.

We had a lot of guests including some crazies, a narc from somewhere, and probably an FBI agent. Someone ripped off our biggest prize marijuana; proof that the agent had done his job.

Thursday: A friend Ron is here. He was an engineer in a subway mine in Washington, D.C. He was in a mine cave-in and is now adjusting. With him is a fellow Élan from Jerusalem. Kay, of Hog Farm fame, is here adding another car to the grand collection in the back. We are going to tighten up some and discourage visitation, crashing, and free meals. Maybe.

Blond Larry gave the wheat a good watering and Goat John watered other fields. I advanced on a few more gopher holes with the water. It is a warm evening. We have squash, corn, and beans up as we enter June.

June 1, 1973: We had many clouds today. Everything is ready for the big meeting. A giant teepee is up and food prepared. Ben, Chapita, Tinker, two friends of Kim's, Vicky and Happy, friend Willy, Stella, son, and Jeff are here. Sundance said at prayers that he hopes our Heavenly Father understands his indulging so much energy in the meeting, having to leave the planting to others. Tomorrow night we sit in the teepee.

Saturday: First thing this morning was pancakes, music, a little smoke, and morning hugs and greetings to every one like on a festive day. Lots of work in the kitchen. About sixty adults and kids here this evening. No cars up at the pueblo; some in back, many down below. That is working pretty well, to keep vehicles away from the house. The water ran again all day.

Sunday evening: As the sun fades, I look over the land and see that I have gotten myself into many tasks. It is going to take a lot of energy to accomplish something.

The other night I sat in the teepee, up with almost the whole Buffalo family and our Colorado family. In addition, Frank Samora, a great and famous Pueblo Indian was here, and Teles Good Morning ran the meeting. Sixty people were in the teepee, plus fifteen or twenty kids asleep outside with John, Sandy, and friends who did not go in. It ran very smoothly. Dennis Long presiding next to Teles as Drum Chief. Bapook handled the fire with Paul Rotman helping him. He apologized for not being fully attentive after doing an excellent job. Eddie Gaudet from Morningstar mesa came too. He is one of the real heavies of our forests.

In the beginning, as I walked around the teepee, it already looked full. Bill pulled me down at his right hand and made room for me between Kemal and himself. I was—am—honored, and hope I conducted myself at least properly. It was real work, as prayer meetings are meant to be. Up all night as the drum passes around, one singing, one drumming. The peyote tea passes around also. If one gets ill, they must ask permission to be excused.

We followed all the traditions and then had a feast and extra special birthday cake. Margy did great, and even cried, when Sundance gave her fifty good feathers for a fan. This meeting was for their family, now of four, still one unborn, but very much alive. They definitely have our support as a family. The peyote church tries to make good families. I encourage that too. We really need it. I need and want it for myself, for that matter.

Also at the meeting was Jonathon, a brother from Bolinas. He was the outstanding singer. During the early part of the day, people sat in the teepee on the sandy floor, on blankets under the canopied alter, relaxed, and listened to songs, drum, and rattle.

Élan was at the meeting. He is a young doctor from Jerusalem, a Hebrew, an Israeli, and we are impressed to see how closely we speak the same language. He thinks a lot of our venture and believes we have a chance to survive and prosper, as I, too, believe.

Last night, June 4, was cold. Most of the beans and squash that were up are dead. The corn? I cannot be sure. Al's corn was all planted about May 15 and five inches deep.

We checked the lead water gate and John turned on several places where ranchers had completely blocked the water. Majordomo Ben Garcia agrees that no one should be taking it all.

Ronnie has moved. I didn't want to see her go. And Sandy, too, might leave. I don't want to see her go. She could do very well with her life here, I believe.

Friday: Sun all day—hot outside. Garden is looking better. The ditch was on full; John and I worked together in the fields. We ran some prairie dogs out of the middle of the field.

Buffalo is a good-sized place; twenty-six irrigated acres can be very productive. Plus there is a lot of potential pasture. Only now am I getting familiar with the most western field. The prairie dogs live mostly around the old ditches that haven't run for perhaps ten years. Fixing up these old ditches is the necessary prerequisite to planting them.

By the time Sunday comes around, I am really knocked out. I rested for the whole day. All the planted fields are well watered and prairie dog hill, a high point in the middle of the property, is the last prairie dog stronghold. A small viaduct and the water will be up there—we are reclaiming the land with shovel and water.

Larry Reed built a skylight to a new height, a great step for New Buffalo. There are about ten more to repair.

Full sun in the morning—cloudy toward evening. At 7,000 feet, we qualify as mountain people. The expedition south came back telling of some hot weather. Here we cool off every evening.

Pepe has returned. He is sharp-looking and very successful. Chuck and Kim have returned from the woods. Joe is here too. Full house.

Wednesday : Michael, Sandy, and some others weeded the garden. Pepe and I finished the viaduct and put the water on the hill. John and I hit the most populated holes. This hill was the hardest to get the water to. Now we can turn it to lush pasture.

Pepe and I talked just a little. He feels very good here, and we are as right on together as ever. From him and the craft guild, he gave me $2,100 for taxes and the kitchen.

Ian: Ian is back and is making it known. A few years my senior, he calls me Sergeant AnSwei. He wants to live in a palace. Me too. With an incredible amount of energy, he washed the dishes, then literally threw out the kitchen sink, got Blond Larry to fix the plumbing and then straightened up the library and our free store. Pepe says that Ian frightens him a little.

Yes, Ian is on a rampage, completely revamping the workroom. He gave away his money to the Learning Center, I hear, and has given his truck to Pepe to go to Wisconsin to see his folks (he is taking Carol and Kachina). Pepe's father was in a brawl and has to have an operation on his forehead. Pepe's going to give them a little money and a visit.

Ian is energy—yelling, whooping—everybody's talking about him. Come down? I suppose he will and he will need a good rest. He has already had a screaming clash with Sundance. Ian, will he stay around? Can he get into some solid work? Maybe he'll just collapse.

Ian didn't collapse; he just left. He apologized to me saying, "You've heard of coke hallucinations." I said, "We love you."

Friday: A cool and windy day. Frost tonight? Most of the house is off to a party in Pilar at Chris West's. I ran a good five miles today.

The kitchen is moved into the circle. The bad viga in the kitchen is being exposed, the dirt and latillas removed. Don is making a skylight for above the stove.

Saturday: The new viga is in. It is a heavy pine log we collected some time ago. More wood is bought for skylights. Three young men on horses were here this evening.

June 16: I remember I once said something negative in talking about Sandy. Shame, I am terrible. I just felt kind of off because she was talking about leaving. Sandy, I really like. She leads the commune in weeding and does an excellent job. She's a great homemaker.

Monday: The roof started going back on the kitchen and the women's liberated construction crew started to mud. Blond Larry dug the dirt and Kim helped in the afternoon. Tomorrow, the broken GMC gets taken away.

Holly cooked us a marvelous dinner and even iced tea for everyone. Neil called a meeting enumerating what he felt we are doing here.

Tuesday: It was exceptionally cold this morning. Very fresh. We were afraid to look, but the garden was not affected. So far, we have a fine garden. Somewhere else, we could look forward to a good harvest. But here, it is too much chance and anxiety; best to grow things that are not so frost sensitive as beans.

In front of the pueblo are the mud boat, a few hoes, and the sifting screen. Kim has been in charge of clean up. He and Michael mixed the mud for Neil, who put it on the roof. That is a lot of mud to haul up there. Inside, the kitchen is being mudded and some are leaving their mark in design on the wall. Carl has been turning out beehive boxes. Who will step up to head sink and cabinet construction?

Our food stamp worker was out to see us. Her husband drove her and her two little grandchildren were with her. I showed her around and it all went very smoothly.

Carl got some advice from the man who cares for the chickens at Lama Foundation. Don't feed them citrus rinds, no coffee grounds, and no tamari. We gave them a very heavy dose of the first, but tamari, no. Also, keep them cooped; keep them around those boxes rather than having them ranging.

I went in the river for the first time in many months. Still, it was just like yesterday, standing at that enchanted spot. The river is raging; it is hard to move along the banks, the river is so full.

Last year at this time, it was warmer and no ditch water to play with. We also had many guests, whereas now we are seeing fewer faces around which we don't know. More together, more family-like, yes. All the boozers are gone, no cars allowed in the front, and we definitely have less of a people-crashing scene here.

Saturday: A lot of guests arrived just at dinnertime. My ass is sunburned. We have fifteen guys here and nine ladies. Kemal is taking care of the chickens now, and he is getting some chicks very soon. Started to mud the back pantry today. We're going to lay out stone in cement walkways in the kitchen and then mud the rest.

Tonight a little storm hit us. Usually we just get to watch the great storms to the south and east. In the sun today it was near 100°. Now the fields are watering on a stormy, fragrant night.

The insects are really coming out. There is a certain section at the lower end of the property, down near the gate, which is a bog, a natural collection place for water. The insects are really thick. The deerflies have a nasty bite. It can be quite comical, watching people run up the driveway, arms flapping, hands slapping, in an attempt to ward off the nasty buggers.

The drought is over. This evening there is lightning flashing every minute or so, but so far away that there is no thunder at all.

Saturday: Strider and I set out in the morning and worked the east side of the ditch that goes up to prairie dog hill. We worked right near Lake Buffalo [the holding pond], where we now have two ducks in the water, eating tadpoles. Beautiful scene. Some people are off to Lama for a party.

Sunday: Very hot again. I was out in it most of the day at Lama Mountain. In this glorious spring the Taos County hip community is doing especially well.

At Lama Foundation, they share a simple outdoor kitchen and have a

Fig. 26. Afternoon volleyball break. Photo by Clarice Kopecky.

concentrated agriculture trip happening. They have set up a small field for best irrigation. It is plowed, fertilized, and has tall peas, barley, clover, and alfalfa growing better than any spring crop that I have seen. Above Cheryl's is the Tortoise Foundation, with an outdoor community kitchen. They even ring the bell for breakfast! Some fifteen adults or so live there. They have established pastures and corn and potatoes growing. The scrub oak is lush all over. Lama Foundation has had more contact with us this year than ever—a strong, mellow, and healthy community. In our own valley, the Taos Learning Center just about leads the hip community in energy.

July 2, 1973: The sink was moved out. We are washing dishes in the newly two-tone painted washroom. Kim looked after some things in the garden. Jesse sorted out another truckload of junk. We now have a volleyball net up in the courtyard. A great advancement for Buffalo physical education.

July 6: Ah! Aurora popping popcorn for her late breakfast.

The Rio Hondo is running very clear. It is still higher than it ever was last year. No houses in sight; only trees, boulders, and rushing waters. It distorts people to have only buildings and asphalt and nowhere for kids to have adventures. Now to share the wonders without destroying them.

Saturday: The water, in the last few days, has doubled the size of the grass. Their vibrant green stands out from the other side of the valley. Almost all of the prairie dog holes are now closed.

John is away for the day, so I am in charge of the goats. Neil, Holly, Strider, Aurora, and others are off to Bapook's meeting.

A little excitement, because both Neil and I are not reconciled to seeing Larry Reed continually showing up, seemingly oblivious that a strong group of us are really tired of him. Larry says he doesn't see what Kemal, Neil, and I do that's so hot. Here we are, putting out a substantial effort. How are we to relate to this one man who neither sees nor respects our effort? The sickest thing about Larry is how he smokes so much and rarely can motivate himself off his ass.

Carl has gone off to retrieve his bourgeois bride, Randa, in California, leaving his five-year-old son Paul with us. Carl is like a pioneer; sets off with his oldest son, truck, tools, and bee craft, looking for a new life. Since he has been here, he has worked hard and felt good—sees the commune as a real fine place. Quite an unusual fellow.

The house still smells from a skunk we shot under the stove in the circle last night. I crawled toward it and held a flashlight while Kemal took a shot. It actually never sprayed.

It was getting dark when I went around the ditches and turned the gates down. I took little Paul with me. With him on my shoulders, we fell flat on our faces when I tripped on a stump. We just looked at each other on the ground and then got up.

Harvest soon—I hate to believe it. Ever since I gathered carrots and potatoes last year in Colorado, I've wondered if I'd be making use of that knowledge this year. Of the four who made last year's run, I am the only one left here.

One of our objects is to supply what we can of our diet using "organic" farming methods. This is written into the papers forming the New Buffalo Corporation, and it is the outspoken and unspoken desire of the hip culture to achieve such a life. We are definitely on the case.

Monday: I spoke with Max and Rick Klein at Lama. Rick signed a paper conveying some described land to New Buffalo. It is decided to get our legal affairs away from Ramming.

Tuesday: Great storm yesterday—the sky, dramatic. We had a meeting about aims, Larry Reed and a new cow. Good feelings basically came out.

We entertained Sequoia's mother, who came in the night, guided by a neighbor. She laughed a lot with us and had a pet monkey—poor thing—grabbed the hot chimney of the kerosene lamp that was on the table.

Wednesday: I worked with Blond Larry on the kitchen floor. John has been taking care of the fields the last two days.

Kemal called Santa Fe and today goes down there to settle this deed trip. We definitely are going to take all our papers into our hands, away from J. R.

Kemal returned before dinner from Santa Fe. Three weeks from now, we should get a deed from the government releasing their claim in our favor.

Neil and crew are off on a wood run. Blond Larry is on the floor job, faithfully, and I am his assistant. Angela arrived yesterday! Beautiful. Larry Reed, true to form, put in a few hours' work after the meeting; then tripped off yesterday, and is off again today.

Here is a note about our meeting the other night. As harvest and winter approach, I stressed the physical task of working to create the life we want. Spiritually, I respect all and give them credit for their devotion. But if some are not making a strong show here, then I feel there is no reason to shelter and mother them. Some thought work was good therapy. Some said it should be done if you enjoy it. Heavens! Never do anything you don't like! Almost no thought expressed that certain work must be done to achieve certain results.

Strider's parents are here; they are very friendly and having a good time.

Sunday: Kemal, Jesse, and Michael bucked bales at O. G.'s and scored some bales for us. Main task now is getting that tractor running. Jesse is stumped with what to do. Kemal got twelve one-year-old laying chickens. Our brother Tucker is back around and staying at the Tortoise Foundation on Lama Mountain. He was here last night and gave us $80. Tucker is definitely right on. Now maybe we are a little closer to that cow; we would be smart to put it together.

I see the neighbors cutting hay. We only have a little to scythe and sickle. Have to get that tractor running. Larry Reed is off to Wyoming.

Monday: Most of the cabbage transplants look good. There is a little surplus of greens in the garden. But cows got into the sweet corn again! Weeks ago, Jim was going to fix the fence. He gathered all the tools but ended up working on the roof with Neil; I never got to it, either. We lose.

Land of milk and honey. John makes delicious yogurt in the greenhouse, and we have finally harvested 120 pounds of honey after great efforts.

Blond Larry and Strider worked on the kitchen floor; just one more day of work and it is done.

Wednesday: Kemal made a big batch of donuts for us last night. He is glad to have found a good family. He is an excellent man.

I put in a few fence posts, and started to track down the carburetor for the tractor. We also have a great flow in the ditch. The season for gardening is short. It is pasture and alfalfa and grains that can take advantage of this weather. After two overcast days, it rained on us as we sat down to dinner.

Thursday—so they tell me: A steer got into the blue corn last night and made a dent; we are taking a loss because of poor fences. On my rounds, I ran him all over the property until he found his hole and slipped out. Tomorrow, we fix it.

An IRS man visited us from Santa Fe. We talked and Kemal showed him around. Said he was satisfied to see that we were not making money, and that we did definitely do exist.

Today started with a rush. George Robinson, fine Christian neighbor and a Buffalo leader for three years, came early to give us some chickens. George happened to meet Tam on his way here. Tam is eighteen, a Morningstar brother and fellow I have always come on warm to.

Perhaps, at the invitation of Sky, he decided he lives here. He had acquired the old abandoned Rambler, with headlights smashed out, no battery, no clutch, and not a single tread on any of the half-inflated tires. And here George was towing it up our driveway! In a quick and heated exchange, in which Kemal and I tried to be sociable with George while being direct with Tam, we settled the matter. We accepted the chickens and George, willingly enough, towed the Rambler to the other side of the Hondo. Tam came up and apologized later saying he meant no harm and didn't expect to be freaking us out.

Larry McInteer has been reviewing the kitchen plans and is making exact calculations along with correct diagrams in preparation for the new kitchen furnishings. Isabel, whom I feel is more a part of our house and tribe now, went to an AIM—American Indian Movement—Conference, spoke with some of the people and invited some up to our farm. Very good.

On Friday I went with Michael and Kemal to see Dan Garcia and his cow. We shook hands on it and she is ours, with calf, when we come up with the bread. That was very pleasant. We bought lumber and supplies for the new kitchen. A number of people fell off food stamps; none has any money to contribute, so they basically live off the food contribution of other people.

Joe Concho, a Taos Pueblo Indian, and his wife were here for dinner. He is about sixty. That was very nice.

Beara said in a discussion that she thought we would isolate ourselves by discouraging certain people from staying here. Not at all. Once in a while, we do have to urge people to do their next thing. We need people who will help make Buffalo a healthy place to live through the next winter. Are we crazy to face it again? Like running uphill, you have to believe you can.

A fellow Scotty brought news from Ledoux. The police are all over the Rinconada area because of some deaths. The banditos, so anti-social, had a shootout around their campfire. Imitation of TV got too real.

The sky is so absolutely clear with a quadrillion stars. On both the eastern and western horizons, great flashes of light reflect incredible storms. In our dark huts, we drink our own wine (Carol's dandelion brew) and smoke a little Mexican weed that came our way.

Next Tuesday night is square dancing at New Buffalo. Yee-ha!

Wednesday: Pepe arrived in a clean pickup with a beautiful Spanish lady, Lenore. He is also pretty broke but with lots of turquoise. Home. Carl, wife, and daughter arrived last night amidst folk dancing and volleyball festivities. Two new cars in two days we get and two new ladies. Angela also returned from Albuquerque.

We got $280 back from Ramming, took our files into our own hands, and terminated our business with him. Good move for us. The new (used) sinks are installed, table saw in the kitchen, and woodwork continuing apace, Blond Larry in charge.

Strider and I did a careful job fixing fences all morning. Jesse installing an exhaust system in the Mind Machine. Feels good to be on top of repairs.

Great storm to the west and north. Incredible yellow sunset. Drums beating, girls dancing, rain pouring down on us with a super lightning show after dinner. You can hear Pepe's laugh all over. Everyone feels good, I think, to have him here with us. Coming up soon is the wheat harvest, fruit and vegetable runs, wood runs, stove installation, skylight repair, plowing and planting, we hope.

I am a lucky man. I have a nice place to stay and good friends around me.

Friday: Our first fruit run went out, directed by Kemal. They were back in the afternoon with boxes of apricots, and they found a source of apples. Both flatbed trucks went to get aspen poles in Garcia Park for the barn. At 10,000 feet, we saw a big piece of our surrounding mountains. Tomorrow we get the cow.

Visiting Smilinghawk from Colorado made a very fine spice cabinet for our new kitchen.

Saturday: Nelly and calf are here. $525 for a cow and now we wait anxiously to see how much milk she'll give. With some wrestling and chasing, we have two more good-looking animals living with us.

I haven't been across the fields for two days. John is not only happy to be left alone to handle the goats, but would just as well be left to irrigate the West 40.

Tuesday: Greenhouse definitely needs repair or we'll freeze our tomatoes. And the stuff we call carpet grass needs to be cut and stacked. In a few days, we can cut the wheat and then the oats! Of course, there is plowing if the tractor ever gets running.

The parts of land that are not watered look desert-like, but the irrigated fields are very green. There is growing season for another three months for forage crops.

Friday: Sunny hot morning. We bucked 250 bales for O. G., got lunch and twenty-nine bales. Now we have forty-five bales stashed. More jobs coming up, plus our own largest cutting. Some oats are cut. We got about sixteen quarts of milk today from our little herd. John making some cow's milk cheese with a primitive cheese press.

Yesterday we stepped into a Van Gogh painting and cut the golden wheat field. Five sickles and two stackers worked much of the day. Incredibly beautiful. Also weeded and watered the cornfield. We have a pretty good harvest.

Michael and Kim are off to Boston. Pepe is going to remodel Michael's room and be settled in it with Lenore before Michael comes back. There is a little controversy over that; seems o.k. to me. I like it if Pepe wants to make this his home, which it has been ever since we came here. Holly has returned from a trip, and we have a big stack of clean towels once again. She's glad to be back.

Sky, our real hardcore hippie, fired some ceramic, successfully using aspen wood and cow dung. It comes out black.

August 9: Hot clear days. A lot of good energy at Buffalo. Davy, Syna, Chamisa, and about nine guests here, a Swiss gal among them. An older couple came up the road, spent the day and night and had a very good time. Very friendly.

The cow we milked three times yesterday, to no avail. She is doing very little for us so far. I believe she's got milk, but she holds it back. The goats are at maximum production. Five gallons a day is what John feels we need to satisfy the commune appetite.

Thursday: Busiest time of the year now, planting and harvesting, and we have little experience and lots to do. For planting we have a plow that we've never used and a tractor still incomplete and no seeds. For harvesting, we have five sickles, one scythe, and we're behind. We still have a chance to come through very well.

Threshing is scheduled at Julian Lucero's farm tomorrow morning. Larry did an excellent job stacking, when we loaded all the wheat into the red truck.

Larry is quiet and unobtrusive. He hardly ever leaves this immediate area except to go to church. I respect his knowledge and country wisdom. He put in the kitchen floor and made the sink cabinets and built the drag. I like working with him.

New trip with the cow; don't let the calf suck at all. She we milk until we get milk.

Saturday: Today we got the carburetor and started the tractor! Two days ago, we had the wheat threshed, 900 pounds! In a neighboring community, Julian Lucero has an old stationary threshing machine; it's huge with belts and conveyors. When folks like us are learning to farm, many local ranchers love to lend us a hand. We meet the family and enjoy the country life. And here are twenty sacks of grain.

We separated the calf and got three gallons of milk. This is the best way. We also had full water today for the first time in a long while. John and Carl took charge.

Today we finished our latest bucking job. We have eighty-two bales now.

Monday: Jim, Ian, and I bucked 217 bales for Manuel. We added $16 and some more bales to our stash. We also picked up more of our oat harvest. At the barn we have a big stack of freshly cut oats, fresh wheat straw, ninety bales, and most of the materials to build the rest of the barn.

Jesse greased the plow. With the acetylene oxygen torch we remodeled a plowshare so that we now have two. We get the tractor to start easily and drive, but it should have more power. New plugs next. We're getting much closer to being able to plow.

JOURNAL TEN

On Kemal's request, one deputy put
his machine gun back in the car.

August 13, 1973: We have at least eight guests for dinner and the night. We're going to ask Lama Foundation for some money. It has been suggested we could get it. I am a little exhausted myself. I'm into a lot of work and determined to keep up the pace. I rested a little in the afternoon and revived very well.

Tuesday: The water is on again and strong. Most farmers up the valley are done irrigating their new cut fields. We are trying to water both corner fields to ready them for plowing. The person in charge has to constantly spread the water with shovel or hoe.

Last night, we visited the Lama Foundation, presented some candles, talked with them at their weekly meeting and got a pledge for $2,000 to help us out. Today, Kemal is driving the red truck for them on a latilla run.

Ian is staying here.

Thursday: Larry on the plow and me on the tractor, we started plowing today! The fellow riding the old two-bottom plow has to lift the plows out of the earth at the end of the run, and then drop them in again when we turn around. If you hit a big rock it can throw you right off, so you have to keep your eyes open. By about 4:00, after many changes, including putting the distributor wires on the right way, we got the machine running with lots of power. It should be a cinch to plant all we want to now. Boy, does this feel good.

At least a dozen guests here this evening. Drums playing, moon rising, warm evening, beans flowering in the garden.

Friday: Last year, Leo and son plowed for us, and we did a fall planting that brought in this year's 900 pounds of wheat. This year we have our own tractor.

Jesse and Pepe put a rack on Pepe's pickup for Kent's hurt horse. Pepe then drove thirty miles an hour into a pothole everybody knows to look out for. The horse went through the floor, had to be rescued, and the whole scene brought back here and repaired.

Strider worked on some jewelry or something. He seems to be lacking motivation lately. The barn remains not worked on. Ian is in and out of here.

I'm broke. So is Kemal and most everyone. Sundance has some money, but he is so tight with it.

Hot during the day. A storm at sundown—a good rain. Carl and I finished the drag Larry started. We hooked the harrow behind the tractor and dragged with Jesse driving. After plowing, this equipment creates a seedbed. Tomorrow we plant.

We bought a new goat, a full-blooded Nubian, a contribution from Sandy. And I got a $2000 check from Lama! Thank you muchisimo.

Sunday: No rain but lots of clouds. I kept right on and so did Carl. Sundance got recruited for a while. I only had to repair the carburetor once. Of course, we have problems and learn things every day. We finished dragging a field and started plowing another. That tractor really has to work on these abandoned fields; they're not set up for good irrigation, and they are full of furrows from an incomplete plowing years ago.

We got three dozen eggs today and twelve quarts from Nelly. Most of the house took the day off.

Wednesday: Yesterday there was a confrontation at Morningstar between Eddie Cat and all kinds of police. Today there was a manhunt in the area that was national news. Eddie was somehow implicated in an "assassinate Nixon" plot. He is still alive and free, I believe, in the hills above Morningstar.

With helicopters and many police in the area, the sheriff was up here, of course. They were pretty friendly and courteous to us. On Kemal's request, one deputy put his machine gun back in the car. Kemal showed them around.

Fellow from the D.A. said he'd been meaning to come up to visit and Kemal invited him to do so.

We planted and harrowed our first wheat field of the season. We rebuilt the drag, once again. Storm clouds came up at night as the sun went down. Now we want rain to bring up the grain and alfalfa. Our newly harvested wheat showed just a little mold, so we spread out sheets in the Mind Machine and are drying in there.

Strider, who has to be at least 6'6", is in agony with some problem in his chest. I don't know what's with him. He does smoke, and the body will try to send some signals once in a while. Beara slopped a mustard-plaster compress on him.

Sundance is putting up a special meeting for Eddie Cat Gaudet, our unjustly framed brother.

Thursday: These past days have been as hot as any we've had. The pasture fields are a mass of hundreds of sunflowers, most as tall as I. They're all in bloom; what an incredible sight. Below them is a lush lawn of grasses and alfalfa, a first year pasture.

We finished plowing yesterday. Finished dragging today, after some tampering. All the equipment worked well. We are now harvesting beans and carrots. Nelly is getting a little easier to handle.

Kemal went to Colorado and bought 500 pounds of corn, 500 pounds of lay pellets and 1000 pounds of trio-mix dairy feed. He also picked up an old horse-drawn disc for $30! Fabulous.

Winter squash is growing. Early tomorrow, I'll irrigate the newly planted fields.

Friday: How do we manage pasture and grain fields in the same area? Will the cattle ignore the grain fields and eat on the lush areas? I don't know. Maybe we can tether sheep. It's impossible to tether a 400-pound steer. We tried.

Sunday: I took the tractor and plowed up Al and Judy's two-acre oat field for them. It's lush summer's growth we plowed in for green manure. I had some homemade beer over at Al's and got really nice, then ran around for about an hour. I found my way to the river in the dark and took a cold dip.

My family had saved me a terrific dinner: apricots, chokecherries, currants, and the specialty, Beara's hot sauce with lima beans. Jesse was very dressed up for Sunday: clean jeans, white shirt with collar buttoned, buffed shoes, and black cowboy hat.

Pepe made a fine necklace. Sandy made beautiful candles and is off with Holly to California. Angela is returned. Lots of people up the road. We sent $30 to Colorado for some pigs. Next to plant a rye and alfalfa field using the new disc.

Our rich house—beans and apricot delight left over, two gallons of milk in the fridge, a big hunk of cheese and three dozen eggs. There's a new bench for the circle room also. The cedar table wedges perfectly between two of the massive support posts.

After tomorrow, Benito is no longer mayordomo. I spoke to him about the water. He was over this morning to see that we got it. I was up irrigating before I could hardly see. We're getting the new fields good and wet. We can do about four acres a day with a fairly good flow.

Under heavy clouds, we got a load of manure after delivering some vigas we sold. Beautiful mists rising on the mountains.

September 4, 1973: This morning, the garden was frozen solid. We collected squash, pumpkins, and beans. Ice on top of all water outside. The new greenhouse roof saved the tomatoes.

Yesterday we gathered wood in the mountains, to the northwest. Tomorrow, big rock party here with the Blue Streaks. Sequoia, Dominique and kid are settling in. Gal named Wind here too.

Friday: We had a fantastic party, 300-400 people and three great bands with the Blue Streaks' incredible electric equipment. Our two flatbeds served as a stage with a big parachute high above for a canopy. Boxes of fruit—a taste of psychedelics. We all felt it was a great time. Joe Cota put together a band on the spot and it was the best. Joe is the most terrific honky-tonk piano player. Really! The wind blew, the dust rose, and the people gyrated in mind-twisting rock and roll. So mellow that the drums even ended about 3:00 in the morning, and we only have about one leftover, two days later. Next day Carl worked for Lama Foundation with our truck. Kemal chased their mules, which have escaped far.

Another wood run to Dangerous Crosswinds, our favorite spot.

Friday night: I am feeling very good. Fire and peyote drum going at Sundance's teepee. I know those people are feeling good, immersed in their medium.

Buffalo looks good. We have a barn scene that is looking together: big haystack, straw, oats, and lots more building materials. The kitchen is just about all finished. The tool shed is well on the way to completion. We even have a newly designed volleyball court. Plenty to do to keep a few people occupied. Food runs to Colorado are coming up soon too. Soon we'll take in the corn and some 200 pounds of honey from the hives. The squash and pumpkins go in storage tomorrow.

Wheat fields are wet and so are our newly planted alfalfa fields. Some beans survived and the corn can soon be harvested. The freeze stopped any further growth of the garden, but the field crops thrive. Recorded! The winter wheat field is up, half planted in wheat that was grown here!

Pepe is off to Minnesota—trading. He is our contact with many who are the new age people of the nation.

Saturday: Finally we had a rainstorm last night, giving us five hours of actual rain. The landscape in Arroyo Hondo now has shades of brown and yellow. The grasses, the alfalfa, and clover still look lush. Our pastures now could be grazed a little.

We got another wood run in, and the barn roof is on. Jody, who left last winter, has returned from many travels including Colombia. Lots of hugs all around.

Monday: Sun rises in a completely clear sky and there's frost on the ground. Before first light, crew took off for apple picking job at Collier's orchard in Los Tuceros, above Española.

We have expeditions out and more due: a close one to Julian's for grain; a day trip to Colorado for carrots and potatoes, and several for apples down in Embudo. Kemal and Michael on Saturday saddled horses, a packhorse, and rode out, headed north looking for game.

We are almost into fall. Six months to go of the hard season. Except for a few tomatoes, our harvest is in. We do have some new greens growing in the greenhouse. Better prepared than last year, definitely. Every day we eat squash, wheat of our own, milk and a few eggs.

Bill Sundance has bought a new truck. He intends to move north to Colorado. Sequoia, too, is rumored to be planning a move. Both are the heavy peyote men. They like their fans and beaded gourds, and from my view, they're a little like priests; a lot of prayer, but little work that comes back to the commune. Smilinghawk and his new bride Aurora are that way too. Beautiful people, all. It's the Peyote Hotel.

Fig. 27. Sequoia, Pepe, and Sundance. From the personal collection of the author.

September 17: Treasury is pretty much broke—last $50 for propane.

Margy will have her baby soon. Mei Hua, Stella, and Catalina are here to help her. Razberry, Paul Mushen, N.Y. Sandy, and Jimmy from Red Rockers are at Buffalo too.

The other day, Larry and Smilinghawk put in a stone platform for the central fireplace of the kiva. Today Larry made a new metal chimney and it is more weatherproof than ever. Kim started work on a skylight, the same that Hog Farm Jason stepped through last winter. John and I stacked the oats, corn stalks, leftover wheat, and a little alfalfa right next to the hay. Country music harmony drifting from the circle. Solid home we have. We're eating well and the singing is very nice.

A different day: Snow is on the mountain and it is freezing at night with one-half inch of ice on water in the morning.

Kemal and Michael just returned, after a lengthy hunt. Tonight we drove up north and picked up the kill, a big buck elk. Seven of us hiked up the mountain and carried the prize home. It takes strength hunting in the rugged terrain. The three horses and two men lost weight.

Now the men are back at the pueblo. We're really working together. Old way, good way.

Four days ago, Margy had her baby at Little Joe's at the Taos Pueblo while a meeting was going on; a boy for our model family.

Wheat is growing tall and turning the fields emerald. More skylights being repaired, corral going up and several hundred pounds of meat on our table—first snow and first elk. Very right on. Feel good—alive.

On the fruit scene, I went with a group to Ramon's orchard on the Rio Grande near Embudo. Our brother is master of 100 trees, mostly apples. We made cider and gathered off the ground 300 pounds of apples and pears, with a few good boxes for storing. Now this is the kind of friend to have. Careful, don't drink too much apple cider!

I have just been to see the family in La Sierra where they are bringing in the harvest at 9,000 feet and planting wheat, using two teams of solid horses. Ismael is my brother from Rainbow Farm, where we farmed with shovels. Razberry is my very close sister from the days of the Pride family. She is now living and loving with Michael Pair, a most marvelous and knowledgeable brother.

We are learning. After several years, we are getting at least knee-deep in the basics. Learning about horses, old truck and tractor mechanics, farming, hunting, mud and log construction. We all hold hands and pray before our evening meals, and we sing all the songs we know. Through it all, we feel our way of life will prosper. It is slow, but we are getting stronger. How to live and survive and what is good and right is becoming less of a mystery. The cold winds are blowing up and our fires will burn another year and we'll do better. We are doing better.

It is raining just a little now. The tarp is back on the oats.

Thursday: Yesterday I helped put up the meat: cleaned it with knife and water, wrapped it in canvas, and put it in the back pantry. Today, early, I walked the entire Llano ditch. I stepped up the flow. The water is good for the alfalfas. Those little plants are doing o.k. even with freezing temperatures most every night. Goats are moved into the barn. John keeps adding stalls and doors.

Michael and Kim went up for the horses. The next hunt is going to start off on next Tuesday and I plan to go along. We're going to start out on foot and have the horses meet us. I'm not going to stay long though, because of the food runs that are coming up. Potatoes, carrots, and apples are the minimum. Chiles and onions would be nice too.

Cut, string, and dry apples, I got into that a little today. The more we do, the better. Very festive. Tam put two double thicknesses of plastic windows in the workshop.

I asked all of the people here to make a contribution to the treasury. We need to cover some immediate things like nails for the barn, socks for the hunters, and brakes for the truck.

Peyote drum playing as the two peyote church long-hairs, Sequoia and Sundance, prepare to part from Buffalo and head north to rent a house in the Huerfano Valley.

Friday: Got $50 from Lama Foundation and Sequoia gave $17. We bought 400 pounds of rye at Mariposa, a battery in town, and fixed some tires. Carl, Sandy, Beara, and I went on an aspen, firewood, and rosehip run to Garcia Park. It's magical in the forests with the aspen trees turning color in the crisp air. Now we can make more corrals.

Monday: America's motorized children. Sunday our vehicles left here five times. Today, seven trips were made. It is like a thoughtless, helpless addiction.

Tomorrow I leave with Kemal and Michael to be dropped off, on foot, at the base of the mountains to start our hunt.

Friday: I returned this afternoon from our camp in the forests. I feel good. Kemal and Michael remain. I left them with a snowstorm coming up. I was the only one to see an elk. So far, no kill. The first day Michael and I hunted, the second day, Kemal and I. We sleep alone at night where we think we might surprise one in the morning. I lay in the cold mists, as the deep forest became light. In the distance I could just make out a lone elk. I watched and drank in the moment, too perfect to disturb. I got to see a lot of mountains and experienced the hunt with Kemal. We found a spot which the elk seem to like a lot. It's like a hundred elk dance there—another world. The elk are up in the highest forests. We ate dried corn and a little dried fruit with a taste of chocolate and had three full-length feature dreams every night under the clear skies on the frosty ground. Tonight Kemal and Michael are sleeping in the snow—really trying hard. It is a difficult hunt.

Saturday: Kim has started on the mudding of the barn. Jesse fixed up Michael's truck, gave him some money, and now it is his. In the spring he plans to truck.

The tractor was used one day to pull Max's wagon out of the Rio Hondo, after our very own father drove off the bridge in a blind drunk.

Jim and Tam are planning on leaving tomorrow with the horses, headed for Kemal's camp in the hope there will be something to carry down.

Sunday: Yesterday and today, most of the wheat and alfalfa got watered. Still perfect growing days for alfalfa. Off to Colorado tomorrow for potatoes.

We have short, Mexican fellow Eduardo staying here. Pat Barrows—Wind—is now a solid part of the house. Carl and Beara are winterizing the greenhouse; tomatoes still growing well.

JOURNAL ELEVEN

*Pepe is out there constantly,
forwarding the people's movement
for the liberation of the mind.*

October 9, 1973: A very cloudy day. Carrots are being sorted and put in the root cellar—a disappointment. We didn't get more than a 100 good ones out of 500 pounds. Jim spent much time making carrot juice from the many rejects. The juice is very popular. Carl already put the cabbage away in sand and straw with roots remaining on for best results. We have chard, rutabagas, and beets still growing.

Big Dave is mudding the barn. Carol made many loaves of brown wheat bread. Michael making spaghetti sauce. Some ladies put up a number of jars of plums. Strider got three tires repaired.

Kemal and Michael are back from the hunt, feeling great but no success. Tam is still out looking for them. Kemal says he'll come back when he runs out of food.

The moon is almost full. Snow is reflected from the top of the mountains. The first ditch is running. You can hear it when you stand outside.

October 10: First snow! Today started off with an abundance of clouds. By the end of the day, we are well into our first snowstorm.

Tam returned this morning in fine spirits. Smilinghawk and Aurora left for praying in Colorado. They're not much motivated by the idea of making

Buffalo together for surviving this winter. Now it is getting close. We're sort of on top of it.

The circle is leaking less. Two skylights above the stove that were terrible are now completely waterproof—Kim's good work. The kitchen and circle roofs still work. We have four wood runs proposed for Jim Root for $200. We owe him a big favor for helping Kemal.

Thursday: Today was fabulous. Lots of people feeling really good. Our kitchen is completed with the big wood cook-stove right in the middle of the room—central heating. Larry cleaned it by burning all the removable parts and hammering and chiseling away at them. Then with the first fire the room took on a special warmth and glow.

The kitchen part of the pueblo points to the north and to the road entrance down the hill. Therefore the kitchen door is also the front door. People come into our heart right away, so to speak. It does keep the kitchen crew in the middle of the action. Full moon.

Friday: Dave, Isabel, Wind, Randa, a guest, and a few kids picked apples at Ramon's dream orchard. We gave him half and brought a lot of very storable apples home.

A peyote meeting is happening at Steve and Dale's at Ortiviz Ranch in Colorado. Smilinghawk and Aurora already went up. Today Strider, family, and Jim went up with the intention of also scoring some food. I gave him $16 for the venture. More than half of what I had. They go with less than little money—no chains, no spare, and no food. Good luck.

Cedar chips got put in many of the mud puddles. Sky worked on the leaky kitchen skylights. Kim and Tam were busy at the workshop. Neil and Holly came home. Homesick. Looks like they're gonna stay together for the winter.

A new day: Some local sages predict a "very hard" winter. For sure, already it is cold; still good weather for alfalfa and wheat. Kemal says Julian has bales, wheat and oats for us. We're going to raise $100 for the purpose by Sunday. Julian has a beautiful ranch.

Agnew resigns. Israel and Arab nations are in another heavy war. The U.S. supplies Israel with arms. Arabs are supplied by the USSR. Here peace reigns. The sun shines on us after our one-day snowstorm.

Isabel and Randa made a showing for us at the co-op meeting. Carl made storage shelves while we picked apples. Very coordinated. John hitched home with Toltec the goat.

Tuesday: Strider left in another dramatic farewell. Nobody is especially pleased with his attitude. Chuck returned here with some pretty good smoke. Holly has been super busy since she returned. Her domestic skills are really impressive. She made yards and yards of cloth weather-stripping in no time yesterday.

All the excellent apples are wrapped and in the root cellar. The carrots Al gave us are stored away. On Sunday Kemal scored the wheat, oats, and barley and that's all put away. Smilinghawk arrived. Marianne and others returned and put up many apples for drying.

Kim has recently become all kinds of energized, really getting into New Buffalo. He made a very nice cutting board. Big Dave worked for us at the co-op all day. Michael made bagels, and Carl, Isabel, and Beara went to Joe Concho's at the Pueblo and helped with the corn harvest and got some stalks and corn. John put posts up for the cow's corral.

Tam put the workshop skylights in. He suggests that we could scam some lumber and bricks from Reality if we want. Maybe we'll build those alcoves yet. They are a good idea for saving wood and heat.

Carl and I were down swimming. The days are sunny and hot; the nights are always below freezing.

October 16: We had the annual meeting, twenty-five members. Officers: Robbie Gordon—president, Carol—vice-president, Max—secretary treasurer. Michael took the papers and sent them to the State Corporation Commission in Santa Fe, so we exist as a corporation.

Great dance in town with Tommy Hancock giving a free show for his home crowd. He promised another boogie, after the tour. They're great! He said Oriental Blue Streaks are doing well in Frisco. They should, after the great send off they got here.

Dave, Kim, and I threw a wood run together. Without any chainsaw, we returned with a good load of primo hard, dry, piñon and cedar. Perhaps one of the last wood runs of that sort; Very little wood left out there. We had a great day working together.

Back at the ranch a bunch of people put up the second corral and a fence around the haystack too.

October 17: Planting information: Corn—Several of our people participated in the corn harvest at the Taos Pueblo, at the invitation of Joe Concho. Isabel gave Joe a fine necklace of serpentine and copper beads she made. I think that was well done. And we have some of the Pueblo corn. I feel excellent about our family going over there. These fields have produced corn for maybe a thousand years. The Taos Pueblo is about that old.

Sunday night: Michael has two visiting girls in his room, plus cute, freckled, redheaded Marianne.

Tuesday: Larry, Carl, and I serviced the red truck. Carl is now living in the greenhouse, since Nelly cow kicked him out of the barn.

Ham, potatoes, and cabbage for dinner, a warm room to sleep in, good land and tools to work with. I wonder when I'll have a woman to sleep with me.

Saturday night: New Mexico around here has attracted quite a few "hippies." I'm getting to know more of them. One of Ramon's partners was Chief Joseph, a legendary bad ass from the east, who was killed in a police narcotics trap about a year ago. Ramon was born in Paris, schooled in Chile. With real long beard and long black hair, he is a sturdy fellow. We've made good friends.

George, a man we befriended last year, had a cow choke to death and rode up here to see if our crew was interested in butchering it. Yeah, we can do that! They had already bled it, which is necessary. George got a piece. Celso, owner of the local bar, got a shoulder, and we got some 500 pounds. Kemal and Michael took care of the cow, with me doing cleanup.

We have milk, wheat for maybe five months, meat for a month, and Bobo on the hoof. Kemal also just butchered a sheep. We have chickens, averaging ten eggs a day. There is another two months of squash and thousands of pounds of apples. The circle is full, once again, of apples and pears to be sorted, wrapped, and stored. Six bushels of chiles are drying along with corn, creating a festive atmosphere. There are carrots and potatoes in the root cellar. Good. That's what it takes. Both trucks are running and I'm ready to do some wood runs. I like it.

Saturday: Lama Foundation gave us a mule. Michael bought a four-month-old sow for $40. Feels so good here in the evening, everyone gathered around the lamps and the kitchen and circle fire.

The treasury is having some success again. We earned $100 off wood runs, $30 from apple picking and sold 100 poles to Chris West's ranch for $60.

Another day: Neil is becoming a knowledgeable tanner. He has made some of the finest deer hide leather. There's a vest cut out; it is white and soft. Sky, our most silent brother, has his craft well set up. He scrounges our workshop area and half a dozen people have eventually found some missing piece over at his clay works. It all works out all right.

Mr. Paul Rotman is here. He's patching a teepee in the circle. We see him and Yvonne a lot, and I like that. They have left the commune, but they're still close with us.

The kids! Noise and so much energy—zam, zam, zam all day. They've got a sand pile, wagon, swings, and the run of 100 acres. The mothers keep a very close watch on them.

We had some guests here from a university in Denver who gave us food and some grass and were very well received.

Tuesday: We started to move some bricks down here to build an alcove on the circle, a wood-conserving scheme. The double door system makes a huge difference with the cold wind blowing. I'm determined to stay on the case so we don't destroy our resource. While we're making an alcove, we ought to incorporate some solar heat ideas.

November 6: *First day this time last year I came here—Yvonne—Yee-ha!*
Neil and Holly got married! Holly said she just couldn't live with Neil like that because Jesus could come any time. They threw together the wedding in one day. Lutheran minister came out with his wife and robes to conduct. About seventy people came. We had a great time with champagne, wedding cake, and lots of really good music.

Thursday: From the north comes our brother Pepe, and from our brotherhood in Minnesota and Wisconsin he brings news. Lots of strong people of ours and of Gaskin tribe and others, putting together lots of fine trips in the country. Grotto Brothers rebuilt Pepe's truck engine to keep this great servant of ours on a safe road. Pepe is out there constantly, forwarding the people's movement for the liberation of the mind. He gives us a perspective and keeps some of our best parts alive and growing.

Dulcimer Dan is here, giving us terrific country music to entertain the visiting gypsy king, and there is lots of family to share ideas with him about what's happening with our world.

Friday night: Full moon. Talk of the comet Kohoutek coming. Pepe asleep on the circle table with his fine blankets. I'm writing by the light of a storm lantern that Carl brought. He has really given us a lot. He's asleep up at the barn again, under a huge stack of blankets.

Up at the barn the billy goat stinks terribly.* John has been mellow lately and has even helped house the pig. He just finished a stall for keeping the animals' feed off the ground.

Chuck and Aquarius Paul say they've given up the booze! The other night when I was sleeping on the circle floor before the fire, Chuck and Paul were standing at the top of the steps in the kitchen doorway and Chuck, looking down, paid me a solid compliment, saying I was doing a great thing for New Buffalo.

In the Mid-East, tanks, planes, rockets, and soldiers are lined up against each other. Russia and America behind the lines with their most incredible war machines. The American government is trying to work its way through scandal and our "democratic process" to reach important decisions. Good luck, world.

Sunday: Pepe and Kemal are off to California. While Pepe was here, he lost no time setting up his shop and getting to work banging silver. He's pleased with Buffalo.

John has been staying with Carol lately, and that has had a noticeably good effect on him—not so grumpy. He is carrying a big piece of the farm work, by choice, and now seems very pleased in doing it. Myself, I sleep with Sandy sometimes, whom I like a lot.

Monday: We sold poles for $70. Brother Ron, whom I have known for eight months, gave me $500. Thank you! He just collected insurance from an on-the-job accident.

November 14: Ron is now part of the family. He first came here in March and camped out for a few days and dug some ditches with me. He's a wounded Vietnam vet, a casualty of the mining industry, and I think he is going to put a lot of energy toward our country scene.

Sunday: More clear skies. Carl, Ron, and I started plans for the alcove. We went up to Taos Learning Center to see their building ideas. They have three houses going up and all incorporate solar heating ideas. Nick has $600 worth of corrugated fiberglass to build a great big greenhouse to be part of the house. He also has a fair number of skylights. Next door, John Kimmey has several kinds of fiberglass in his roof and a grow hole inside.

Carl and I went down for a swim. We're feeling great. It has started to snow.

*Male goats emit an oil that gives off a heavy, musky smell.

Monday: There are three male guests in the circle. Wind has a friend, Barbara, staying here. Diane is returned from Florida. Randa and Marianne left for Boston with $15 and their sleeping bags.

A word about my sister Wind. Wind is pretty and dark-skinned and has very quietly become a major part of our household. It came a time for her to settle for a while and she fell right in with us. I hear she knew Sandy. She has a great compassion for our new kitchen. I never hear her complain. She is pleased to play a part in a miracle. Wind is a lot of the muscle behind the constant cleaning up that is required to keep our very heart looking calm, orderly, and working. She has much the same vision that I do.

Jesse went out riding to burn up some gasoline. This place is like an airport with him coming and going four or five times a day in his no-muffler rig. Now he is royally stuck miles away with the snow coming down and no change in sight.

Beara is not here much these days. Her room is a shambles with the door off and a hole knocked in the back wall. Not very nice. She did put a dozen sculptures and relief paintings on the walls. Such a great artist. Beara is cute, but with her tangled black hair and dirty bare feet, she's like from 20,000 years ago. The storm is over and we see the snowy peaks. Still a month before official winter.

November 23: We had a great Thanksgiving party and feast. Tam, Jesse, and I spent a good part of the day getting Jesse's truck out of a bad hole in the hills. We tried a lot of tricks. Ian's heavy-duty bumper-jack did the job. Now the lanky cowboy is back on wheels. He and Diane are going to get married tomorrow! He's sporting a new sheepskin jacket and is clean-shaven except for a little mustache. Unfortunately Jesse's mind is not so much on making the commune a viable place to live.

Here's a little something about New Buffalo. At Buffalo we have two groups: the religious ones and the not-so-religious ones. Aurora and Smilinghawk are our most handsome peyote couple, in fine Indian blankets and moccasins. Aurora is an exceptional looking woman, thin with a severe hawk-like glance. Smilinghawk is tall with always well-kept blond hair. They live separately in a teepee, and are the least participant in the pueblo maintenance. Isabel is now one year in the peyote circle, and she likes it a lot. Larry is very much a churchgoer and tries to celebrate all the important holidays in the teepee. He is also one of the handiest men around the house. Sky, too, is much infatuated with the songs and drum. Almost everyone here has been to a few meetings and honors the Church, at least somewhat. I've seen some really fine things in the teepee. I also share in the annoyance most feel toward the churchgoers every once in a while. So much energy goes into their church and preparation. While I am working on getting the house and shop tight for winter, Smilinghawk makes one of his rare appearances in the workshop in order to make . . . drumsticks. He likes the place for sure, but his mind is on the rattle.

These peyotes don't smoke marijuana, and they do offer their prayers to Jesus Christ. Holly and Neil are quite Christian, but the rest of us pretty much care as much for Buddhism and Judaism and what have you, as we do for Christianity.

November 25: This morning dawned clear and cold. Ron and I finished pouring the foundation for the alcove.

In the afternoon we had a very beautiful wedding with Reverend Grabener officiating. John was best man, and good friend Alfred Hobbs gave away the bride. Jesse made two fine silver rings out of a silver fork in the tool shed this morning and then helped with the cement. He got dressed in clean jeans, black cowboy shirt with white embroidery, and his black hat. Diane was very dressed up in white lace and a flower garland on her head. They were married on an improvised altar, before the newly sculpted buffalo on the adobe wall. It has the buffalo skull above it and a buffalo robe on the floor beneath.

The ditch is finally off. The whole stream today had a covering of ice with beautiful patterns covering the gravel. The water can't find its way down the ditches anymore, because they fill up with ice and the water overflows.

That was a very good water season. The snow is now collecting for next spring. Last year it didn't melt off until the middle of June.

Kemal and Pepe have returned. Pepe says he's going to stay put for a while and work on his craft. We'll wait out this comet thing together. We're as close as ever, and he and I feel good about the way our lives are taking us.

November 27: The mountains are white—white and cold. Today is Pepe's birthday—thirty-three years old—our grandpa. He is working on his silver in the candle room. I finished up the alcove doorframe. Carl and Larry zeroed in to mix mud and lay bricks. We put four courses on. For warmth we sealed up one door to the giant circle room; that makes a noticeable difference.

Wednesday: WE PAID THE TAXES! Isabel did the transaction at the courthouse. They have the number of rooms down. Somebody in some office ruled that we don't have to pay for 1972 or 1971 taxes. Too bad New Buffalo stopped paying. It took over two years to prove New Buffalo owns this land and to get the taxes paid. Pepe, Kiva, and I raised tax money when we first came here, but we were never able to pay until yesterday. Congratulations.

Four more courses went on the alcove wall today.

Saturday: Jesse and Diane have left; hip life just wasn't for him. He is returning to the fold of the man. What are his plans? I don't know. He's going to want a job and a kind of normal married life. We love you, guys.

Feeling good. I negotiated with Alfred for the Ford parked at his house. It's ours if we want it to restore the Bird truck. It will give us a mobile unit in the best hippie tradition.

Larry has taken considerable interest in the portal. Today the roof vigas went into place. John takes excellent care of the livestock without much interference from me.

I know I feel it; we have a powerful thing going that is bigger than any of us.

Monday: About four inches of snow fell during the night. We brought the '48 Ford over and put two wheels on the Mind Machine, and started it up. Sounds pretty good.

Thursday: Neil is sick in bed. Lately his life has seemed one continuous cup of coffee, punctuated by as much tobacco and dope as he can smoke. Not surprising he's ill. Such a big strong man, yet he just can't seem to get into something to make his energy grow. I'm really sorry to see it.

I ended up making candles today. Kim just made a marvelous big bead loom. The starter is back in the Studebaker and it seems to work.

I saw the comet this morning. Uh-oh! What's going to happen?

Sunday: Kemal, Lama Billy, and everyone got Rupert the mule out of Buffalo. We had to knock him unconscious with drugs, pick him up and put him in the truck. Recently Rupert kicked Kemal squarely in the chest, sending him airborne against the corral fence. I think it was a near death experience from the expression on my brother's face, so we had to get resourceful. Are seven people carrying a sedated mule resourceful? Anyhow, we got the job done.

Surveying the fields, I see the alfalfa is as green as ever. I think about what to plant where. I'm anxious to do it. By planting time, I'll be plenty ready. Now to get through the winter.

Tuesday: The days keep getting warmer. Larry finished putting the Plexiglass roof on. Next, mud and canales. I bought some mahogany planks for the door.

Pepe's been working steadily on his silver, casting and hammering. While his shop is open, at least one person a day does work with the tools. A lot of his working time is spent showing technique to people who want to make all kinds of things.

Neil and Holly are trying to manifest a change; they'd like some money to come from some direction. Yesterday we immunized the herd against blackleg disease.

Thursday: And there went the comet, a complete miss. Just as well.

Neil and Holly just left for Mexico. Pepe gave them a valuable blanket for a present. They wanted to leave. Yesterday Neil sold that blanket for $375. Nice present. So they've got their ticket. Good luck. Pepe gets the room and I'm back to just me in the candle room.

The chickens have started producing again; average about twelve eggs a day. We only have 200 pounds of wheat left. We eat perhaps fifty pounds a week. With our own grinder we make bread and tortillas every day.

John finalized an agreement to buy four pregnant goats. He's got new ideas for the barn. Really going to be into it come spring. Lots of work.

Sunday. Ten days to Christmas. Our winterizing is almost completed. The big heat stove is all set up and working in the circle. The solarium roof is mudded-in tight.

My friend Ron sold candles in town. He made $12 in three hours and gave me the money. Super cooperation. What can I say about the commune trip? From my view, it is happening excellently. In six months from now we'll have a real dairy. By next summer, we should be able to sell enough milk to pay all goat expenses. We should be able to do the same with the chickens.

JOURNAL TWELVE

Our most obvious spiritual connection; we work more to serve each other and find a new path, than to accumulate personal wealth.

January 5, 1974: Here I am freshly returned from a New York visit. Kemal and I were gone two-and-a-half weeks. My mom Clarice is fine and considering moving herself out here to Taos County.

Back at Buffalo the animals are all fine. The Mind Machine is being worked on. All the four vehicles survived that -22° night. The woodpile looks dented.

At the last boogie there was a rumble. A group of local kids jumped the Mind Machine. Sandy, Ron, John, and Rebel got roughed up, and Pepe got stitches. Came home with bullet holes in the top of the van. Terrible.

The Lutheran Relief Fund has come to our aid, once again, with fifty new quilts, very fine-looking and warm.

Pepe has a new gigantic hat. He looks sort of comical in it. He's finished another belt. His last one is on sale at a fancy shop in town.

Monday: Wintertime it is, long prepared for. I really sleep solid at night.

There are two new people, Rebel and Kay. Rebel has lived for years in the area, mostly at Morningstar commune. Now that he is here he's hustling to pitch in. Very good. He's strong and tough, from Virginia.

Kay is staying with Pepe. Very nice-looking—slight young lady—a member of the Egyptian Vice Lord's Chorus, I believe. She's putting $100 in toward food and she's helping our resident artist Pepe.

A big controversy arose when Kemal and I went to butcher our calf. John says it is better to save him until next September. Sandy and Carol would have been upset if we'd gone against John's desire, and it seemed a little tactless for us to just go ahead. So we still have our prize steer and we're vegetarian until we get some meat another way. Ron is out hunting alone.

A number of adults have colds. We have been keeping the circle and kitchen warm. I'm using my own separate eating utensils. What else can we do? Add a little meat to the diet and people could cut out smoking tobacco so much.

Three hitchhikers from Boston came in and camped for a night, refugees from the city. They're in good spirits, long-haired, sort of raggedly clothed, and like most, not very prepared to start a new kind of life.

Tuesday: Another five inches of snow fell last night. The scene is incredibly beautiful with so much white ground and all white sky. We put down dry straw for the cow.

A visitor bought half a sheep. Tonight we had a taste of it with our millet, carrots, and cornbread.

I have felt just a little uneasy on coming back—something missing. I ran for several miles in the thick snow. Kim and I cut wood. How long will the woodpiles last?

Now we are in the throes of winter and our long-staying guest, Smilinghawk, has moved to the pueblo. He burned at least a ton of wood while all the rest together were burning less. When he could no longer make it in the teepee, he moves into the house. There are many people who wonder why he is here.

His circle is the peyote. These people I feel close to, so that is why, as yet, I have made no particular issue with their blond-haired boy.

I mentioned to Pepe about his attitude toward driving the Mind Machine every time he gets a desire to. While I was gone, he deserted it, out of gas, on the mesa. Kim, whom Pepe relates to very badly, had to rescue it. We had a short heated exchange.

In the morning, Kim was right back on the case. He got the Bird truck started with the six-volt battery. Then Carl stepped in and retarded the timing just a bit.

Nelly cow has a shitty attitude. She is giving two gallons a day. Every day we have fresh yogurt. John says last month the chickens averaged sixteen eggs a day. This month, a little down.

Ron is back after two days in the wet snow and in pretty good health.

Friday: Moon above us in a perfectly clear sky. Temperature reads 0°.

Our animals can eat over 900 pounds of grain a month. That's a lot. This spring we should get a much better idea of how much we can produce. With milk sales, we will buy grain and be self-sufficient in that way.

This spring we're going to try for full operation. The way the winter looks, we'll have the water. The big effort will be to plant alfalfa in most of the remaining fields. All will be accompanied by a grain; oats is the standard.

Tuesday: Pepe is feeling a little restless– kind of uptight—wants a better scene here.

Sandy just cleaned under the sinks. That looks good, and the sinks do not leak, thanks to Larry our ace plumber. Sandy also just recently repainted the kitchen with tierra blanca.

Larry is much like an encyclopedia of useful knowledge—very handy. About plumbing, cars, carpentry, adobe construction, astronomy, etc., he can put you way ahead. He's also our living history, since he is the only one who can tell about those times five years ago. Super level headed—no upset, no temper, not exposed. He even had a drink with me and a few of the other fellows the other day. Very down home.

We had a bunch of kids over for a while. Big Jim Gaskins and three other people are our guests. At John and Kim's suggestion, we had some beer tonight. We got to feel very good.

Pepe had a long "discussion" and a few harsh words with Isabel. However, a small council reprimanded the "down the road bit." Nevertheless, Isabel is going anyway to Colorado; Aurora is going to go, too, I hear.

I'm feeling great, actually. Each day I try to dig up a few wheelbarrows of cedar and piñon bark and put them on the main paths that are fast becoming a quagmire of mud. For walkways we have two-inch deep water next to four-inch deep wet snow on top of two inches of super mud. The woodpile is an abundance of this material that makes excellent walkways.

Kim put up a basketball hoop improvised out of a piece of wood and a bell housing.

Thursday: Pepe had a few hasty and harsh words for Sandy and Kemal today. He wants results right away. He wants certain perfection out of the people around him—demands it sometimes. He is very definite in a lot of his opinions; I certainly have my clashes with him, too.

I can see where there is a clash between Pepe and Sandy. He is excited and could fill a million hours with the things he sees to do. Sandy is—though always with a smile—a little bored sometimes. She is one of our most chronic smokers, very high energy, but only some of it coming out in things she likes to do. Still, she is the toughest chick and loves her home here.

The workshop is fitted with new doors and is completely enclosed. It is better arranged than ever. We have a big honey extractor, table saw, a small propane casting furnace, acetylene-oxygen tanks, plus all our hand tools, the free store, and workbenches. Now it has a lapidary machine, too.

Twenty eggs from the chickens yesterday. Great.

Randa is thinking of returning to California for a visit. She is the newest one to the scene. Half a year ago she never would have dreamed she'd be in the midst of a commune helping to cook and clean for up for twenty-five people. Carl, her husband, is now sleeping outside in the coldest weather. He stays up with the animals on the platform. He is great.

This is the hardest time when we need the best diet, but we were stopped from killing Bobo (not for long) and this upset our winter supply plans. John just loves the steer. He can have gold medals, praise, my love and help, but he can't have the steer. Next year we will have all spring and summer to prepare, but right now our diet needs improvement. Nowadays, I stay in bed an extra hour, just so I don't use up too much energy.

Tonight I'm just too tired to argue. We partied the last two nights and I got very nice indeed. Five guests here from Colorado going for their third day, and a new arrival from Minneapolis; Lucky is his name.

Sunday: The days continue to be clear. The uncared for walkways are all mud. About an hour after sundown everything is pretty frozen solid.

We are much more prosperous than last year with a full house and guests piling up. Big Suzy from Lama and Eddie are here. Handsome Billy is staying a few days. People from Colorado are still here. We're not only mellow, but we've been showing these people a good time with food, drink, smoke, and nightly entertainment. Kay cooked a great lasagna feast for all.

Monday: Nice and quiet this evening. Sandy very thoroughly washed all the kitchen counters. Carl watered and swept the circle, our living temple. All the colds are about gone. No kids coughing. No smoke from the circle fire anymore because of the new hood. Much better.

I keep working on the walkways adding cedar bark and chips. I remember Morningstar last year; to get to people's doorways you had to wade in at

Fig. 28. Billy at Taos craft market.
Photo by Clarice Kopecky.

least six inches of mud. No efforts at all did I see to drain the water or make pathways. Now I've become rather fond of making them. Just like a kid making dams in the rain.

End of January: Rain, yes. It started last night. Big snow in the mountains. Several places in the circle leaked pretty badly.

The vehicles are staying put. We're set with food and wood. Just keep the place straight and dig the winter scene.

Wednesday: Very cold day. Before first light Kim, Rebel, and Kemal walked out of the pueblo with their guns and headed north in the 0° morning.

Kemal's rifle froze in some manner. He was disassembling and reassembling the gun while watching the deer.

Our men are hardy; but yet, no success. Kemal and Kim didn't appear until dark. Tomorrow we hunt up at the barn.

Sunday: I led Bobo up to the cedar tree. We observed a quick blessing, and then Kim shot him once. Kemal cut the throat and I caught the blood. Quickly we had him gutted, skinned and halved. In the kitchen the carcass was cut up further and hung in the cellar.

Carl is preparing the tripe, and the head was boiled, and the meat went into posole. Chopped liver was made, which we ate right away, and Kim prepared the tongue. The meat fleshed off the hide was fried; that's mighty tasty. The blood, mixed with kerosene and linseed oil, went into the candle room floor. Old way.

On Saturday, twenty-two people in the Bird truck went to a "sort of" outdoor party at a ranch in Colorado, on the windswept snowy plains. We danced to the drums. Sobbing, Yvonne passed out on the dance floor. Foaming and slobbering at the mouth, Tam, obnoxiously drunk, tried to pick a fight with me and was bad-mouthing Buffalo. I hit him once and knocked him down when he attacked Carl. I pissed a little blood this morning from a kick he gave me. Bad as he was, we took him home with us. If nothing else, we did give the folks at home a beautiful day because of our absence. Last year was very different; Tom Brown was here. I shiver to think I lived with that guy.

I was just realizing the necessity of a tractor last year, and now we've got one. And we have a barn and livestock and a big crew who want to see this place produce.

February 1: Kemal and I talked to Leo Vigil about grazing some cattle here. I felt, rather than refuse him as I did last year, we should try to get an offer and help him out. We've had no livestock for so long that we've got some very good graze. We share the place with whatever weirdo comes up the road, so when our good neighbor wants to share the land in a practical way, we should do it.

John, "of course," is very upset; he is unreasonably anti-cattle. We did discuss it, he and I, in a pretty cool way this morning, but he is adamant and calls us buffoons with our heads up our asses. No one wants Buffalo turned into a desert. The answer to overgrazing is proper grazing, and we need to know.

Several believe cows eating and shitting is beneficial, especially at $5 a day, and we are helping one of our neighbors. Every year is hard for farmers with very little land holdings. Leo knows sheep and he knows the land. His 95-year-old father lives right here. Leo has no job in town; he's one of the few men left making a living off his land. I like him and I want to do him a good turn. He has helped us.

John is very intimidating. Still, I rather give consideration to Leo and sweat it out with John. Will John quit? I doubt it. Tomorrow we go to Beale's and buy more goats.

We had a few nice guests lately. One Spanish fellow, Victor, cut wood for the circle all day. Fellow Mike Pots, quiet and young, cut kitchen wood and is sweeping the circle. He brought us a little grass.

We separated the baby goats as soon as they arrived. They're living in the sand-candle box in John and Carol's room. They get fed three times a day and are so energetic with their long legs, floppy ears, and inquisitive eyes.

February 5, 1974: Wind is in the mountains, staying at a friend's cabin. Several went hitchhiking to town for the movies on a cold, cold night. Leo's cattle have been here for three days now. They prefer the graze surrounding the cottonwood tree.

Friday: Definitely a change of mood here, for the better. We cleaned all the vigas in the kitchen and oiled them. The vigas are dry pine trunks without the bark. They are beautiful.

Six quarts of milk the goats are producing. John is running all around; it is possible to help him. Tonight I went through the paces with him, helping to wash bottles and buckets, find lost things and feed the kids. It is also necessary to stay aware of which goats are which, how healthy they are and everything else. Oddly, for a person on a commune, John does not like to share this work.

It's February and it is COLD! Carl lit a fire in the root cellar yesterday. The temperature has gone down too far. The chickens average eighteen eggs a day.

Sunday: Kim has an offer to build some benches in return for six months free rent on a booth in town. He sounded excited this morning. Seems like Kim is going to do his part to make it happen. Lots of people beading and doing silver and copper jewelry.

This is the start of a spiritual age. Look at all these spiritual people. Pepe, a great spiritual leader, recently levitated to the far north reaches of Petersburg, Alaska where he was taken in by the Indians as an honored guest.

The spiritual age is also reflected at New Buffalo. We had a seminary student with us, Mick, now our neighbor and soon to be a father—a real revolutionary from Leadville, Colorado.

The peyote church is a super example here. Smilinghawk is quite devoted to the Church; he is even going to be adopted into an Indian family. To these people ceremony is no joke.

Justin, George, and Max were much into the Church. These were the leaders. Of course, we don't really have any leaders, but these people were important in Buffalo's beginning. The style of house is a connection to the spirit way. We live in a meetinghouse. Tonight the drum was playing, as it often does. We even have some of the most eligible peyote maidens living here at Buffalo, Isabel and Aurora. We do pray together every night holding hands.

Spirit is also in the jewelry craft, for this is a fine embodiment of a culture's symbols. We wear Indian head nickels, which have the buffalo on the reverse side—our own symbol. Our vehicle has paintings on it from three Indian cultures; painted on in fine colors and figures by Pepe. The most obvious spiritual connection—we work more to serve each other and find a new path than to accumulate personal wealth.

The twenty-seven cattle are easy to herd and they keep to the areas far away. The goats are going to be mischievous though, when we have greenhouse, garden, wheat, and oat fields to keep them out of. Leo Vigil was surprised to hear we had goat kids. He said, "They'll freeze." I told him they lived indoors at night. Leo's great chore coming up is lambing; he has 400 sheep. He wants to hold onto his alfalfa because sheep are going to start lambing early this year, so he'll have to bring them off the range.

All his cows look pregnant, as does our Nelly. Next, we've got to get Petunia the pig knocked up. She's quite wild and moving her definitely presents a problem. We have a real farm, just what I like. Wind is very fond of the pig.

Mid-February: The wintry scene is melting away. We've heard meadowlarks lately. Carl and I walked the fields. The best sight is the green shoots of grass and the thousands of alfalfa plants very near the ground.

The store where Kim is building some benches, is right on the historic Plaza and is coming along great. The booth is built. We get free rent. I made more candles. We could be making the money we need through our own crafts. Crazy little Mike from Lama Foundation gave Rebel $100, and we bought a money order for Stokes' seed order.

Wednesday: Perhaps a storm is developing in the mountains. Only the wheat fields now are covered with snow on the steep north facing slopes.

Our biggest shopping trip was today. We have a new relation to the food stamps. We are recognized as one family—one application. Our food stamp lady, Mrs. Vigil, is fairly helpful. I am grateful.

We were drinking coffee today with one of the federal agents who was up here once on a search. We laughed about how we were tearing up the plants as they came up the road. We met the fellow, Jim somebody, in Chuck's Gun Shop.

February 25: Pepe and Kay returned—glad to be home. In thirty days they were all the way up to Alaska at a wedding with the Indians for Dan Irish and his new Aleut bride. Pepe's no longer taking any drugs—no drinking, no smoke, LSD, or coke. So his trip has helped him make a good move.

Last night about ten hitchhikers with backpacks showed up. Today from Minnesota came our great friends, Bill and Phil Grotto, and about seven others in their 1953 school bus.

The fabulous young Mr. Pots has started sleeping in Randa's old room. He is the kind of person that brings new life to our scene. He wants to improve things; he's action-packed and disciplined. He likes the boot camp, tough aspect of our life.

It's drying out here. Most of our snow is gone. A few bees are out. Tomorrow is three weeks since we put those cattle on. It's quiet tonight at Buffalo. Our Minnesota people left. They want to get where it is warm. It's so much fun to see our friends from all over. Kim and Michael, our two good brothers, are off to Mexico.

Coyotes howling here in the valley. Star-filled sky above and no let-up in the drought.

Wednesday: The days are longer and the weather fairer. All seeds are ordered for the garden. Today I oiled all the tool handles and did some repairs.

Ron is wearing the new concho belt, one of Pepe's very best, and he treated a bunch of us to see a movie called *State of Siege*. We took in the ice cream parlor and the new bar. Very nice. He also made a $200 present to me.

March 2: We have to decide where to put a milk room. Maybe use Ian's old room, the closest to water. Concentrated energy—this is a catch phrase of mine. Use the structures better rather than keep building. The Tortoise Foundation this year, too, is going to try and swing over to agriculture, away from building. The Learning Center, too, will pretty much have to stop. Morningstar and Reality are both pretty much gone; they were only buildings, with not enough of the rest. Too much construction; it is a problem all over that people build and build.

Today we ended renting the land to Leo's cattle. Twenty-one days credit we have, four sheep, and we helped out our neighbor.

Wednesday: With John, Carol, Rebel, Tam, and Sandy, we took a look at our finances and at the letters from the state engineers. We're asking for a rep to come up to look over the situation.

We're just about in it now—Spring. Tractor is ready for plowing, disking, harrowing, planting, and spreading manure. The time is near. Felipe Cordova at the Mariposa ranch has already prepared his spring wheat fields. He is about the biggest rancher around. He's a fund of information for someone like me who is quite ignorant. And he's so happy to offer us a drink and sit in his big house and talk about everything. Petunia is over with his boar now.

March 6: Rebel led us on our first manure run of the season. Best haul ever— composted sheep manure—pretty dry. We brought a full load, about five tons. Had to use the chains to get in and out, and had to use the chains in our own fields.

We got poles and the calf corral is up. Carl already threw out five pounds of alfalfa seed.

Brother Ron, now departed for Washington, D.C., is due back in two weeks with his son.

Friday: Town trip—went with Rebel, Tam, Carol, and Marianne in the newly washed Bird truck. Bought food, seed, and handy things like scoop shovel and the wrong kind of chicken wire. And we got seed: brome, orchard grass, alfalfa, and spring wheat. Also priced fiberglass. Figure we want sixty sheets.

We made a new hitch for the plow and tested it near the barn. Carl and Reb are working right beside me, and Tam is in there too.

Marianne, Wind, and Carol will not let the kitchen slack. Sandy, too, works hard for us—she looks nicer than ever and isn't any less moody. Kay stepped in to cook last night, and Isabel, soon to depart here, puts in her time.

Saturday: Quiet at the pueblo. Beara and Diddy are among our guests.

My consciousness is really getting into farming practices. With Rebel,

Carl, Larry, and John I have long discussions. I am intoxicated with such things now.

Today we got some actual rain and it snowed on Lama. Great. We can postpone earth preparation until closer to planting time. That leaves the soil bare for the least amount of time.

Sunday: Here we are in the middle of a blizzard, snow coming down thick. Carol making date-apple zoo-zoo cake. Plenty of wood in the pile. Now this is the "right on" weather.

Boy, oh boy, we're back in the farming business. The Heavenly Father smiles on us and does not forget us. Though we missed a good chance last year to plant all the fields, we won't miss this time.

The fires crackle and the wind blows, the snow hits against the windows. Many of our clan are sitting in a teepee on the Morningstar mesa. Sky and Aurora put the meeting together, and Sky is singing twice as loud as ever.

On the romance scene, Rebel's heart has been slightly roughed up by Sandy, who took a liking to friend Billy. Reb, to vent his feelings and with some quantity of beer in him, let the air out of Billy's tires in the night. He pumped them back up in the morning by hand pump, and we passed humorously through one of those episodes that can involve a tussle or two. While I was talking with Reb last night, he told me how he had been so drunk once in 1970 when visiting from Morningstar, that he drove through the gate instead of opening it. Then he took the gate to Morningstar. Rebel the "vandal."

Wednesday: Clear days have followed that storm. Ground is still very wet. We should plow a big field perhaps by Saturday. First we need to get the tractor back together. Looks like we have enough chain for the bald tractor tire. Larry's been cleaning ditches and made a device for determining a three percent slope. He's a genius. It's like basic Egyptian geometry. A three percent slope neither erodes nor silts up!

Today we settled with the state engineers for 23.2 acres with water rights. This is the first time that this water right business has been clear. The fellow from Santa Fe was very friendly and told us of some up-and-coming court cases involving water on the Hondo.

In service of the community, Nellie, from Lama, poured some candles. Phil brought Kemal's three-year-old pregnant sorrel mare down here. Chickens are ordered. Strider and Beara are planning on being at the Ortiviz ranch, which is to become a corporation, quite like New Buffalo.

Thursday: Out front we now have cultivated soil protected by guard posts. The posts have already served very well as hitching posts for visiting horses. Kemal now is much into his horse. He's going to develop a fine skill. A run for cottonwood is in order.

We cut a few tops off some 55-gallon drums for garbage, and to catch rinse water. With a barrel outside the door, one can carry the water from the sink to the barrel. The new milk room needs a sink and a drain installed.

Both washing machines are out! The best one is in eight pieces in the tool shed. The stripped gear has to be removed. So where's Michael and Kim? The backlog of these jobs accumulates when some of the helpful people are away.

The pastures are turning vibrant green. The plants in the greenhouse are growing extremely well. We ordered some Russian olives and elms. We've got ourselves into a lot. Now the ground has to be made ready.

I'm going to help milk. Carol might pick up a big part of the milk responsibility too. This to me seems the best industry for Buffalo. We can't produce market vegetables or corn or beans—too risky and too dry. We probably can support a nice herd of goats and cows.

Our place is alive, busy yet quiet. Kemal is making housing for the young chicks, John cleaning house for the girls at the barn. Larry and Tam put in the new ditch that comes off the first ditch, goes to the barn area, then below to above the courtyard, and next, behind the west wing and past our greenhouse (did you get that?). Pepe quickly created another concho belt while Kay was beading. Aurora busied herself with something. She is an outstanding case of someone who stays almost entirely out of house business of any kind. She makes herself a fine blouse, but doesn't want to get those pretty hands very dirty!

Mike dug holes in the courtyard for some of the seventy-five trees we are expecting. Last year I made a small attempt at landscaping. This year we are making a major change by adding a lot of planting right near the pueblo.

I finally repaired the alcove roof; aesthetically, it could be taken a step further. I hear Tam got the brake lights to work. Carol filled in again, at the last minute, and cooked us some dinner.

Our new ditch is going to bring life to land that has been crying for it: the courtyard, the west wing dump-grounds and the greenhouse area. This ditch will put about thirty prairie dog holes in range too. It will not be such a major undertaking this year. Those gophers are starting to come out now.

Recommendation: No more money on booze or dope. Put the money into the kitchen for food or useful items.

Ron returned tonight from Washington, D.C. He survived but was not fitting in at all. Now he's back and will be a hard worker.

March 16: Nelly dropped a healthy bull calf. She ate all the afterbirth and her udder is so full. We're back in business. Five or ten more and we'd really have something. Gas filter is jerry-rigged into the tractor.

Carl and Mike put up the greenhouse fence. We had salad out of the greenhouse tonight. The aphids are gone; a dressing of compost did them in.

Ron finished digging the new summer outhouse; a screened in facility further from the kitchen is a very good idea.

March 18: Today Kemal, Ron, Rebel, and I went on a manure run to Carlos's up at San Cristobal. He was not home but Mrs. Trujillo was very friendly. This is another outstanding ranch where we have been welcomed. We then went to the Valdez ranch and Mr. Marcus said we could take all we want. Got a full load and then we stopped and had lunch with Ben Garcia on the way home and gave him a little of our score for his garden.

John got Tam to take the Bird Truck to the Talpa mill to buy lumber for the calf.

The fertilized places look much superior to the other places. Do we plow this week? John cautioned me about planting the wheat field early, because once the sprouts are up it is going to cut the goats' grazing area. John has been herding them almost every day. I think we need to start plowing.

Our apples are finally gone, but still there's three sacks of dried ones. So our apple stash got us through the winter. That was great work.

History: Janet is staying here with her two kids. We were recounting tales of the banditos. We spoke of Mongol, also called Funky James, who was here with his woman two days before he was shot dead. We talked of Ritchie whose funeral was held at Ojo Sarco; Pepe and Leslie were there. Chief Joseph was mentioned. He was killed in a gunfight with narcotics officials in Santa Fe. There also was a fellow Barry who died. We got to talking about Lobo, who maimed brothers Joey and Jimmie (shot in leg and hip) and then shot himself. Jimmie was once Janet's old man, and is the father of her younger boy, Shoshone, who is with us now. They were caught up in a Wild West fantasy with nothing constructive to do. Lost souls.

Earlier in the evening, Reb was telling stories; Poncho came up, our cowboy-prospector friend from Deming. "Poncho," he says, "was killed in a gunfight with Mexican federales!" Jesus.

Some of the scenes around have been rough. I hear tell where Indio, our revolutionary Chicano brother, once took some shots at the pueblo for some wild-eyed reason. Once a visiting hippie here, completely naked, ran down into a neighbor's house and destroyed their television while they were watching. They took a few shots at Buffalo, too. But now, with our friendly attitude, Sandy's five-year-old Jason sometimes watches TV at their house after school. We also ran through the catalogue of local livestock that have been killed by people's pet dogs.

For guests tonight there's a young fellow with his girlfriend. She is slight and quiet. He is in some sloppy pants with sneakers on and shaggy hair. He has a bag of food for his dog. The girl is a little ill. No bag of corn or dried fruit does he carry, but a bag of dog food—lack of consciousness—just as a rich man may ignore the poor and may squander millions, so the poor man plays the same fool and thinks not of how he can help himself or others. Such irks me.

March 21: First day of spring and no party this year; instead, a day of preparation. John worked on the calf house, Rebel and I dragged the disced fields, and Carl worked on hives. Marianne cooked all day to make us a splendid dinner with salad out of the greenhouse. Got Petunia back with little trouble. Hope she's pregnant.

I am now going to try and handle the cow. John never liked her but has dominated the scene. It's a frustrating situation, a cow that delivers as much milk as a goat. She's got milk, but she won't let it go. John was really fit to be tied last night. No more calf on her; we should have done that right away. I'm just going to keep milking her and hope I'll have her releasing her milk.

I celebrated spring with a few miles' run. I am getting a better breath. I feel just a little tenseness. Tam is sometimes uptight; most everyone emanates it once in a while. John is not pleased with Kemal's horse.

Big party at Lama. John and I left early and got home just in time to do the milking.

Friday: In the morning the Mind Machine went to town for a big shopping. It took the Brown house gang home, too, with all their groceries. This afternoon it took twenty-five people to Max's birthday party. She sounds great.

Toltec gave birth to three kids at milking time. They're all standing. The calf is now in with the male goats.

Saturday: The clouds are rolling overhead and heavy in the mountains, keeping the mountain snows cold and our ground from drying out. Rebel and I worked together on the planting. John came down and threw the alfalfa seed and Larry drove the tractor.

Pepe almost has one more silver belt ready. When finished it should be worth near $1000. He works on them and then usually gives them away or has someone else sell them. Ron still has the last one.

Mike mudded half the floor of the new milk room. He also mudded two holes in the kitchen, in need of repair for months. Kemal worked on the chicken breeding room with Smilinghawk's help. He made donuts after dinner.

March 26th or so: Larry and crew dug the irrigation ditch going below the greenhouse. Ron now has sworn off drinking. Rebel scored a regulation basketball hoop, backboard, and net.

I put together a map today showing all the fields and their crops and planting dates. Larry suggests we should plant some green manure crops in some of the fields. Field peas and oats are about the best ones I know of.

For some reason, a prairie dog was near the pueblo and a dozen people were chasing it. A visitor skinned and ate it after I did the poor creature in.

Tuesday: Carl and I went on a run across the valley. We saw several hundred acres under cultivation, mostly alfalfa. Some had an extremely green plant that was drilled in and is probably rye. The wheat from our seed also looks green and healthy.

Today we spread the manure piles and sawdust and added 400 pounds of rock phosphate on the upper garden site. We had difficulty with last year's weeds, which clog up the plow and create an immense amount of work. On the other piece of upper garden, we drove the disk twice, and it pretty effectively cut up the weeds. Now they can be gathered by rake or fork. May 8 was last year's main date for planting oats, alfalfa and pasture, so we have some time. The tractor, thank goodness, is running well. The big drag broke somewhat, when we flattened the plowed and disced garden.

The Hondo River is still running low. The run off from the mountains has not really started yet. Good.

Mike Pots made worm beds and fertilized tree holes. Kemal is getting the chicken house ready for breeding as well as a laying house.

Kim and Michael are still gone. Sandy and Wind are leaving tomorrow for California. I don't know what makes them think we can get along without

Fig. 29. Lower Arroyo Hondo. Photo by Clarice Kopecky.

them. That leaves five women here and eleven men. Marianne and Carol I hope will stay mellow and keep up the kitchen so well. Aurora, she's a bit like a fluttering bird caught inside.

Just two guests here. I hear there were two motorcycle rowdies freaking people out in our kitchen today. We have one far-out, weak, skinny freak, who drools and stares, around here somewhere. He once gave us $100.

Thank God I feel strong and have family who are feeling good too. We have the ball rolling now to see if we can make the farm produce.

March 28: I hear Ben Garcia would like some plowing done. We certainly should take the opportunity to work with our neighbors and give them a hand if it is in our means. Next Tuesday the tractor is due to go to Jonathon's. There is the post office lady's garden, too.

I'm anxious to prepare another field. Manuel Martinez, across the way, says he's put out his oats already. We have five major fields to be planted yet.

Reb has cleaned up around the workshop; very neat and orderly we are. I certainly like it that way. We'll be working on the ditch soon when Manuel tells us. A week's work for six guys—no small task.

Friday: There was a party over at John Kimmey's. We got an excellent taste of the best birthday zoo-zoos. Micky Long was there and asked if our plowing was for hire, and a household just below Micky's, asked for help. I hope we can do all these jobs. I do not believe every two-acre farm should have a tractor; rather those places that do maintain farming equipment should be willing to help.

Today, Carl, Kemal, Pots, and I got the truck stuck at Carlos Trujillo's. With a heavy load we sank right into his new little causeway. Carl had to go get the eight-ton jack. We threw off three-quarters of the load and drove right out after only six hours of pretty tough effort.

Our tire on the tractor is low. Our pressure gauge is broken. Our air pump was given away a year ago. We do have a hand pump. It is hard to say what will go wrong next.

The goats are doing well. John seems happy. He's feeding five different age groups of kids.

Sunday: Cold and windy. We took apart the tractor distributor three times and the carburetor four times before we found a very obvious clog. Reb and I finished the plowing in the moonlight.

Next day Rebel and I plowed most of the day at Ben Garcia's. The tractor worked excellently. Ben and family treated us to coffee and lunch and a very sociable rest from the wind. Next, bring the equipment over to Jonathon's. From there it will go to David's near the Learning Center. We saw Leo out plowing for several neighbors today.

April 2, 1974: We woke to a storm this morning; I made a few candles, Marianne baked us another cake. John is a bit ill. He watched as Carol and Ron fed the goat kids in the circle this morning with bottles while the snow blew outside. The little goats scramble for that nipple with such energy and desperation.

The couple staying here for three days from Texas left. The Frenchman Jean Pierre left, the Puerto Rican Chino left. Some clown Gray Horse came from a Las Vegas mental hospital to "join the commune."

Wednesday: With the surge of work has come a little earning; we sold a load of good quality manure to Mr. Duncan and family for $40. They want to buy some milk, too. Pepe sold a belt and pitched in $40. $30 came from plowing and more jobs coming up.

Thursday: On the stormy day we made our fastest batch of dip candles yet. Mike mudded a big piece of the circle floor. Marianne, after washing the morning dishes, made us maple walnut biscuits. She and Carol uncomplainingly have kept the kitchen most together. Front pantry is all cleaned. The Mind Machine picked up the chickens from the Feed Bin today. Ron scored a lot of chicken feed for only $10 in Questa.

The family at Buffalo is at a new stage. We're looking forward to a very good planting season. There will be croplands that dependably support the dairy every year. We will have a milk room too. New Buffalo was built with the expressed intention of creating a community that helps support itself through farming. Now we have a practical approach to this goal. When the consciousness only saw annual crops such as corn and beans, it could not create a farm year to year, because the area is so dry and cold and drought-prone. An acre or two of these, we'll do. But primarily, we're creating hay and pasture.

All the farms in our valley are basically into hay, pasture, and livestock. Mountain people all over the world depend much on their animals because what they eat grows in the mountains. The locals only grow small areas of corn and beans.

Saturday: Larry drove the tractor and Smilinghawk rode the plow. First Jonathon's patch was done in about twenty minutes, then off to David's. Later Larry came back and disced our orchard.

On foot, I visited Reality and Morningstar, which are just ghost communes now. It is like visiting an ancient ruin only the day after the last inhabitants left.

Tuesday: What can you believe? This morning Ron says the silver concho belt was missing! We had it too long. Still, where is it? A mystery.

"Worst of all," says Tucker, our brother Ian apparently shot himself in the head with a .22 pistol and now is very dead. Tucker saw him. Ray found him. This does not seem right either. Terrible.

On the lighter side, we have a late evening visitor who has a great big teddy bear with him and a little grass.

Pepe is quiet, keeping to himself. He has a .44 pistol, which he says he's going to inlay to double his money. With Ian dead and the belt missing, I might feel better if Pepe was closer to the family and not inlaying pistols.

Pepe does not care for Michael or Kim. I don't think he especially likes Ron, either. With all these people, I feel real kinship in the commune movement.

Larry's been re-routing irrigation ditches. Now with the fingers of water we are improving a great deal of the ranch. As we run in the fields, we see the hawks fly above the arroyo with the little river, headed for the canyon of the Rio Grande.

I feel a little uneasy. This is not too good. Ismael has gone back to city life and Pepe, my closest brother, not getting it on so well in this revolution he says he is for. But in his very active mind, he must have some ideas brewing. It is not the every day affairs of this house as it is with me; it is something far removed. Pepe is a messenger; he travels and absorbs people's culture into his art. I have called the hawk with Pepe; we have run the streams to the beaver ponds. He took me places I couldn't go alone; ours is a special bond.

Ian dead and the belt gone; Ian was in our family but he left. Damnation if the tale of suicide is true. He was a good man and could have made himself most useful in prospering this life. He did not, though.

It takes a long time and many tests to find our brothers. "Brothers, find your brothers" is a call of our time. Any movement worth its salt has its disappointments, its betrayals, and its opportunists. Whose mind is so subtle that it can see every mind? I know there are some I don't see. I hope for my brothers and sisters to pick up on the blind spots.

And today I saw Tucker; a man I have great trust in, and he told me he had seen Ian dead on the floor. This is a tragedy for his children and a tragedy for our family. It happened over on the Valdez rim.

The "revolution" is a thing on our minds. As we haul manure we talk. Sometimes I have Kemal describe to me all the kinds of food he can remember. Sometimes we talk about why we work, what we see in the future.

The wind is blowing very loudly tonight.

April 10: On a cold day with snow in the high peaks and clouds above us, Sky shaved for the first time in five years. Afterward, he went on a peyote wood run with Larry and Smilinghawk in the Bird truck.

Gurney plant order arrives. Fantastic. Right away, we started to put the plants in: three roses out front, and black raspberries in the courtyard. All the Chinese elms got planted. Russian olives and the asparagus tomorrow.

Ron gave me his last $100. He is a solid brother, working for the same things I am for. He believes that our life is a practical way to forward brotherhood and world peace as I do. He is serious and works at the tasks at hand. He has contributed several thousand dollars to our impoverished scene. Some people scoff at money, but he understands, as I do, that it is a very great help to have a little. Our goatherd and our barn owe much to him. And the smooth functioning of our house, through the past hard winter, was helped very materially by this man.

The belt has returned. I hardly believe it, that someone ripped it off. "No retribution for those guilty," says Pepe, is the price for its being restored it to us.

The commune has a long way to go. Our craft scene is not backing up the day laborers. Sky's first moneymaking scam in years is not coming off well. It would be beneath the dignity of the pampered Aurora to sell anything. Here again, we miss Michael and Kim, who are now gone a long time. And Sandy and Wind are gone, too.

Ah, but we still feel good. Garlic plants went in, garden plowed, another big field out west plowed, trees in and abundant snow in the mountains. We've been wearing jackets these last few days. The weather is so right on; it is like a miracle. All day the sky was dark over the east. The ground is still wet, excellent for plowing.

Friday: Good Friday as they call it here in Christendom and a windy one. Today in town, I went for broke, buying 150 pounds wheat seed and forty pounds of pea seeds, gasoline, gloves, antifreeze, and a few snickers bars.

Kemal started to plant the oats. Asparagus and more garlic in with Kay planting. Then she dove into the dishes when she had to come inside, out of the cold. Ron and I planted a few trees. Pepe took the one rear brake cylinder on the Mind Machine apart; we'll have to rebuild it.

Sandy, Jason, and Wind are back! Sandy wasted no time getting busy. In California she sold a necklace she made, a silver and serpentine piece. Not more than a few minutes back home and she presented me with $40 she had earned by selling that fabulous necklace.

Pepe created an incredible piece today; $50 worth of turquoise and silver into a bird with wings and tail on hinges of silver. Exquisite. Yesterday he made two rings: one to Rebel and one for Tam.

Sunday: In the kitchen Sandy, Kay, Carol, and Marianne were cooking, and Pepe was bending over the sink, so that when the Easter feast was ready, every dish and pan was clean. This morning Carol made exceptional cheese pastry, and cream cheese cake from our creamery.

Wind is right on the case with trees; today she exhausted herself planting.

Tuesday: Very busy. Many of us went to work on the diversion up the river with some locals. We all worked hard in the water. Had a great day.

At the house Sandy colored candles, Kay fixed lunch for the crew, and Tam fetched it. Carl pruned the orchard. Community ditch cleaning Saturday.

Wednesday: Clear and warm—great for working on the ditch. A few hard days' work moving rocks and we're aching to get on that tractor to plow and plant. Certainly we are learning a lot. The dairy took in ten gallons of milk today; Nelly up to four gallons plus. We had whipped cream on fabulous ginger-walnut cake.

Sky and Aurora are off to Arizona. The first money Sky's earned in two years, $50, and he uses it to get away. He and Aurora, I imagine, are going to find some other scene. They are our two most unrelating people, rarely talking to the non-peyote crowd. But they are spiritual and take good care of themselves.

April 18: *Sunny days and beautiful ways. All our men were working hard getting those fields in order. The women, more or less, took it easy today with a few jogs to the river. Another ditch crew went out but didn't have Rebel and Arty with them this time. Reb doesn't seem to like the idea that the women have exercise sessions; says there are rakes and shovels in the tool shed if we really want to exercise so badly. Oh well. I hope Arty comes home, or we'll just have to get someone to feed the calf.*—Writer unknown.

Sunday: Little Aaron is sick; his cough is worse. A few days ago, Janet had him on a blue-vervain tea fast, and he went in the cold river. They returned home and Janet had us drive him to the hospital, because she thought he was having a heart attack. Just as the truck was out of sight, I heard the story of the fast and swim—food fetish—he'll be better soon. Janet still has got the boy on eleven kinds of tea.

Yesterday Sandy drove the tractor with me on the plow.

JOURNAL THIRTEEN

I am now mayordomo of the Acequia
Llano de la Madre in Arroyo Hondo.

April 22, 1974: This evening is truly warm, one of the very first in many months. "More ditch cleaning tomorrow," says Al. It should be running Thursday. None too soon.

We seeded another field. It seems that the powers that be have postponed the ditch opening one more week. They are showing their authority by keeping the water back. They have certainly not showed their ability by getting the water on.

Tam and Kemal plowed. Finally the patterns are looking complete, and we have a definite idea of what should go where; wheat and alfalfa for most places, with a little brome. Plant tomorrow in the morning. Our test plot of peas is up.

Eight new colonies of bees were given homes here by Carl: one queen and three pounds of workers to each new hive. Carl gave them honey water right away.

Tam made arrangements to purchase the fiberglass for $240. Ron started digging out the site, so it will be slightly underground. That will be a major step to get the hothouse in.

Kemal, in fun, threw some books through my open window in the morning, onto my head. He then heaved a boulder into me while I was cleaning the sewer. Oddly enough, it didn't make such a big splat.

Pepe, in not so much fun, shoved me around the kitchen, after flying into a quick rage at Marianne. He smashed his fist into the table, startled everyone and frightened Marianne into tears. Then he had to grab me and push me around when I suggested he was being rude.

Five more Buffalos worked on the ditch. I stayed home to plant and plow. Only one more field left to do. All the fields will be transformed. The gray and yellow landscape will soon be green and only on the edges a reminder of what I looked at for two-and-a-half years. The field of wheat we planted March 20 is up very nicely.

April 26: Gas bill—one month overdue—broke. Wood run went well. Got vigas, poles, firewood, and two small live cedars. The Studebaker ran flawlessly.

Back at Buffalo, water still not on. Carl, Randa, and Pepe working in the garden. Pepe just finished an elaborate woodcarving and another silver concho belt.

Friday: We're certainly ready for the water. We planted another field of peas and oats and put in more irrigation. Reb switched over to mudding, and he and the fabulous Mike did a big section of floor. It's going to make a real change here, caring for our very center. After hours of labor, Larry and Ron unplugged the drainage pipe. Well done.

Our local commissioner, Al Kaplan, said we should have water next week. This weekend a delegation from Hondo is going to the upper diversions and try and get more water down to our ditch; Valdez and Desmontes ditches have been running for three weeks. Now it should be our turn.

Tam now has his own vehicle.

Saturday: Though the days are long now, it was not until sunset that most people put down their tools. Our fields lie ready; the sky does not give us water. The community is slow in getting the irrigation moving. I for one will take action next week if we do not get the opportunity to start our fields.

The wheat is most critical. The spring crop is threatened by too late a start. The water has been running for weeks in the Atalaya, Valdez, and Desmontes ditches. Meantime, we are very busy working the earth. I feel sort of weeded* now to the soil—a new exuberance.

April 29, 1974: In the afternoon, the water finally came on. The Desmontes ditch, about five miles above us, which was taking most of the water, is off completely for cleaning.

---

*A pun on "wedded."

The water is near raging. All our four gates are open and all the ditches are on, dividing up the water. We started to water the new fields, but took the water off them, as it got dark. At night, it is on the established fields. At least nine of us took turns.

Some friends arrived and also Steve Raines. Steve was part of the original ten-man team that made 16,000 adobe bricks the first year. He has stayed with the scene and now lives and works at Libre.

Tomorrow, early, we can get back to that water. Just now, near midnight, I unclogged the first ditch, which had shut itself off.

Wednesday: Yesterday was Kachina's birthday. Party brought about twenty kids between two and four years old; quite a sight with a band and lots of friends. There was more than enough food and cake and it rained moderately for about half an hour. At the party Pepe was the clown; earlier he was in the fields with us irrigating.

Today the irrigation proceeds. It is difficult to start fields because they need constant attention or the soil washes out, a big reason for perennial crops. It is too much erosion to be irrigating a field in its bare condition each year. We had one washout the night before last, when the first three gates got closed and all the water went to the last gate and overflowed on one wheat field.

Starting so many fields is a ridiculously big job. I've run myself a bit ragged keeping up with it. Today the situation mellowed back to just regular hard work, after that first frantic day watering seven new fields.

Full, full days of work now.

Thursday: We have pretty well carried through another job. The irrigation came on; our fields were planted and got irrigated. After this year, we'll have more established fields, which is essential for this little farm. The irrigation head gates we installed last year are serving us well now. The prairie dogs have remained eliminated.

Petunia's feed needs to be ground, the sink must go into the milk room. We're still at the elementary level of getting to be productive.

Carl and Wind have been just about continually on the job. Larry, too, has been doing many hours in the fields; his specialty is erosion control. He has resurrected a hand pushed machine that can cultivate and lays out furrows. The lower garden is almost all planted. Kay has done a lot of the planting.

May 1, 1974: Carl, Kay, and I planted our first corn of the season—white and a little patch of blue—four inches deep.

Rebel the vandal strikes again! In an uncommon fit of anger, Reb cut the rope for Mike's trapeze. Now that wasn't very nice.

Speaking of clever moves, Ron finally sold that silver belt and got badly burned in the process. So, we are back to being pretty poor, but without the promise of this windfall. Never the less, we can make out with little money for a while longer, I'm sure.

Pepe has four pounds of raw turquoise and a lapidary machine. It's a lot of work to cut those stones.

Tuesday: The hay fields look emerald. Records for milk being set in the barnyard! Sometimes there is a bit of an uptight vibe around, but basically we are enjoying our life together. The whole house is working out. We bottled some beer yesterday and much of the planted garden got mulched. The volleyball net is back up. Larry and Smilinghawk put in the foundation for an horno—an adobe oven. Pepe went to get us in the movies—*Bite The Bullet*—but was too early on the set.

We passed some beautiful country in Desmontes when we brought some thin vigas to Little Bird's house. She paid the gas and we shared some wood.

Here's a new reverse; a state trooper brought a young lady up here. Along with her, Alan, kid, and Tufique are here; they are family. There's a couple and a single guitar-playing guy, too.

The Circle growing. None of any of the visitors brought so much as one cracker as far as I know. Doesn't make things any easier when we cook for twenty and serve thirty. But we do like to see the people.

Thursday: We're working right up to the critical time for planting beans and corn; By May 15 we've got to be ready. The main ditch has been dry for us for five days now. In Desmontes they have much more water and in Valdez also, because they are right on the river.

Pepe, Kay and I saw a movie, *Executive Action,* about the Kennedy assassination. That movie gives an historical lesson. The deciding blow that convinced one conspirator to go along with the killing was Kennedy's taking 1000 advisors out of Vietnam. I am realizing more and more that the elite who control the economy are going to have to be gotten off their throne. Land of equality with such disparity is farce. More and more I believe, that in my lifetime, I should see some major change take place in this area.

The commune is a natural alternative to the lifestyle of consumption. I've still got a notion in the back of my head, that this may play a role in the future of this country's economics. With roots in the soil, with people being close to some essentials, there would be less insecurity about the often-slipping numbers of jobs. With more working people not so dependent on the jobs offered by the big corporations, we would perhaps be able to depose those people who guide our economy into such conspicuous consumption.

Friday: Señora Medina says she planted corn today, five inches deep. Neighbor Al says another delegation will go to Desmontes. It is the talk of Arroyo Hondo how they cut us so short.

Tam did one of his everybody love me numbers at the dance and is now sporting two black eyes. *"Fuck you Anshway. It's a bunch of bull. You weren't even there and Tam got his face beaten in."—Tam.*

In the afternoon, neighbor Simon Vigil, a cousin of Leo's, came over to see if he could get us to plow with our tractor. Sure enough, we went. His mother, about eighty years old, helped plant. They dropped corn, bean, squash, and sweet pea seeds in the trough behind the tractor and got a whole field planted in two easy steps.

Sunday: We're scheduled to get water next week. Desmontes cut down their ditch according to Al, who saw it happen. Then Valdez adjusted some gates. This should give Arroyo Hondo more water. Hopefully tomorrow, there will be enough to run the garden ditch.

Monday: We got a little water. This is overflow from people above us. It is the difference from Desmontes and Valdez cutting down their gates a little. Just what we've been wanting to happen.

The wheat is a good six to eight inches tall and makes waves in the wind.

May 13: Busy days. Some are off to make some money at the Chama movie set. Actor James Coburn was up here and told us they'd be hiring extras. Some of the girls were all a flutter, and Carol mischievously pulled up Marianne's shirt, exposing breasts, and asked Coburn if they would do!

Wednesday: Dry, dry, dry. With a week of almost solid sun, the temperature is up to 90°. A good rain would be very welcome. We got just a little water today as we did some planting: beans, three inches deep, also a few squash, fava beans, corn, lettuce, beets, and chard. Still holding off most planting of the beans, squash, and corn.

Ben Garcia is mayordomo. We need him and there was a new meeting about the Valdez, Desmontes, and Hondo ditches. Al has been chasing around in his VW. He's almost late with his own garden, which is a pressure on him. He showed me some papers. He says the Llano ditch has 640 acres or so and Atalaya about 600. Desmontes has some 1500 acres and Valdez, 300. There is a proposal to have three locks on the controversial ditches' head gates.

Thursday: All the germinated zucchinis have frosted. The very frost hardy alfalfa has sprouted all over. I marvel at the complex unfolding of tiny leaves. Some one told me, Al fal fa is Arabic for "father of food."

Today we got a piece of the water. Some clover and alfalfa is bushy enough to cut. Nelly should get some. John lets her pasture in the late afternoon near the barn. So far, she has just stayed in the clover. We painted her back with some turpentine this morning, which we read is a cure for larvae in the hide of cows.

Ben Garcia, the mayordomo, was here for a few minutes. Janet ran the ditch this morning and met him as he was coming down stream.

Janet and Beara put potatoes and peas in. Carl put in most of the remaining onion seed. Wind planted the asparagus seeds near the strawberries, where our very quiet visitor Paul prepared the ground. Wind also has seeded a few of the little cultivated plots near the house.

May 18: We were very together to have had our field crops in when the water first came on. If we had to start all our fields now, we'd be in trouble. Comfrey is doing well. Jerusalem artichokes and asparagus are sending up more sprouts.

In our kitchen everyday we are served excellently. Carl often cooks the morning porridge and Carol makes lots of bread, usually. Marianne, it seems, was getting into too many hassles with a few people and has removed herself for the moment. Janet is quite right; that we have gotten into a pretty strict division of labor. Kay, Sandy, Randa, Wind, and Carol take most responsibility of the kitchen.

A few people went to Chama to be movie stars. Oh well, another fantasy down. $20 a day for hanging around. Pepe having fun, seeing how often he can get in front of the camera.

May 20: Froze last night—a quarter-inch of ice on the water trough. Peas and corn look smeared in the field. NO corn planting before May 15! The alfalfa and clover are only slightly affected. Ron and I finished planting the white and posole corn.

Wednesday: We got $322 worth of food stamps. Very nice. Some of us went to the movie production in Chama again. Sky and Aurora put their things on Carl's truck and moved a few miles away! I wish them luck.

May 24: Latest news Friday: six SLA [Symbionese Liberation Army] radicals in California were killed. Terrorism in Israel—machine gun killing of school children—Israel air attacks on refugees.

On the home front, Pepe and Ron got in an argument, which ended by Pepe kind of stomping Ron, with Carol trying to break it up. Ron has a gash under an eye. Pepe left the scene to take Kiva home. Ron looked a sight with his face all bloody and us all standing around with Pepe screaming, challenging any of the rest of us to try him.

INSTANT KARMA—Pepe's ankle is broken; he is in pain. I took him to the hospital to get an x-ray. Tomorrow for the cast. Ron has conducted himself very nicely for us by being very mellow behind it. Now that Pepe's temper is back down, he's his usual amusing, laughing self. This was a bad one, though. Pepe should have controlled his anger. Not very nice for us to watch Ron, one of our main men, get raged on. Perhaps Pepe should say grace less often and practice a lot more.

I had a great day. Planted one row of lettuce with Sandy, sold $40 of manure to Duncan. Duncan said his El Medio ditch meets once every four days to divide the water. He makes the point that our community must be organized before we can approach the other communities for more water.

Ben is not happy with being mayordomo because some people are heavily on his case. Rumor has it he quit. I told Al that I'd volunteer to be mayordomo if no one else is willing. Another manure run went out to raise some money and brought back news that Ben Garcia says we'll get the water sometime next week, for forty-eight hours.

Kay has tied one off tonight. Carl, Janet, Larry, and Mike irrigated in the dark when the water came on at last light. Louisa appeared and disappeared.

Monday: Another hot long day with a few clouds. John got some alfalfa bales. Pepe got his cast. Three rows of lettuce came up that Sandy planted. Tam said yesterday he was leaving. Good luck to him.

Thursday: Since Monday I've been irrigating with Manuel on fourteen acres of his. He sure is a hard worker; right on the case and very mellow too. Talkative. I've been working in exchange for the cream separator and as a favor to him.

Tuesday we went at 5:00 p.m. to the Desmontes head gate. Cristobal Montoya is their leader, and Don Gonzales was there, too. From Hondo, Marcus Ortiz is our head spokesman. Al, Manuel, and a couple of others and I from Hondo were there. Desmontes did close their gate some; they were taking an outrageous amount and still end up with very good water. They don't really give us satisfaction; they should have taken a one- or two-week penalty for having had so much. Took about one hour of bargaining. Ortiz and I then moved some Valdez rocks. Since our Llano ditch is the least water, all others should come down a little.

Yesterday Ron and Rebel did a big piece of the circle floor with red mud and Elmer's glue. Carl put a bunch more seeds in. Still no rain and each day windy and getting hotter.

Thursday: Tomorrow, the water. It is officially ours for the first time this year—the whole of it. John suggested a meeting and a group of men discussed the watering plan for tomorrow. This is actually the first time since I'm at Buffalo that we've had such a situation. The first year was a bad drought, and the ditch was off. There were actually no fields in any crop, except for one-eighth of an acre of alfalfa and brome. There was also a dead corn patch with one row of shriveled onions all around it, out where no one knew to look. The next year was very dry, too. Still, we planted a garden and I started to learn about the ditches. As I helped tinker with a few rows of beans and peas, I admired the big expanses of green in the valley and wondered what could possibly be growing out there. Now I know and we're well on our way to having the same green fields here, too.

Last spring was flood instead of the usual drought. We still only had about half of our fields planted. This year we're farming our twenty-three acres of water rights. Tomorrow, we will start to try and water the whole thing. We were right on it this spring, so that the day the water came on, we had all our fields waiting and for two days we watered. Like a hockey player moving the puck, we constantly spread the flooding water to cover everything while washing nothing out. Dozens of shallow ditches bring the water to different areas of the land. Like a giant freight yard, we can send the water anywhere we want.

What's the matter with Pepe? Always ready these days with a bad word for someone. With the news today that Kim, Michael, and Marianne were soon to be returning "home," he sharpened his temper and told several of us that he was going to make sure that those fuckers know that there's his kind in this world, too. He just can't wait to kick someone with his cast or wrap his crutch around someone's neck. Nice attitude. And really it's these young folk that give the commune life. Oh dear. So God bless us and help us as we ask in Circle. As we are overcoming our problems on the economic level, we are also faced with spiritual problems. These three people were long ago accepted as part of the Buffalo home team. Matter of fact, Michael was here long before the Pride family and is a good friend of Max.

Tonight there is a big storm in the east. The lightning flashes very frequently, but there's no sound—far away. Water tomorrow.

May 31: Today we got up before the sun and irrigated. Carl went and broke the dam so we'd get the water.

Ben Garcia was here this morning. Said something about me taking an official job with the ditch. I am certainly interested. Tonight Celestino Medina, a neighbor, took the water under Marco's authority. We had the water under Ben's authority. Al, Celestino, and I went to see Marcos. Marcos said he's supposed to be sharing it with us. If we are to do two farms at once, we're going to have to get more water from Desmontes, Valdez, and Cañoncito. I'm sure things can be adjusted.

Saturday: I kind of dragged myself up before sunrise. Carl was up at the ditch when I looked up, and he went to get the water.

Señor Ortiz, Nasario Jaramillo, and Al came over this evening, and with no one especially meaning it to happen, except Ben perhaps, I am now mayordomo of the Acequia Llano de la Madre in Arroyo Hondo; an official of the State of New Mexico. A small town and a small honor, perhaps, but incredible to me nevertheless.

I have no fear of it or apprehension. Though it is a paid office, it is pretty much volunteering to do a difficult job. By the theory set up, the commissioners are in charge and hire a mayordomo. I am willing to learn and take advice, and I am very interested in learning about farming and watering systems. The water is vital. One of the first things the commissioners suggested was meetings; I have been in favor of this. The Desmontes ditches are way ahead of us on that score. Some have a reparto de agua every day.

The commune gives me a great advantage; I have enough brothers and sisters doing the survival trips with me that I can devote some time to a community job.

June 6, 1974: Al and I went over all the ditches in the Rio Hondo Valley. Desmontes ditch was changed recently, by vandals, to favor Desmontes. One

Fig. 30. Arty AnSwei. Photo by Clarice Kopecky.

Valdez ditch had been patched to favor the south Valdez rim, about three farms, that's all. We looked at the Cañoncito ditches, with seventy acres against our 1000; they are being much favored.

At Buffalo the crops are in. The sewer roof is back on. The front end of the red truck is in the air being worked on, Larry and Carl doing the job. The circle floor is ready for its slip-coat. The crew is Reb, Ron, and Kemal mixing up batch after batch of mud.

I'm getting a real good look at Hondo agriculture. I can see how the water rights have been slipping. I can see how people are planting. And I am proud to be a part of the scene. I hope I can help our neighbors by taking such an interest in the water. After a week on the job, I've helped reset the gates, and I've met most of the farmers.

Friday: Today I could definitely see the difference that cutting back the Valdez ditches made. We're only asking consideration and equality. We were at the point, where on a normal year, we could hardly function. And now we have rain, hours of it, gentle but pretty heavy. It is a week since we irrigated, so it is well timed for us. All of a sudden, a new situation. The fields are well watered by the rain and the river is up ten times or something, from the snowmelt. The Hondo is raging. This is the first heavy precipitation since that snow in

January. Our diversion dam is holding and the ditches are full. I ran in the rain. Happy. Will it freeze tonight?

We have truly been smiled upon. All our crops survived, even the tomatoes. It never got very cold and the morning dawns clear and hot inside of an hour.

Monday: Kim and Michael arrived today, home to a prospering scene. Sandy and Carol mobbed them with hugs and kisses. And Marianne returned the day before. She broke back into the kitchen with two strawberry-pineapple cheesecakes, made with our own cheese.

Larry worked a little on the new outhouse seat and floor. John and Sandy dug out the trench for the new pigpen. Of all the wondrous things, a tall, blond gal is staying with Rebel. All that effort and devotion does get returned.

Monday: It was very hot until some clouds came up this afternoon. The earliest spring wheat is getting its seed heads. There are alfalfas all over. The fields, with steam coming off them in the morning, are quite potent.

Busy here at New Buffalo. A number of friends and guests arriving, including our long-lost president, Robbie Gordon, whom only Larry has ever met. Robbie has enchanted the white walls of the circle with his mandolin playing for several evenings. Lenore is quietly popping up all the time. She gave me $85, which we spent quickly. Lenore is a goddess, and sometimes she wears nothing at all.

Being mayordomo is taking time, three to four hours a day, and fairly often I'm pretty tired when I cross back into Buffalo. Hunting party is back—no kill.

Wednesday: Went on a wood run with Mike and Kemal. Leo cut our clover for us.

Thursday: Another fabulous day. The asparagus seeds are coming up. The garden growing slowly. We got the buck rake back from Tony Medina and for $55, Kemal, Larry, and the Boston boys bought a horse drawn mowing machine—two more pieces of farm equipment. They are beautiful!

Had a good day on the ditch. Talked to a lot of people and made decisions. And it's summer! Oh, spring is gone and it's time for our party.

Saturday: Hot day. We had our incredible open house party. Two very good bands played until dark. Five to six hundred people—whirling, dancing—$300 or so of beer, some LSD, a few drunks. John had the goats out all day by the river; brought them in with no problem. The drums played all night. Lots of people camped down by the cottonwood tree and pasture.

In the morning we were up early, anxious to see the party over and the leftovers gone. We cleaned up, took down the stage. Carol was scrubbing the counters by 5:30 a.m. and Sandy sweeping the circle—urge to get back to normal instantly. Just one fellow, who is your city junk and booze bum, we asked to speed his departure.

The boys bringing in the hay. Others out with hoes, weeding the garden. Back to being this farm that we love.

Drunks and heavy booze—Duh—one drunk had to be taken to the hospital. Our own Paul and Chuck both passed right out, after guzzling as much as their brains could take. One drunk threw up in Mike's blankets. In general, the drunks have that bad motherfucker mouth; talking about smashing, always just slightly away from violence. To me it shows weakness, and the more I see of it, the less I like it. That's one reason we're so anxious to close down the party in the morning, because we don't want that particular vibration.

Thursday: There is a petition against the development of Kachina Village. They want our water. I wrote a letter to the Forest Supervisor, expressing concern. The circle floor got a red slip-coat and looks really great.

Tuesday: Our ditch is way down. I'm giving Buffalo some water today, and Rebel is going to be on patrol. I'm glad to be off for a day; I've put a lot of time on the ditch. I was in a little argument with Melacio. I guess it has to happen sometime.

Desmontes has a very good stream of water. Other communities are still maintaining the level they are used to. In Hondo, we have a crisis with very little water. The only solution I see is that they have to turn off every other week or whatever is fair. If we don't get these solutions firmly made, then our agriculture is constantly threatened. The other guys hardly know it is a problem down here.

Cut more hay. Petunia is in her new pen. Kay is returned and happily reunited with Pepe.

July 10: Pepe and Kay have left, but Kiva has moved back in—with Kemal! Kiva's horse is here, and Kemal's is soon to give birth. Petunia gave birth to eleven piglets.

JOURNAL FOURTEEN

This is our school—how to get along, how to cooperate with near and far neighbors, how to solve difficult problems, how to confront fellow humans without the situation developing into a brawl.

July 15, 1974: This is the middle of summer, beautiful and quite perfect. There are clouds and the hope of rain. Crops look good in the fields, and this family is as together as any group I've been with.

On the other hand (en cambio), there is the ever-unresolved crisis with the ditch. To resolve it is to guarantee the future of this tiny pocket of agriculture, Arroyo Hondo.

Our harvest should be one of Buffalo's best. For the winter we have four sheep, eight pigs, and three goats for meat. Bozo the steer we're going to try and raise to full size. We will also be able to pasture some cattle here in the winter for trade, maybe beef. Carl says we've got honey coming up.

Our main crop will take several years to reach maximum. At least it is clear now—the vision—the alfalfa is in, but we have to let it grow. Alfalfa is like an underground bush; you can keep mowing it back. But it takes several years to achieve a decent size.

Around 4:30 p.m., Larry, Kim, Michael, Kemal, Ron, Rebel, and I took the newly repaired Mind Machine and went to the Desmontes head gate with two heavy-duty digging bars. Several times in the past we were disappointed in what we got. This time, we gave a demonstration of what we considered a fairer sharing of the river. Some men from Desmontes were a little aghast. We got into the rushing water of the Hondo—clear, cold, a couple of feet deep —and rearranged boulders to adjust the flow. This diversion from the river is several hundred years old.

Now that we took the bold step of really reducing the Desmontes water, we are obligated to do the same to Valdez and Cañóncito. Only with those ditches off, some of the time, are we going to get enough water to do the second round of watering in Arroyo Hondo. If there is so little water that people must accept a loss, then the communities each should take a loss.

I am committed to the struggle. To give up or to lose means to give up the farm here. I believe there is enough water for all if worked well.

This is our school—how to get along, how to cooperate with near and far neighbors, how to solve difficult problems, how to confront fellow humans without the situation developing into a brawl. God bless our efforts and let us find good solutions.

Kiva is going to make this her home and settle in with Kemal! Kiva was once my high school sweetheart in New York. I had a two-hour subway ride to see her radiant smile. Here in the high desert we are an eternity away from the Bronx.

In a surprise move, Kay is back living here and Pepe is a bachelor again. He's up for a flash quite often.

Friday: This evening I put another blanket on. It is getting a little cooler, days are slightly shorter, the plants are rushing to develop their fruits. Some of the wheat is getting distinctly yellow; it is drying.

Marianne just showed up, and I hear Angela is in Colorado at the Red Rockers. She is such a beautiful woman, and what was wrong with me that I didn't pick up on her more.

Saturday: I got the water headed down to this end of the valley and we picked up beautiful, high-quality hay and lots of it. The smells are intoxicating as we gather and stack the windrowed harvest on the flatbed truck using our pitch-forks.

All of a sudden, we are pretty much home free. The corn can go without another irrigation—the squash too. The wheat is turning yellow and the ker-nels are full. The oat fields look uniform. The alfalfa looks fresh, over a foot tall. We live in such abundance. A bunch of poor people, we are still able to scrape up what we need to patch and glue this scene together.

Fig. 31. Kiva and Kemal. Photo by Clarice Kopecky.

Thursday: Clouds and tiny little rains. One good head of water in the ditch. Thinking more and more about the Kachina Village sleaze. It is a very real threat to the agriculture of Hondo.

July 25: Big storm but still no rain. Mike's birthday today—big feast in celebration.

I drove a "Stop Kachina Village—Save the Water" float in the town Fiesta today. It's a beautiful float, put together on our Studebaker by a bunch of young local people. They did the work at El Centro—the old TLC*—getting together, clarifying the issues, and taking action. STOP Kachina Village; that is our object. Reason? It's them or us. The water in Hondo has dried up to the point where another big user would take the slim margin away that keeps us going.

Rebel is fixing the skylights with plexiglass screwed and glued down; the circle and kitchen are getting leak-proofed.

Meanwhile, Kiva and Kemal are settled in their new pad: new rugs on the floor, low bed and very nice-looking. From the cave of a wild and slightly mad bear, to the comfortable and warm space of Mr. and Mrs. Clean.

*Taos Learning Center

Monday: A little rain in the afternoon as we harvest with sickles. We're cutting the oats green with the kernels still immature; dough stage, milk stage, I don't know. John says this is good for the goats.

Lots of guests. Yesterday, there were twelve strangers all at once. A couple from Ottawa, Canada also.

Tuesday: Kemal, Carl, and I went to see Ron in Valdez. We'll be able to pick seven apple trees of his. Back home John, Carol, and crew are harvesting the oats. A pretty girl, Peggi Sue, has materialized and is painting skylights. Mike doing more mudding on his wing. Kids' room getting mudded, and a new floor going in the room Neil and Holly used to have.

Wednesday: Wood run went out; had to hunt through the woods and carry to the truck. I am very conscious that it is a dwindling resource. For the moment though, we have got the tools and strength to go to the more remote places, where there is still dead seasoned wood just lying around.

We got a heavy load. With a rope over it once, it was well packed. Put Carl and Michael and the spare on top of the pile and had beautiful ride home. The truck engine carries the load perfectly up and down some rough terrain; the load and the body are one, making the truck handle much better than when empty.

Monday: It rained for real, from Friday until Sunday. There's mud in the road and a good watering for everything. We've been getting more guests. Seems Peggi Sue is going to stay on. This is more like it. I think she knows Michael from Boston. Young, blond, perfect figure, and she is just an explosion of sunshine.

Doctor says I'm cured—hope so. Walking down the back road, holding Sandy's hand, I told her she's the only gal for me now. John and Carol seem pleased to be together, and Kemal and Kiva are set up to last for some time. Kay, in the most on-and-off romance of the year, has run off with Pepe today.

Tuesday: Larry and crew finished the winter wheat harvest; the sheaves of grain are in the truck. The spring wheat is also ready to go; it should be kept separate.

The alfalfa grows incredibly fast. There are many acres now, a far cry from the old barren, dusty fields.

The kitchen is providing food for thirty people a day, with lots of our own garden produce. John always has cheese in the works.

Ceil and daughter Kaiya are visiting. This new gal Peggi Sue is just a gift from heaven!

Thursday: This morning the sky was full of clouds. Carl and I gathered in all the oats off the first field and stacked the bundles. They were easily covered with a tarp. The bundles allow the grain to be stacked and unstacked to keep it out of the rain. Best to keep grain dry. Carl cut the wheat that was left. After scything a bunch, he ties a bundle and props it up so the kernels continue to dry. This method has been going on for 10,000 years.

   With the rain, the pressure is off for irrigation. As mayordomo I keep having to find people to take the water. We can let it return to the Rio Grande also.

Friday: RAID! Last evening, just as Nixon was resigning, we got raided by three cops, two FBI's, backed up by a few carloads of state troopers, who stayed in the parking lot. Kemal took the rap and it cost us $60 to get him off. One long-haired narc chased Reb around and drew his gun on him. Rebel then gave him the slip through the kitchen. They left after an hour. All agree—magistrate, cops, and us—that we were foolish to have that pot so out-front.

   Kemal is wonderful.—Written by Kemal. He is indeed. Paid Washam Gas and Electric bill, which broke the bank.

Saturday: Beautiful day. I went on the ditch and talked to everyone about Augusto 18 junta en Arroyo Seco; Learning Center will go in force, too.

   Kemal took the 550 pounds of wheat to Julian's. No charge because we're going to help Julian with a wood run. Julian, a neighbor, has that huge old-time stationary threshing machine; you have to bring the bundled wheat to it. Then in a flying, shaking whirl, it separates the wheat kernels.

   Wrote a letter to the *Taos News* about Kachina Village. Kemal talked to our Desmontes friends about it. In addition, he found some fruit trees to pick.

   At least twelve guests here. Guest scene has been pretty mellow, but almost none of these people are food-conscious enough to contribute something to our kitchen. Very good though, the way people for some reason feel a part of the place.

Monday: Hot sun all day. Fabulous for our hay that is cut and lying on the ground. Tomorrow morning we windrow, gathering it up with the buck rake.

   Carl, Kim, and I helped Leo repair an old Ford tractor; the problem was the points were not set. His hay is coming in late, but looking good. As we harvested the spring wheat we found nice alfalfa fields. Because alfalfa starts out so small it is usually planted with a grain crop the first year. By the second year you should have a perennial alfalfa field.

Thursday: Kemal got Michael and I to do a wood run, third day in a row. We were tired, but went through with it and then took the load to Teles Good Morning at the venerated Taos Indian Pueblo. He fed us in return.

More wheat is getting harvested. John brought in the oats and another truckload of hay. More second cut to come in yet. We're working hard. In appreciation, Kiva cooked us a super fine chicken dinner.

Saturday: Crystal clear mornings and nights. First slight frost a few days ago, definitely a change in the weather. Our corn and pumpkins would like another month to grow.

Big volleyball tournament at La Lama Foundation. There were four teams: The TLC, Tortoise, Lama Foundation, and New Buffalo. We won every game. Fabulous party with lots of friends, food, a little beer. To the games today we brought a big bowl of excellent goat cheese, John's finest. We also brought half a sheep and a giant garbanzo bean salad. Max, Paul, and Chuck all there; Pepe, too, who refused to ride up with us.

Pepe's part has changed considerably. It is like he's got a personal vendetta against our furry freak brothers, Kim and Michael. They are from Boston—Easterners. He's already plastered Ron. Now he fought with Kim. His pleasant mood and smile is like a guise; he jumped on Marianne and then me in the kitchen—a little berzerko act. We certainly can't have a tight group with this fellow. Pepe, our dear leader and my good friend. Just a passing phase, I hope. Kay has fled the situation.

Kay got jealous of Pepe chasing the girls. She thought she could rope him in. No, I don't think so. Then she comes onto handsome Kim for revenge and Pepe gets mad and throws some punches at him. Who writes this stuff? And Kim is so important to us. He's young, bright, with big strong arms. And he is mellow, hard working, thoughtful, and he's the farming type!

Tomorrow we travel to the big junta to show opposition to the Kachina Village and get support for our development proposals. Kay packed up and split for California.

A new day: Several of the kids have taken to sleeping in the main circle room. Jody has swept it several times.

The BIG news is La Junta. Several hundred people came, an excellent presentation was made, and the meeting was very mellow, orderly, and solidly there to say "no" in no compromising fashion. The gathering was carried on in two languages. This was an historic meeting where more inter-community action was taken than has probably ever been.

Already, all kinds of environmentalists and Sierra Club graduate school ecologists have made effective opposition to the rich men's development. Now the farmers have spoken out very strongly. Hopefully, this will be the shot in the arm that the agriculture needs in our communities to get the water better used.

Seems the cow was in heat again, because old Toro jumped the fence and has been having a very amorous time with old Nell!

Wednesday: We are basically finished with our grain cutting as of yesterday at suppertime.

August 23: A little frost this morning—touch of snow in the mountains. One porcupine killed last night. The unfortunate critters love corn. More hay coming in. Wheat to be threshed today. We helped cut Kaplan's alfalfa. Wheat harvest is in! Last year, 900 pounds and this year, 1800 pounds!

Saturday: The wheat is all over the place; the back pantry is full of sacks and there are ten sacks in the milk room and 500 lbs drying on Michael's floor.

Hay is in and it didn't rain. John un-domed the stack I worked at yesterday. He's got two out of three stacks molding, and now it is set up to catch more water than ever. The oats too, have got lots of exposure, instead of minimum exposure, and they're set up to catch and hold water too, instead of running the water off. This inability to work with John is getting to be a problem. I just don't feel right when it rains knowing our hay is getting soaked.

Saturday: Peggi Sue, our new zoo-zoo queen, has settled it with her mother to stay here. I highly approve. Kemal is mudding the floor in what was Jesse and Diane's room to give Kiva her own space.

September 1 1974: I was up early to see the garden and to check for porcupines. There was ice on the alfalfa leaves; they were not damaged, however. Pinto and pole beans just about dead.

But the garden is a success; plenty of sweet corn now and peas and carrots to eat as you walk around. Lots of tomatoes in the greenhouse.

Monday: Cooperation, that's what makes us happen. Larry was a little stumped as to how to unclog the drain. I dug up a section and then we snaked it clean. All back together now. Pretty soon, I've got to head for New York to help my Mom move out here.

September 3: This is autumn weather; garden getting hardened off. Short thunderstorm at night. Clouds this morning and a cold wind blowing as we disced in the wheat seed. John and Mike cleaned out the barn. Peggi cooking all day for us.

We have water on the newly planted field to insure its success. Last night, near midnight, Kim set the water to the farthest west field. He took a lot of time to set it right. Where the water goes, the alfalfa improves instantly. We have so much graze now, our animals could not possibly go hungry.

New escapades: Kemal fucked up and stuck an ax in his leg—had to have 4 stitches!— Kemal

Friday: Today Ron brought his son to Albuquerque to return to his mother— great having him here. Carl and Janet are off with the four kids to score pinto beans. Also in the news, Carl gets hero of the month award! Yesterday he very coolly spotted two thieves picking our marijuana in the last light of the day. He took it from them and they split in a jeep.

Quiet in the baking sun. I have lost all sense of dates. Sandy scrubbing the cabinets, Carol washing an immense stack of dishes. Some grass (the mowing kind) was moved up in front of Sandy's room. Now Kemal is doing some landscaping. We have raised paths and slope the rest so it can be irri-gated. Already we've had water to the center of the courtyard dust bowl. With irrigation ditches we can get it to most anyplace we want.

Mike has been working hard on what was Max's, then Janet's, then Kim's room. Janet is up at the pit house with Carl! Carl no longer sleeping alone at the barn. Romance in the piñons. Everyone's got a room—no vacancies—no one in the milk room now. This room is for food only.

We had our quick and very proper annual meeting. Robbie, Max, and Carol are the new board; they are also the old board.

Sunday: We cut alfalfa with the repaired mower. Kiva and Kemal went to make an apple deal.

Robert Mondragon, the Lieutenant Governor, has come out with the best statement yet against the Kachina Village. He put the issue as farming verses the developers' interest.

Fig. 32. The New Buffalo pueblo seen from the
western fields. Photo by Clarice Kopecky.

September 9 or so: Took in our last hay cutting today. I'm dreaming of alfalfa in the three acres above the pasture. Soon to New York for me.

Monday: Our world spins on. Through it comes Tom Kelly, known as Walking Horse. He has been fulfilling dreams at a momentum he has built for years. He climbed to Mount Everest, took acid with Tim Leary, met Ringo Starr, was in jail in New Delhi, presented a filmed documentary about California's Vacaville State Prison (where Leary is now incarcerated) to a UN council of some sort. Tom hitchhiked through the Khyber Pass and rode horses with the Afghanis. On Mt. Everest he jumped into an unfrozen pond and had to be rescued by some locals and brought back to life by a woman shaman. Yes, that sounds just like Tom.

　Walking Horse treated us to some psychedelic brownies and I am feeling quite high. Up late. I've done a little wrestling and running with Tom. So good to see him. He and I are much on the same wave of some reverberating echo, that sounds down through the consciousness of humanity. Some go off down chasms and chambers and many actually stay too much in one place. I'm feeling good—glad to share it with this man who shares a mystique with me. He's been doing great. Strong man.

Food stamp trip must be arranged again. Lots of red tape. They want to fill out volumes of paper forms: new forms, file forms, long forms and new improved forms. Do not want a disagreeable argument with these people; they have jobs to do.

Called my mom and she quits her job October 4 to move here to Taos from New York City.

Wednesday: Kemal and Michael out on a high country adventure, with the first snowstorms of the season hitting the mountains.

One Week later: More clouds—still no rain. Michael and Kemal returned. Kemal stabbed himself in the forearm while butchering the prize. Nine guys in the Bird truck went to the mountains, and with backpacks marched up to 11,000 feet, packed up the entire elk and brought it down. We reached our base camp just as it was getting very difficult to see. This is a real boon for us. Bird truck took us home; I proudly drove.

This converted bread truck, also called the Mind Machine, I have driven in thirty states. It has been to see the Rolling Stones in Altamont, California; it has been to Johnson's Pastures in Vermont, and I felt good then and I sure feel good now.

Thursday: BROKE! Wood run gas money went to get us to the north hunting grounds, so we need to sell some candles. I hate to truck the streets for a few bucks, but I will.

I worked in the kitchen, helping butcher the elk. Sandy was in there putting up applesauce from our latest apple run. Carol joined to make dinner. By evening, there was no sign of the butchering.

I am experiencing my first real harvest season. In the afternoon, Carl and I brought in the five supers, which are our honey harvest. Not enough for all our wants, but a real harvest nevertheless. The extraction process was set up in the kitchen. It's going to take a few days to get it done.

Mercy mission to Lama; they have some sick ones. We gave them a five-pound cheese, elk meat, candles, and we acted the good neighbors to see what was happening with them.

Pepe gave us $15, which broke our crisis.

October 1, 1974: *Heavy frost almost every night. Land looking dry as cloud-less skies and cool breezes bless our scene. Early evening harvest saved our squash from first hard frost. Hard north winds blew all day.*

Tomatoes were canned in three days. Sandy, Janet, Michael, Peggi, and Carl all pitched in; I guess about fifty jars were put up with six more lugs to do. Aromas in the kitchen are strong with big pots of steaming tomatoes cooking down on the great iron stove.

Sold two pigs to Pepe for $40. Mudding crew well under way past couple of days with as much as six people working together.

The kids' room is coming together as Janet began the New Buffalo School yesterday. She's hoping to teach some reading and writing. However, some of the kids can't tie their shoes or blow their nose. She says Carl is help-ing her. He wants to teach them how to work.

Corn and bean harvest began today. Oats below just finished being har-vested after John sounded the word that they were at just the right stage. Kim led the barley harvest, which looks good. Threshing next.

Everyone working very hard and well together. Spirits seem higher than they have for some time. Shorter days, longer nights. I think many are look-ing towards quieter times this winter. Kitchen doing excellent. We must really consider ourselves wealthy with all the blessings, which have been given us.—Writer unknown.

October 10: Art returns with mother, car, and a little U-Haul of possessions. It was sort of a grueling ride to New York and back. I pretty much avoided cities on journey east. Made a quick, boring trip.

My mom is staying in town—too rough out here. She's feeling great, though. After New York, she steps into a whole different scene, full of young people, kids, and surrounded by our own home produce. She's already found the Friends (Quaker) Meeting in town and is blending right in. Clarice has left everyone she knew in New York to be near her son.

Kim and Michael are plowing. Sandy and Carl are filling the root cellar. Potato run is all done and Kemal went and helped Julian. Carrot run in and our own carrots getting stored, too. Plenty of pears and apples to eat.

John has been into mudding, too, and the pueblo is just about completed! It is in better shape than ever before. If not kept up the pueblo melts back into the earth.

Such beautiful days—fall colors including lots of greens now that we have fields of alfalfa, meadows, and wheat. The perennial plants look so vibrant in this weather. Aspens and cottonwoods all yellow. Winter soon. We planted the last wheat field.

Tuesday: I'm feeling very good. Looks more beautiful around Taos Country than I ever remember it. We went for those apples today. I brought along my Mom for a beautiful day in the country.

Sunday: Carl brought in about 150 pounds of onions, which are braided and hung to dry. Kim put away some excellent heads of Chinese cabbage. They look more successful than the regular cabbage for growing here. Pumpkins in too. By some lucky mechanism, I'm now interested in packing and sorting apples. Sandy is cutting some for drying. Our honey stash is two cans, 120 pounds. Not a lot, the way we can use it.

Sandy's made a batch of candles to trade for wax with Lama. Colors are better than ever.

Oct 23: We had rain last night. The rye is coming up now and the field is taking on an emerald hue in the evening light. Apples are all sorted; best two grades get stored. Our root cellar is just about full. Carl and Kim bringing in another 100 pounds of our carrots and a 100 pounds of potatoes.

Peggi Sue is very pleased to see the chicken feed room filled again with grain on the stalk. That barley has excellent full heads. We grew about two months of our chicken grain supply this year.

Sunday: A bona fide rain started just after dawn. Had a party here last night with some young Taos Pueblo Indians and friends from La Sierra. Good music. This morning, breakfast of potatoes in our leaky kitchen.

Kemal worked putting in a floor for Cheryl at Lama. Sandy went along and dug up some plum trees. I made a new shovel out of two broken ones. Moved some more lettuce into the greenhouse and some more grass around the pueblo. Deep down I always want to move more grasses and plants around us.

We got an apple press from Badger Mountain. The new winter wheat came up in five days.

Oct 29: Yesterday was Kemal's birthday. We had a regular party and celebration and a most fabulous feast: marinated elk shish kabob with rice and almonds. Now Michael is baking a super cake.

Wednesday: That was a regular storm we had and it has turned cold. The mountains are all snowed in. Big fish-fry dinner of trout, mostly from Mike. The smells waft down to Kim using the corn shucker in the circle. What a great invention.

Friday: We step outside and see the frigid, snow-covered, mountain panorama. The new kitchen door has weather stripping and with some work, closes well. This is the first time since I came here that we got it to shut and stay closed. Only took three years.

The big stove is cleaned, painted, and installed in the circle, and the one door is sealed shut. Snow during the night. Cold.

November 4, 1974: Stormy sky finally cleared just around sundown. We hooked up the circle stove for the first time tonight and put springs on the doors. We can still have the open fire for ceremonies, but the stove gives more heat for less wood.

Michael cooked cabrito and potatoes for us, and to celebrate our new circle kiva, we're going to have a band here Thursday. Surprise. I feel so good that we've got our central place so together. It had seemed so cumbersome to care for the big room, that Max once suggested taking the roof off. I don't know how serious he was.

Wednesday we had the most fantastic party; Sutro from Silver City (about a dozen people with bus and small truck) played with some locals joining in. We had a fire in the center, plenty of food, over a hundred friends, some LSD. The music got to be really incredible. First on our new floor.

Friday we did a wood run and got a full load of cedar. The cedar is the best burning wood for the cook stove and is kept for the kitchen only. The same day Kemal got nine plum trees and a few more apples.

We've butchered two sheep from Leo; Kemal has it all put away.

I did some work on the road below. With the ground so wet, it was easy to work on. We've come a long way from the swamp that passed for our driveway two years ago. The road did to cars what flypaper does to insects.

We've received our tax notice—$302 reduced! Great. Kiva has a fund started. This is the first time since I arrived that the ownership has been regularized. Three years it took to re-establish our claim. Now we'd best not let it go. Lucky contributed $25 last night.

November 11: Very frosty morning—absolutely clear sky all day. Rebel's been helping out in the kitchen a lot—made chicken salad. He had the whole place cleaned right after the party. Kemal wants me to mention that he is wonderful. So true.

Mike makes sure there is a big stack of split cedar in front of the kitchen every day. Very quiet, our Mr. Pots. He's out in the local wilds quite a bit lately; very well tuned into the surrounding country. Mike is like a young soldier: short hair, clipped sentences, very busy, works on the group projects.

Carl made some new shelves for the front pantry giving us room for more pumpkins.

John has the goats out most every day. Michael and Peggi Sue are both off to see their relatives and have a taste of that fine life in the bourgeois city.

November 12: The day after we did some chicken house repairs, the hens laid eight eggs. Hopefully this will start a continual rise. Larry McInteer is returned. We're glad, and he's glad to be "home." We do have a full compliment of men. Just like I said I would be, I'm tight with Sandy.

November 16: We made $15 selling candles and Reb sold a necklace for $25. Kemal sold that bolo, and he worked for a few days, too. Omar gave us a $5 donation.

Sunday: Under an absolutely clear sky Reb fixed up the pig shelter for winter. Carl put some support poles under the root cellar roof, so it can be built up further. Sandy colored the new batch of short tapers.

Kim and Rebel got busted for having fishing poles. Rebel got away, but Kim got brought in. My mom bailed him out, $35, and brought him home. John's birthday tomorrow.

Thursday: Still one full month before the official start of winter. Our alfalfa graze is about gone. We had another flare up of the old horse controversy this morning.

To me the horses demonstrate that there is future potential for cows. What the horses eat, in the future can be eaten by cows. Of course, a horse could be sold for a cow. To broach this topic though, is difficult.

With steers to butcher, our food scene would change greatly; we could get off food stamps. If we could sell one or two steers or heifers a year, we would have a reliable income that would cover our taxes. The more I think about it, the more urgent it seems to fill in this missing part of our farm. We're going to trade Leo for a heifer, we hope.

Kiva's birthday, Janet's birthday, and Pepe's birthday all coming up.

Saturday: These birthdays are really getting to be big things. Rumor has it, another electric band, Family Lotus from Santa Fe, is going to play.

Doubtless, we'll have some company. I think Kiva is looking forward to it.

Last year we had a controversy over bringing on a herd of cattle. This year it is completely accepted. Growth toward cattle is our future. From last year, we have grown toward horses instead.

November 25: Absolutely clear sky—warm in the sun—near 0° at night. Sure enough, on Saturday we had another fabulous party with live electric band and lots of food. Everyone at the party agrees it was a great time.

Yesterday we put the animals in the fenced-off lower pasture. I feel a relief not to see them on the wheat fields. The lower pasture is no solution, however. It is already heavily grazed. Kim, Rebel, and I talked with Kiva about her horse and about the farm.

A lot of people at Morningstar had horses. Before people spent money on the farm, buying necessities or stock, they spent it on their personal horses. Reb says he probably spent $1000 on his horse before he gave it away. Morningstar is now deserted. To me it is that same attitude; each feels devoted to his or her first possession. Before they think of what does the farm need, they think, "I want a horse."

We have an epidemic—flu—what a pain. Janet is disabled and in the cave. Still, they keep those kids closed up in there. Mike, who doesn't even have a stove in his room and was wearing a tee shirt yesterday, is fine. He gets a lot of fresh air.

Last night, Kim cooked up the rest of Mr. Dick, the grown billy goat we had to get rid of. Very good.

November 30: Wednesday was Pepe's thirty-fourth birthday. We celebrated over at Jody's with lasagna and a sauna. Very nice. Kiva came late with pumpkin pies.

The procession of crazies does not stop here at Buffalo. Two traveling monks passed by; all they can spout is bible talk. No money, food, or blankets; just their weirdness to offer.

Sunday: A very pleasant day. We took brother Tahiti and his stuff up to his new house, which is Dave Gordon's old house. With chains it was no trouble. While up there and Duncan gone, we took the opportunity to do a wood run for scrap lumber.

Morningstar is crumbling; still, it could be rebuilt easily. We were happy to be helping, putting on chains and starting our rig with the tractor, and we scored a culvert so we can utilize the wastewater at our outdoor faucet. Mike continues to supply the kitchen with wood. For himself, he takes none. This year, he doesn't want a stove. These American kids can be tough.

Leo brought us two sheep. Carol has made some incredible coffee cakes for breakfast tomorrow. What a clever girl! Larry says it's gotten to -20°. I believe it.

December 3, 1974: Today we paid land tax of $151.52 to Taos County treasurer for half of 1974. This is historical. Our history became very confused after 1968. We came very close to having New Buffalo auctioned off. We picked up the thread, though, and our legal corporation is secure now.

Yesterday Carl had to come up with some craziness. He took little Leah out of school where she loves to go. Rather than be with little girls her own age and our sister Adriana, she has to stay home with the boys. We were upset.

Eliminate Washam gas bill! Larry is figuring out how to heat water with our present wood stove.

Saturday: The snow is melted. The grains are exposed again, and I'm sure glad those horses are not just running wild over Buffalo anymore. It's the worst to have animals on those wet fields because they sink right in.

Kiva came here after two years' absence because she needed a home, and she found a man—our very own Kemal. And we are all very happy for our resident Turk, for we know it is wrong to spend a cold winter in bed alone.

In discussing the horses, we are working out our ideas of commune: of what we, and those to follow, are to do, to make our "dream" a reality. I want us to create an economic enterprise that can continue without the overseer of a private owner.

Some of our anxieties resolved themselves in a meeting this evening, which was a good affair—the meeting of minds. Sometimes we tend to clash more than meet, and often we avoid the issue. But we can't avoid making communal decisions and with limited resources and a big barnyard to feed, we have got to face our problems.

We do have a problem: too little grain and short on hay. John doesn't want Peggi Sue to give the chickens hay.

Because of our shortness on grain and our lack of experience, it seems we have chickens and pigs on half-rations. We could cut the flock in half, but don't cut the food. Do the same with the pigs. Sell half the litter, and use our livestock to solve the problem.

What we miss are more practical crafts, like the making of shoes, pants, rugs, sheepskin jackets, chairs, quilts, etc. Kim did work as a carpenter; we do make candles and three or four people have sold jewelry. Kemal's making knives. John is making cheese. So we have the start.

Our real hope is the farm. With a farm behind us, we'll have a new life. That's our problem now; to make it until the farm is really producing.

How much milk? "We got over 600 gallons from Nelly and over 1200 from the goats," says John. We could double these figures next season. And if we raise the bucks, we could buy a real milk cow, which could triple our cow milk production.

Well, good luck to us for this winter. We do have a very good group. I'm sure glad things aren't like the past. We may have tensions and problems but no laggards, and we all want to see Buffalo be a farm that can support us.

December 11: Pepe took another pig. He said he'd give us some money soon. I am making some bottle candles while Mike completely cleans the stove and Janet thoroughly cleans the kitchen. Kim is trying to fix our new refrigerator.

December 18: Well, even with all of our abundance we took a few dollars from our Uncle Sam—food stamps. A little more cross examination each time. Seventeen people went in. Janet has quit welfare and so has Kiva. For the commune this is just as well.

We did a giant shopping. This is the most food we've had at Buffalo since I've been here. I remember selling candles every week and bringing home bananas or something, because we were always a bit hungry. About $10,000 a year for us twenty people (and whoever comes up the road and needs to be fed) for food and all expenses is our present standard, I estimate.

Back home, Mike was cooking up a great batch of fry bread; he ground the wheat, cut the onions and rolled the dough. He's right in there. Kemal is tanning some hides. He and John have two goat hides pretty well broken.

December 20: John has negotiated a deal with Lama Foundation for 100 gallons of milk to be delivered in June. And they have advanced him $200 to buy alfalfa. Doing business with Lama is very good. They are our mystic brothers and sisters. In the Sangre de Cristos of Taos, it is they and us who most carry that commune mystique.

Under a completely blue sky, Leo brought his twenty-seven cows.

JOURNAL FIFTEEN

Where is the dream to improve the lot of mankind?

December 22: Kiva arranged a party for baby Jonesy. We had a big cream cheese birthday cake, Reb's chicken salad from seven of our own chickens, balloons, and some friends.

Larry and Carl cut off the top of a piñon and set up a big Christmas tree reaching to the ceiling. Larry has spent several days with the kids making decorations.

Amid all this love Saturday afternoon intrudes a funky pickup, racing up the driveway—Indio and two friends. Indio is all beat up and has a .45 pistol strapped across his chest, crisscrossed with a bandoleer of cartridges. Hostility.

An argument ensues right away. I yell quietly for Reb to get his rifle; Rebel's on the periphery. I go right up next to Indio, ready to wrestle if necessary. Big fellow Leroy gets out of the driver's seat and aims a .45 automatic at Ron, who has just stepped out of the kitchen.

Rebel appears at a window with rifle. Indio sees where it is pointing and very nervously starts saying, "let's go, let's go." A few more words about how they do whatever they want, and we better clear out, and this is "theirs" not "ours" and they drive away. Pleasant. It's over as fast as it started. I let out a deep breath. That could have gone very badly.

December 23: We butchered our first pig, fifty or so pounds. I'm not enthusiastic about the pigs. They eat too much grain. As it is now, we are completely out of grain for them. We don't want to use up our wheat stash, so we went ahead and butchered Petunia, our big pig. Two little ones left. Killing them is a little shocking and shaving them a bit of work. But we have our own homegrown pork; the first I have ever had. One thing, it sure is popular.

Christmas dinner to be cooked by Kemal.

December 26: The night after Christmas, a little storm has turned the scene white, crisp and cold, a good sign. Still not much snow, but the streak of warming days is over for a while. -15° last night.

Chickens are up to three dozen on Christmas day. Someone put a wreath on their door. Now if they can only keep it up. We're hoping to sell five dozen a week, at least.

Pumpkin pies were exceptional! Homemade eggnog, another first for me. We drank a few gallons and had a regular Christmas Eve party; two quarts of rum in the nog, and that was it; no booze on Christmas day.

Lots of plastic goodies for the kids, and some homemade ones, too. Carl made a beautiful wooden cradle for Leah's new dolls. Rebel dressed up as Santa Claus.

Michael Glassman is back to resounding cheers! Now we've got the whole present Buffalo family together to wait out the winter. Merry Christmas. First time Michael's ever gone away and come back to find the same group. That's progress for us. Michael was not enthralled by the society he saw. He's glad to be back.

Much of society worries about food and shelter. Our own prospects are better than ever; things are swinging our way. One segment of society sees fear and despair. For us, it is hope and the promise of a future not dominated by the present culture that we have dropped out of.

Just to top things off, it is snowing heavy on this day, our present from our Heavenly Father.

December 28: Cold—12° below zero last night. Leo's cattle are still able to feed well. I gave Nelly a little hay in her pen. Chickens hit a record three-and-a-half dozen.

We started the trucks; all but the Mind Machine started right up. No place to go, though. We just keep them in running order. Mike washed the dishes and made pea soup and fry bread. Winter boredom is setting in.

Sunday: The full moon on the cold snow creates such a mysterious light. I ran for miles, the snow crunching under my boots. I walked among the trees, covered in snow. It now is coming down again.

There is quite a bit of pigweed standing out of the snow, some wild sunflowers and clover, too. Sleepy grass is plentiful. The fields are just blankets of white.

After dark last night, the new Ortiviz big boys, Neil and Strider and their wives, Holly and very pregnant Beara, pulled up the driveway. They're missing one window and are a bit frozen. Great cheers and commotion. We know our home is solid when we can receive these people and keep them warm and well-fed in this dead of winter. And winter it is, just as we like it.

Monday: Rebel took the kids out to the movies the other night. All the young ones are in good health. Thank God.

Our wonderful washing machine is working excellently. There are people in the washroom constantly, scrubbing and cleaning.

January 1, 1975: Happy New Year! And here's a storm to celebrate it. I feel good and even kind of exuberant being here.

Razberry, Saafi, and Michael Pair are visiting. We have two guys, Sam and Bill, off the road here for the second day. Leo was over to look at his cows; he thinks they're doing fine.

Complications! In the deep night, here at Buffalo, Beara gave birth, got high fever and was taken to the hospital. Delivery was too funky—spur of the moment—hospital in the kids' room. She's too anti-establishment. Doctor said she could have died in the next twenty-four hours. As is, I guess everything will be all right. She's at Holy Cross Hospital. That little woman has got some trials. She'll make it though. Baby is all right, so far. God bless them.

January 2: Thanks to Holy Cross Hospital. It's a very modern medical establishment, which has never refused help to anyone that I know of. Bring in some poor folk and they take 'em right in.

We played volleyball on the cleared court yesterday. Mike has repainted the circle. We have a government-paid lawyer, Em Hall, working on our water rights problem.

Sunday: Clear days. Neil and Holly are here for an extended, enjoyable visit. Janet and Strider in town to be close to Beara, who is recovering.

Larry did some chiseling on the washroom floor to get it to drain better.

This is going to solve our problem of a puddle in the middle of the floor.

The kids are jumping all over me and are full of pranks. Kids in the city must be hard to handle, with no close-by outdoors to play in.

We got a refrigerator out of the dump for a smoke house. Pepe taught me to cut a hole in the bottom, connect with stovepipe to a covered fruitwood fire twelve feet away. This provides cold smoke for best taste.

Tuesday: Chickens' heat lamp went out and eggs went down to eight! Peggi sold some six dozen and bought a new bulb. Now to see them come back up again.

January 8: Such the quiet peaceful life. No alarm clock to get us off to work. Not much pressing to do, actually. Folks meeting in the kitchen.

Pepe returned from another spiritual quest, and he's a single man again. He's not going to stay in Questa, and therefore said we should get our pig back that he didn't pay for. He gave us back the pig he did pay for and 200 pounds of corn into the bargain. So we started the Bird truck and got those pigs. Kachina came along for the ride. She was conceived in this very truck. We had a nice little time grabbing them—Kachina squealing in delight, the pigs squealing in fright.

Today it is three weeks that Leo's cows have been grazing here. We'll probably try for six. I can see where they've been eating. There is a lot to go. This will be the first time in Buffalo's history that the winter graze has been used to capacity.

Speaking of history, we're at record low booze runs, record low town runs.

Thursday: We are a bit stretched out, only a few weeks ahead with livestock feed. Not really the way to operate a scene, to be running to town every time we get $10. We were out of laying pellets for a week, which killed our production, evidently.

Snow, snow, we're immersed in a real storm again. Just got some hay yesterday. Good timing.

Neil, Holly, and Strider got Beara and baby and drove to their home in Colorado. Good luck! Bad timing for them all around; Came down in a frozen state at night—birth in the wrong place. Now they make a run for it in the blizzard. Good, good luck!

Saturday: Real winter, -25° last night. We can't start any vehicles today.

Mountains of the Sangre de Cristo are as white as I've ever seen. But it is still nice inside.

Some cows wandered by our Chinese elms and ate about half of each tree! Oh, terrible. A few Russian olives also eaten. I covered some trees with burlap and old clothes for protection. Still no agreement with Leo about our pay for his cows grazing. We'll have to go talk with him.

Ditch meeting last night. Al is commissioner, again, and Manuel Martinez also. Very nice group of neighbors. We're sure lucky to have that Rural Legal Services lawyer working for the Arroyo Hondo community. That Reynolds, the state engineer, sure is a bum to have given Desmontes the priority. They'll never get it, though, I think. Equal priority is most likely. They're willing to settle for that right now. The issue won't be contestable until March at the soonest, says our lawyer Hall.

Larry has created a plan to convert our propane heater to wood. He needs the cutting torch. That sure would be a very good move. Rebel is going to sell a pig for $30.

The alcove really works well. It is definitely an intermediate temperature there, and at night, it helps hold the heat. Though it is the coldest weather now, the circle is very pleasant and does not require any raging fire.

Now is the time, a real winter, when the horses add to our long list of animals needing cash outlay. Kemal has said to me he can't hustle the money for the chickens by himself. I suspect those horses now may have to be fed for a month. The non-horse owners have definitely made their opinion heard; nevertheless, we have got them. As poor as we are, still so much energy goes into these "fun" things. Ron came home with some good grass this evening, which several of us were glad to see (and smoke).

The kitchen will be newly white tomorrow, painted by Michael with that remarkably white tierra blanca which comes from a vein off at the west end of the property.

We need a new broom. Luckily we fixed the push broom or we'd be out entirely.

Kim and I finally got the tractor and red truck running by about 2 p.m.

January 16: Monday night Davison showed up with part of the Huerfano Valley band and a group called The Eagles. They'd just played two nights near Albuquerque, and are playing Santa Fe tonight. We gave them Sandy's room, Peggi's room, and Kemal's room, broke out a ham and made them feel welcome.

Tuesday night, we had a party with over 150 people. Good sounds and also Leah's birthday! What a great time. They even did one number with me singing an Odetta song, "Motherless Children."

This party attracted a few "friends" who ended up taking over at the end, with a drunken loud and obnoxious psychodrama, which included Dennis Hopper, famous local movie actor, holding a gun at a thin Spanish fellow's head. And Yvonne, drunk, adds her act to the show by grabbing a knife from the kitchen wall and charging the steps toward Dennis because of some wrong he did her. Of course, we removed it from her before she hit the circle floor.

As the party went on and these fellows drank two gallons of wine and a quart of whiskey, I could feel the tension. Dave, some others from the band, Mike, Davison, and I stayed up until our "guests" left. Very unpleasant for the few of us. We just let them have the floor until they finally left. Most everybody had a good time at the party, though.

Kim, Mike (who has quit marijuana), and Larry do not as a rule come to these parties. Very good to see Davison. He is one of the original members, a solid part of our family who stays close. Five-year-old Chamisa is with him. Three other youngsters are with the band, too. We feel good if we can entertain these people well.

I thought the new snow was going to cut off the graze, but evidently not so. Day to day, you can hardly see the cows' effect. Nice to know we have so much.

Friday: Dennis Hopper appeared and apologized for the incident the other night at the party. That was decent. Years ago some members here had refused to have New Buffalo used as a set for the movie *Easy Rider*. So Dennis may have had a little grudge. At the party Reb helped collect for the beer run and stuffed $17 in my pocket. We like that. With it we bought gasoline and another maul handle.

The deal with Leo is ten more days for the cattle in exchange for a tan heifer, part Charolais. Kemal is satisfied, Rebel says fine, John thinks we're getting the short end, but he's not making any stink. I think it is a fair deal, and we get a heifer—Buffalo's first beef cow. If we'd started getting one a year eight years ago, we'd have a herd now.

Michael's friend Sarah just arrived on impulse from Boston—very good impulse. There is another girl, Michelle, who is here for the second night. She helped out cleaning the kitchen.

January 20: Warm it feels outside at 15° above zero. Mud thawed around the house. Our walkways are drier than ever, since we built them up.

That was adventurous of my mom to go from New York to New Mexico. She has now found a cheaper apartment in Taos. She'd rather have the money for her crafts. Just like a young girl, she's not afraid if the house isn't fancy. Her richness is in music and having good friends.

Mike has got himself a stove. He has been living without one up until now. No fire for him, no fire in hogan, no teepees, no fire in the grain room, no fire in Kemal's room. Still, we're not going to have much wood left over. Fifteen truckloads a winter we use now about. Not good. This year we've been using less.

We got a response from that article being in *Penthouse*; one short letter from a fellow in prison in New York, who sends us hope for our continued success. Like ripples, news of us—the vibration goes out—and we get a feedback in return: this one from the very down-and-out segment of society.

January 26: Really getting warm. Some of the grass in the courtyard is exposed, much of the walkways are dry. Mike has gone off to join Rebel in search of knowledge, going to check out the Guru Maharaji.

Dagmar the goat—her cervix is sticking out because she's so full of kids.

January 28: Beets keeping well. The apples' taste has changed a bit, but they are still crisp. Lots of good potatoes left. Recommended: Don't store the apples and rutabagas in the same cellar.

Leo took his cattle today. So we had twenty-four head for forty days. And in return we have a 400-pound tan heifer; she's a real beauty. Yesterday, we worked hard. We had to chase her at least three miles before we got her in the corral.

Mr. Carl is into keeping us supplied with alfalfa sprouts every day. This has become our basic green. We get most of our vegetables from our own stores.

End of January thaw: I had to open up some irrigation channels to get water off the road. Ron has been putting wood chips and bark on the walkways.

Daddy Dave is here, and after cutting some wood, we got him to tell us a bit of our history. Dave is from Pittsburgh and knew Rick Klein there.

Rick had come out to the Taos area to look up Max some time back, because of his interest in poetry. Rick, after inheriting some money, wanted to help start a commune. He was living in El Rito, where also Justin, Joanne, and a whole colony of hippies were living.

Dave came in with some LSD, and the fellows started looking at some pieces of land. Rick was willing to put up $50,000; Max thought it was a great idea. Bob Wertz, an acquaintance from Pittsburgh, came over to Taos area, too, having somehow heard of the undertaking. Another personality was Steve Hinton. He, wife, and four kids were living in Taos.

When the nucleus group came to look at this piece of land, they saw a mountain lion—a good sign. They liked the site and the price was right. They decided to buy. While looking at the site, a fellow, George Robinson, and wife, came over in a white Chevy. They were camping around the area and were soon brought into the group.

They bought some teepees and a $5000 tractor. On or about June 21, 1967, an improvised peyote meeting was held around a fire in the open under the full moon. A coffee can and plastic top had to serve for a drum. Fellow Randy Rand was there, who is a good singer and was the drummer. Steve Hinton carried cedar. This was our official beginning at New Buffalo.

A kitchen and latrine were soon established. While the fellows were out getting teepee poles, a neighbor, Eliu Arellano, made the first 1000 bricks. From then on, the Buffalos made their own bricks. The east wing went up first. The circle was dug out and the back pantry was then the front pantry.

Only a few lived in teepees that first winter, the others moved inside.

Rick Klein, quite soon after the start, left with his wife Susan; it wasn't quite for them. Rick had done his part. He didn't want people thinking it was "his" commune. The corporation was formed right in the beginning, and now was on its own.

Names of some other people in the beginning: Paul Burner—very athletic; Brian Anderson—a very good carpenter; Laird Grant from San Francisco.

There were lots of big windows in the south wall of the pueblo, and the east wing was all one room, not three as now. The circle was higher and had a loft. The west wall was unfinished and was filled in by a big stack of hay. It was that first May after the first winter that the hay wall caught fire, and much of the building was destroyed. That also was a pretty wet winter, and there was a good flow of water in the spring.

Quite a good harvest of beans and corn were brought in at least one year. A pretty great flow of people also started with the first spring. It was after the fire that Larry McInteer came along. He's been here off and on since, and is therefore the one living here now who was here the soonest. Pat Raines and

Steve Andur came in soon after the beginning. Aquarius Paul helped make the bricks.

The Pride family and I appeared after the fifth summer. Only six people were living here—quiet, kind of down, no wood, winter coming on. Justin had just moved away with, I got the impression, a sort of bitter taste. The scene hadn't succeeded yet, though it had served a lot of people. The farm part was hardly anything; baked naked fields, twenty pounds of onions.

Bob Bomsy was here, a rather strange and disagreeable fellow; Steve was here, trying to hold the legal ends together. Also there were nine junked cars where the barn is now and a few chickens. George Robinson had also left; Max was living at Lama and rather tired. It had been a very spiritual, hard-working and hectic five years—lots of people—so little knowledge. That was five summers, and a farm had not been established, although many of the right ingredients had been put in place.

The summer of '72, my first here, was dry. We attempted a small garden dug by shovel. That fall, Leo helped us put in some wheat.

Summer of '73 was very wet. The wheat was good, and we put in five patches of pasture and alfalfa and ran all the ditches and eliminated the prairie dogs. That fall, we put in more wheat and alfalfa.

Summer of '74 was fairly dry. We put in more wheat and alfalfa and had a good garden harvest.

Now we are headed for the '75 growing season, where we are going to look like a prosperous farm. After eight years, we've had more than a thousand people come through; several hundred have lived here. Out of these are some fifteen adults, all turned onto developing a successful ranch, who are at New Buffalo now. Quite a story.

The sky cleared last night and froze all the water. This morning, winter is restored. Very good. We have the entire Huerfano band as houseguests. They brought grapefruits, oranges, eggs and grass. Had two passers-through spend the night. Pepe came over on horseback for dinner. Never a dull moment. Seed order is in.

January 30: Major thaw down here—our pond overflowing—several ditches running strong. We let the new heifer out with Nelly and Bozo, and she stayed right with them. Beautiful to see them grazing our pastures.

Storm through the night—lightning right around us—heavy rain turning to sleet. It looks like a great year for agriculture.

Circle is really leaking; dirt just isn't thick enough nor the drainage correct. I took over fifteen gallons of water off the circle floor. A few buckets, strategically placed, get us through it. In the morning, we're getting some real snow. If we can, we'll shovel it off the roofs before it melts.

February 1, 1975: Last night, just at dark, two young travelers, Dave and Marty, knocked on the door to find shelter. These fellows, unlike that "mountaineer" Bill who was here weeks ago and lost his bedroll and fell off a cliff, are more knowledgeable—headed north for ice fishing. It's nice to open the door and offer these people a good meal and shelter.

The band has gone this morning; we enjoyed having them. Last night, for a farewell, Kemal cooked up one of our twenty-five-pound hams, and we had a real feast. We accepted these people from the Huerfano as family and show Davison that he gets the royal treatment having helped start New Buffalo. The band put on a good show at Martinez Hall, while they were here.

Friday night the temperature finally went down and froze the whole muddy scene. The world looks so beautiful; mountains, clouds, meadows, cedar trees in the snow, and I'm fascinated with looking at our graze.

February 4: Oliver and Harold Sanchez were up here yesterday to say "Adios." Oliver is headed for the Job Corps and Harold to the Air Force. We wished them luck and told them to write. They'll be missed next volleyball season.

I've been reading about the old times. Last year, we were plowing by March 20. Most plowing was done in April. We may have to plow earlier this year to take advantage of the wet ground. I read about the family, the sickness, the booze, the odd collection of trips; so few of them tuned in with farming.

Through all those times, we had the spirit and conviction to stick it out. Kemal, Neil, Michael, Kim, Carol, Sandy, and I have been here a long time. Rebel and Mike Pots were on the mesa across the valley.

I'm glad we could do it so happily. I'm glad it's over now, and we are into a higher plane, a more productive stage. I am stronger, and my days of such complete ignorance are behind me. Thank God.

February 5: Kim showed himself a real master chef, with his lasagna for Ron's birthday. Loads of chocolate cake by Peggi Sue. I played guitar for several hours.

Got a letter from Rebel and Mike who are with the Maharaji. Hook, line, and sinker—they're enthralled with the whole shebang. They want Ron to join them. Just like Pepe, they expect half the continents to be flooded. They expect the whole world will follow their guru.

World peace, brotherhood, service to your fellows, respect for teachers, love for God, group consciousness: these things I am for, and they are found in many ways. It seems rather narrow and naïve to expect everyone to give up his or her good leaders and solid beliefs to follow one way. Peace does not require it, nor prosperity, nor art. Anyhow, these fellows are not expected back for a month or so. In return for their devotion, they are housed, fed, and lectured in Denver.

Certainly does conserve wood to not have all fires going. Fuel is a major problem. If we can gather several years' worth, that is a partial solution until we find another solution. If we make the wood last longer, we won't hit the problem of not having it. Same for every resource we take from the earth.

February 8: John started building a small house for the soon-to-be arriving little goats; I got into helping. With no plan and a variety of pieces of wood, we started. Quite a comedy really, with John getting upset once in a while. Neither one of us is very good at this.

Money just isn't coming in. I have a few dollars toward cutting torch fuel. Heating water off the stove seems one of our most practical steps. The propane is our biggest money drain.

The worse mud stage is past; the road and courtyard are starting to dry.

Carol makes a regular thing of baking now; loads of rolls and eight loaves of the best bread, all excellently done in our wood stove oven.

Sunday: Quiet day. Peggi Sue Plough cheerfully cooking and baking in the kitchen, as she often does. Such the beautiful country girl.

We have a farm income now. John charges $10 a shot for buck service. We always have two or three neighborhood goats in our pen. This money goes right back into alfalfa.

February 11: The great thaw continues—ditches catching the melt. All the fields are soaked. It should only be so wet in May. Still around 10° at night. The plants sit dormant. Every day I think of spring. I sharpen saw blades, cut some wood, run a few miles—things to fill in the time. Every day I go out in the fields. I watch the cows graze, and I look at the many plants. I can feel the wonder there, which will be evident when the sun brings the scene to life. In the greenhouse already it is happening. Chard and onion greens are growing

Fig. 33. John with kids. Photo by Clarice Kopecky.

fast. We received our Stokes Seed order in the mail.

Our cedar wood is lasting longer than we thought it would. The piñon is down to around three truckloads' worth. Wood is only a stopgap measure until we can get something else together or grow our own. There are still lots of ways to further insulate the buildings. We burn up a bit of kerosene here, about five gallons every ten days. No electricity in the rooms yet, only in the kitchen, washroom, and dairy room.

John has the new goat house almost finished. He bought a heat lamp, electric cord, dairy ration, and barley for the pigs.

Pepe comes over quite often. I gave him some pieces of meat for him and his new family He's making an incredibly ornate silver belt now. Nick is creating a butterfly with some 100 stones inlaid in silver. Terrific craftsmen. Great that Pepe found himself a good home with the jewelers' commune at TLC.

They live very graciously—shoes off—lots of fine things around. Though cold, their house is a real castle. Adriana is a dominant influence, and she is truly a princess of these mountains. She speaks Spanish and is related to the Indians. Industrious, pretty, clean, she radiates a lot of love. That sure is an ideal place for Pepe to land for a while.

February 13: Cold nights, but the thaw continues. I got back into clearing bushes and gathering rocks off the field below the orchard. Peggi and Kim received a few dollars in the mail, and a bunch of us had a night on the town. I got a tooth pulled for free.

Lots of help to the neighborhood happening. Kim helped Leo put oil in the transmission and adjusted the clutch. Ron is helping Manuel string barbed wire. Larry took the red truck and pulled out a hippie badly stuck on the mesa.

Kemal caught all three horses, and he has the colt at the barn where he is starting to train it; first time the horses have been caught in three or four months.

Dagmar gave birth to two big bucks, and Toltec squeezed out three kids. They sound just like little babies. John is watching them closely. It's good to help them find the tits and make sure they know how to suck.

I decided to try putting cedar cross-sections in some bad spots in my floor. I'll cut some tomorrow with Sandy. She's very good at cutting and splitting wood.

I finished preparing one place for plowing. I'm feeling good and looking forward to the next day. I want to be so immersed in the work, the movement. I'm just getting to see, once in a while, what it could feel like to be really alive. Super energy—strong—clear. I exercise, run, dig with shovel, swing the maddox, fix the road and build new ditches, garden, transplant trees, milk cows; year upon year of doing this stuff should bring me to a good state. People who are cut off from the land, when they become out of work, there is nothing for them to do. Land to the people.

February 16: The first ditch that has a little falls near the orchard is running strong. Sounds quite loud in the still night.

Toltec the goat, poor girl, had a dead kid in her that she couldn't get out. Today John and Carol tried turning it. Finally, with a full leg out and part of another, Kemal took over and got it out. It was a very big kid. Toltec is sort of in shock; she took the operation very well. John gave her vitamin C and penicillin. It was the hands of Doc Kemal that did what was necessary. That's four kids for Toltec. Three of them are doing well. Dagmar has enough milk for all five.

The baby goats are in their box with the orange electric light on. It's a cold time of year to have them born. John is into February births, but they could be avoided. That orange light is a bit freaky. So we're having problems, and we're dealing well with them. We've gone through a lot of trips with John, and after a while, we should find it easier to work together.

We have three young ladies as guests; one of them is Kathleen, Ron's girlfriend from West Virginia; he's very glad to see her. Sandy gave the girls her room, very graciously. Sandy also cooked beets excellently and made rice that was super. She cleaned the washroom the other day, which was getting terrible with pounds of mud on the floor. Kemal cooked the last big ham, and Carol made bread for Kim's birthday tomorrow. Yeah! Kim has really become one of our main men. This is his third winter, a regular veteran.

February 17: Storm continued in the mountains. The Morningstar mesa, in front of the mountains, still has a foot of snow. After cutting wood, I got into working the road again. I dream about digging. I am immersed and happy to be so. Nelly and the calves are hip to the crested wheat grass. We could get a lot more growing on Buffalo. Toltec seems to be fine.

February 20: Carl has been selling some rutabagas and squash at the co-op. He made $12 last week. We will get onion sets with the money. If we had more beets and carrots, we could sell them, too. We certainly have a lot of potential here.

Friday: John has got his routine, now that there are kids to feed and some goats to milk and bottles to wash. Carol regularly helps with the feeding.

Dixie, now our biggest goat, has dropped two does. Great. Dixie never was pregnant last year, so this is the first milk we're getting from her.

News from Ortiviz: Susie Creamcheese and Jeff were just here. They're buying two more milk cows and two beef cows. This is just the direction I'm trying to push us. They've always been more agriculturally ahead. With twenty acres of alfalfa, they've had a big head start, plus 190 more acres, and members who are dedicated farmers.

Water flowing strong—still plenty of snow on the steep hills above us. I continue fixing ditches each day.

Kim gave me some money that he got from his family. I put $10 to kerosene and gasoline, $10 for Mind Machine registration, $8 to John for hay, $10 to Kemal for Washam Gas. I got a pair of cheap gloves and tape for the axes and maddox, and cream cheese for last night's "after swimming" rolls.

Kemal says goats are a personal trip here; the cow is my ego. As though economics was no consideration. As though the goats weren't the best things yet, even if the herd is ungainly. These goats are productive, and that's all the difference in the world. And what should the commune do? To me, for six years I have understood that the business of the little communal group is to achieve production.

I believe we are supposed to achieve real production with extra for trade. To me, it is a challenge. I've known we could do it, even before I could see how. I hung on through those tough years with certain faith. Now I can see much more clearly what the elements are we need. We have them in the works.

I'm broke and John is broke, too. I have wax, though, and the goats are covered for nine more days. It would be good if we could sell a pig, say for alfalfa seed.

One of Kemal's objections to group decisions about the horses is that we can't seem to make group decisions about the goats. This is a problem, I definitely agree. Selling a milker or two would set us straight for a while, but there is the point that over the milking period, the goat gives a lot of milk and this is what John is aiming for.

The goats are an industry that can be passed on; a resource that derives from the soil, once the alfalfa comes in. The commune is just a bunch of houses and people without an enterprise. Such communes fail. They fail to sustain the people, and like Reality and Morningstar, they cease to exist. The goat scene is no small part of Buffalo. It is an answer to what I believe is our most pressing task, to develop production.

Ortiviz has a little bit of a similar situation. They have four horses now instead of nine, and are getting four more cows. They have come a long way from Ben Eagle's herd of horses. They're thinking of having only two people on food stamps next growing season; everyone is pretty much agreed. I want to get that way too, where there is so much farm produce, we feel secure and wealthy.

We have a British guest who has been seeing some different groups in the States. He was just at Ortiviz and spent two weeks at the Gaskin Farm in Tennessee. Now that is real inspiration. The Farm has 700 people on 1700 acres and is going to be producing on 500 acres! They have groups starting other farms. These people are very close to us in what they're looking for—simple living in the country: home industries, vintage vehicles, and a big emphasis on farm production.

We got a communication from a fellow in England who has the spirit, too, and a group. So far, they are still in London but trying to buy a farm somewhere. We are still very small, but can look forward to a great future.

February 25: Rebel and Mike are back. Rebel with a gal Gerry and little daughter. Great. They're happy to be home.

Carl and I looked at the beehives. All can be divided this spring. They have an average of six frames of honey each to see them through the rest of winter. Only one perhaps doesn't have a queen. Carl really knows his stuff. A very cold tonight.

Wednesday: Last two days, Sandy, Kemal, Kiva, Gerry, Reb, Peggi, and I fixed up a new rental in Taos for my mom, $100 a month, plus heat and electric. It isn't nearly as good as we might like, but the other place is just too expensive. The new landlord has my mom footing the bill for redecorating his place and making it nice and livable. I hate being at the mercy of these people.

Back at the ranch, Carl, Janet, and kids loaded up their truck and left for a new home in the bright moonlight. For two years Carl was a great help, and we surely confirmed him in a new way of life. Now we'll have to do without this wonderful person. And we'll miss Janet, too. Without the kids, it is sure to be a lot quieter around here. Of course, we just gained one more. Plus, little Chamisa is here with Davison. Michael and Ron are off to the Grand Canyon.

Rebel moved the bunk beds out of the milk room and into the kid's room. He put Gerry's cook stove in, so John can be separate from the kitchen if he wants. It will be a good place to make cheese.

As soon as we got back, after two days of house-fixing, I went back to road repair. Sandy came along with a shovel. Back to town tomorrow for more painting.

Last day of February: On a hot day after a 19° night, we moved Clarice in one quick haul. Bye-bye to that plush, warm pad. We did a pretty nice job of fixing up the new one. It now has white walls and clean wood floors. I hope it will be a good place—warm enough and no odd smells. Mom's been good about having to shuffle around and find cheaper places to live. She's quite lively. I just really wish she wouldn't smoke. Sandy, Kemal, Peggi, Kiva, Gerry, and Reb all helped out a lot, and she sure feels good about that.

March 2, 1975: Sun hot today—no shirts. The main ditch is thawed out, flowing in a fast, full stream of very muddy water, heading to the Rio Grande. The water isn't of use now, since the ground is wet.

John talked to Kemal about getting the horses out of the pasture. Fine, but where to put them. Not only do those horses eat, but also they attract this one neighbor's horse. When cows get in, we can chase them out easily, but there's no getting rid of that horse. John is going to buy hay. He received $75 from his Dad, and expects $300 more.

I laid out some more pathways in the courtyard, and transplanted my first grass plants (not pot) of the season.

Pepe had a bad scene with some Seco Spanish guys who threatened his life with a gun after picking him up hitchhiking. He's o.k., though, and came up after he got back to Hondo.

Kim has been spending hours in the greenhouse. At least five people putting seeds in. We certainly could handle another greenhouse.

Tomorrow I have a date with the judge because I got caught in the Bird truck without a safety sticker.

Here we share driving and maintaining the trucks and tractor. We share cooking and shopping. When we mud, it is a joint operation. When we get wood, it is a variety of people who handle it. When we irrigate, no one tries to do it alone. When we plant the garden and order seeds, it is a group effort.

More and more, the dairy scene will become a group effort, too. One feature that was obvious to me, and Reb, Ron, Kemal, and Michael, was the goats weren't getting grazed. Still, somehow, we left it to John. I was relieved of milking Nelly. I once milked goats, but somehow I don't anymore. This is a feature of the "commune" that will change.

March 3: In town I registered the red truck, and Daddy Dave and I had it transferred to my name. Davison owned it for two or three years now, and it is someone else's turn. Cost $16. Kiva and Carol got food stamps and shopped. Gerry collected a check, too; she gets aid because her former husband was a policeman killed in the line of duty.

Kemal and I slaughtered two pigs at the barn. We brought them down to our butchering place, and Kemal did the work. We also sold a pig for $45.

Ron sold some more candles for fencing nails and supplies. He's been working on the fence between our neighbor Al and us.

I pulled out a perfect box of apples today. Great. The beets and carrots are keeping well. Now two hundred-pound carcasses hang down there, too. Kim cooked up the feet and the head. I'm getting the itch to be planting.

March 6: Very windy today. The colors stand out so fresh with rain. Last night there were heavy clouds and rain on and off. Plowing is being discussed. A lot of people don't want to plow this early and then leave the soil to be blown away for a month; this postpones having to plow. Kemal suggests we can get the irrigation water whenever we want, instead of waiting until May 1 like last year. We should clear it with the commission, but I don't see why not.

Gerry's car left again. Since this gas-saving vehicle has arrived, it has helped take care of a lot of business.

We made a new gate and parking lot by the pasture. No gate at the entrance. This should make more cars park down below—a new look. I worked there with a shovel making a road, little by little. I also brought up two more wheelbarrows of grass. That too is little by little, creating gardens around the pueblo. Michael spent all day making sausage. What a great cook he is!

March 9: We're in a real storm with icy, slushy snow on the ground and a heavy snowstorm in the mountains. Sandy dyed the candles, Carol took the kids to the movies, and the boys took Frieda, the pig, off to get bred at a farm in Talpa. Also, they got the Mind Machine an inspection sticker! Great.

We had an electrical fire in the chicken house. Good thing it wasn't at night. We put it out with water and shovels, and we'll have to replace a viga. Those chickens gave only five eggs. What is wrong with them? Don't they like excitement?

March 10: Clouds lifted from the mountains, which have another foot of snow on them. We've been treated to this glorious winter scene numerous times. Super Beautiful dropped two bucks.

Ron sold candles and bought a handle for the hole-digger. Kids got to school and back.

Larry has laid out a new ditch to come down behind the barn. These ditches, zigzagging down the slope, greatly increase the amount of land getting water. They can have many trees alongside them, and they help all the natural things. A great improvement.

Tuesday: We're in a blizzard and can't even see upper Hondo. Soon the sun will come out and we'll have instant spring. This is very right-on weather.

We have two guests for the second night, a young couple from Ohio. They're in Peggi Sue's room.

The chickens haven't resumed laying and average only four eggs for sixty birds. They get approximately seventy pounds mixed grain per week. They also get laying pellets, alfalfa, table scraps, oyster shells and toasted eggshells. Floors kept pretty clean—nests have straw. They had a heat lamp and a white light until recently. They need the light.

Now both big horses are pastured next door. The colt spends his time on our adjoining pasture. In the future, I am realizing, it will be a good policy to concentrate exclusively on animals that belong to the commune. Without this policy, there will be constant conflict between horse owners and those who are trying to manage the graze for production.

The main ditch is flowing with clear water. I ran for the joy of it.

March 13: The storm cleared and the mountains again are revealed in their winter splendor. Snow report says snow is 139 percent of normal for this date. Kids running around all bundled up.

Kim planted one-quarter ounce of yellow Bermuda onion seeds in two trays in very carefully prepared soil. These then will be transplanted. He thinks it's early to plant sets. They should be planted with the top out of the ground, when the freezes are lighter.

Ron's fence is done around the orchard. He's charmed by the spot and anxious to see it in grass and trees.

We bought wheat. Our stash is gone but lasted a long time. Next year, we hope to over produce.

March 14: Kim was down in the garden starting to turn over the soil with shovel. I went and said, "let's plow it." So he and Michael got the tractor rolling, and we plowed the lower garden. Also plowed a better ditch along the road.

Michael hauled some manure with Larry, and then he, Reb, and Kim started putting in the irrigation. Sandy planted garlic up by her room. The strawberries and alfalfa are starting to grow.

The Maharaji group showed a film here, and a few people spoke thankfully of how they've benefited from "receiving knowledge" as they say. The music, the staging, the pitch for world peace, brotherhood, no castes, no prejudice—this I dig. We served apples and someone forgot to bring the cookies.

We have an on-the-road guest headed nowhere special. Billy is the name. Each night now, I am anxious to get into the next day's work. Taxes, propane, electric bill, alfalfa seed, gasoline stash still not together.

Sunday: Kim is at least as entranced by the soil as I am. He's been sifting and collecting fertilizer for the onion rows, adding a little rock phosphate and sand. Most of the irrigation for the one section is in. Michael and Kim both seem to have a good eye for what is a level row. Larry has been very busy too, laying out the new ditch. He's spent many hours on those beautiful slopes.

Fig. 34. Jonesy on the red tractor. Photo by Kiva Harris.

Sundance the goat dropped a buck and a doe. We have six milking now. Chandra will drop soon.

March 19: Yesterday, I took my mother Clarice and girlfriend Sandy out for a drive in the country and a visit to Carl and Janet in Cañoncito. While out we got a dozen cherry trees, two pear trees, a box of strawberry plants, seeds for a wild spinach and some parsnips that, like Jerusalem artichokes, keep in the ground over winter and can be harvested in the spring. Also brought back some weed for the gang. Jason is staying with Carl and Janet's band of kids for a while.

Went over to see Ramon at La Bolsa Ranch. Like us, agriculture is their main thing, and they have the possibility of their little farm supporting them. They've finished their plowing and grain planting. They, too, have a sign asking people to park out front and walk up to the orchard.

John had the goat family grazing on the wheat; the cows and the colt came too. Kemal and Michael put the new roof piece on the burned-out chicken coop and got the red truck stuck in our own ditch. Had to get a crew, tractor, and build two bridges to get it out.

I spoke with Lucky at Cañoncito, who used to live at the Hog Farm. They were so overrun by horses that they could never cut their hay. Farm went defunct for some time. Now four people are trying to put it together again. They have no farm truck, no money, no wood, and no seed. They're a long way from being a communal farm. The land did get paid for. They might develop fast.

Kim came to the rescue in the kitchen. No one especially wanted to cook dinner. He filled in by making terrific soup using some parsnips, Jerusalem artichokes, and Hubbard squash.

March 21: First day of spring! We finally made it.

Chickens! O.k., now, we've got a textbook about feeding. According to them, we have the birds on half-rations. No wonder no eggs! To feed them inadequately is a waste.

Saturday: There are ten bucks now, drinking five gallons of milk daily. Why are we raising so many bucks? Because John doesn't want to see a few young ones killed or sold. He's big-hearted but unreasonable. Money is not so plentiful around here, and our one resource, milk, is tied up in raising more goats that we'll have to buy more hay for.

The alfalfa fields are really growing now. Crested wheat, brome, timothy, and orchard grass now give some graze. A few weeks and the graze will be well ahead of the animals. I love to walk around and see all the plants coming up. It gives me hope for the future.

So, it is a little difficult to make all the ends meet, and our farming is a little cockeyed. Still the place looks great. Circle is always clean, so is the kitchen and the washroom. Sandy cleaned the floor again.

Peggi Sue, recently returned from Oregon, made cherry upside-down cakes for Michael's twenty-first birthday.

March 23: The field below the orchard is ready. With the March winds blowing, we put a load of manure on, picked up some rocks and disced it. Ron is the most adamant about our not plowing. Too early, he "feels," and thinks the wind will blow away too much soil.

Kemal and I brought the cows up to the barn, captured each in turn, and gave them a treatment with kerosene for this mange they have. Nelly is really difficult.

I see that O. G. has already plowed. Orlando Rael's field, plowed by Leo, is done; now Leo is just about finished with someone else's place. A big piece

Fig. 35. Goat John with the kids at the barn.
Photo by Clarice Kopecky.

on our side of the highway is completed. Custom says plow by the spring thaw when ground is wet. Get that early start. One factor, we can't do everything at once. Start soon and we're surer to finish. Just a little matter like gasoline; we need to scam it as we go.

Kemal sold his saddle and bought thirty pounds of alfalfa seed and six pounds of smooth brome grass seed. That's a big plus for us. Alfalfa seeds are tiny.

Wednesday: Plow? No, we didn't. We even had a meeting. For the two pieces that had chamisa removed, we will wait until April. Irrigate if it doesn't rain hard and then plow. I think Rebel feels we'll get a deeper plowing by irrigating first.

Kim and Michael planted and watered all our garlic and more onion sets. I had to stop a break in the main ditch, about one-half mile from here, so we could get the water. I know just where to go.

So after a day of a little disagreement over plowing, we had a friendly discussion. There are some places we can start plowing without any bad feelings.

Thursday: I ran the new ditch in the wind and rain. In the afternoon it turned to snow. By morning, it is cold, with two inches all over and still snowing. Ron predicted this and says it's not over yet.

I look at our mangy cows huddled in the wind. Kemal bought his mare a bale and left it down there. Now the horse is Ron's in a property shift stemming from the loan that bought the mare in the first place. Kiva's horse is at the barn in the cow's manger and has been fed generously the last few days, so I was able to give the cattle a little hay. John had just enough for the goats' breakfast. We are over-extended. John got another few bales on credit.

April 8: Phil, from the farm in Colorado, passing through, suggested I go with him to the Huerfano, and so I went on the spur of the moment to see my many friends.

I was away for ten days—didn't spend any money. All the time I was at different communes, basically the same scene as here. Great luck hitching back in a blizzard.

At Ortiviz, the place looks great. They have a nice little farm with one milk cow, a heavy milking beef cow, eight loose goats, two calves, six horses, ducks, geese, and chickens. There is hay from last harvest and quite a bit of graze left.

The Custer Creek runs right through the place, 280 acres with 30 or 40 that can be developed more. An acre of winter wheat is planted and another acre or two is planned for spring grain and alfalfa. I saw lots of crested wheat pasture, and a big spring fed pond.

Like the Shire, little houses are here and there where the people live: Peter in a cave on the side of a hill; Jan and Ron below him; Neil and Holly in a teepee at the low spot in the land; Tomas and Phil in the blue school bus on a knoll in the alfalfa fields; Jeff and Susie are in their new, round, single-room house among the trees in the horse pasture; Beara, Strider, and Angela in the adobe, which is "downtown," near the road. The barns, tool shed, storage area, equipment yard, parking lot, and root cellar are near the main house, which was a school. It has a pottery shop and is used as a milk room. Deborah lives there, too. A communal bath and washhouse is planned for part of the green-house being built. Libre has the same plan for a spot on their land.

Susie is the heavy organizer, it seems. She joined up with us when we left Bolinas some years ago. We went a lot of places together.

People eat in small groups and have fairly frequent meetings. Everyone knows who's doing what, different tasks are divided up, shopping is planned. Except for Ron and Jan, they're quite a close family like us here at Buffalo.

Some of the neighboring farms are very picturesque and have beautiful, lush pastures. Cattle are the principal industry of the valley.

In Faracita, thirteen miles from Ortiviz, are more friends on a farm the size of New Buffalo, a hundred acres with twenty-five acres of old alfalfa.

They're right on the river—good bottomland—good water rights. Tall Paul and Mei Hua, Arnie, Lyn, and Brook have got the scene well in hand running the water, fertilizing the garden, plowing. They have renovated the old farmhouse and have four horses and many chickens. I spent some days there, and I feel very close with Mei, Paul, and Arnie. We drank home brew and sang until midnight each night.

There's a sort of shuttle between Faracita, Ortiviz, Red Rockers, and Libre. From Ortiviz, I went to Libre on horse, on to Faracita by truck, back to Ortiviz, then hitched to Libre and drove to Red Rockers with Dave to pick up a stove. The Red Rockers have mountain land: piñon forest with meadows. They've been working two garden areas for years. Their population of ten adults has a lot more continuity with the original group than ours. Nancy, Winny, David Henry, and Vicki are originals. Peter and Pat maybe too. Hickory, Marianne, and Reggie came later. They have a big communal dome with music room, kitchen, washroom, living room, a kids' area and loft for sleeping. Outside there is a model workshop and vehicle repair shop. They're a very close family.

At Libre, my good brother, Steve Raines, who was a Buffalo original, showed me around. Ten pretty big dwellings are scattered here and there in the forest and on the meadows. Three acres are developed for growing. Clear mountain springs with pipes and cisterns make a very efficient water system.

New members are admitted to the commune on a formal basis by agreement of all present members of the commune. They don't want anyone to build without first being accepted. Daddy Dave is living up there now. There are several houses, which are unoccupied.

Libre has some excellent carpenters and very fine houses. The parking lot and junkyard are in one place, not at all scattered over the land. No driving house to house.

The biggest agricultural endeavor projected for these families is the planting of fifty acres of barley at a farm in Westcliffe [Colorado]. In return for labor and seed money, Red Rockers and Ortiviz are going to get some of the harvest. At Ortiviz, they fixed up a hammer mill to make their own dairy ration from the barley.

Seems the commune scene is doing well. Still, of course we have our problems; short of money, poor vehicle condition, the give and take between more communal and less communal. Basically all these things are small compared to the reality of a close family, lots of energy, and resourcefulness. People seemed happy to me; a little heavy smoking by some. Kids are free and have lots of room, food, and friends. Feels great to be there; they're all family to me.

And now I'm returned to Buffalo and the warm circle of friends, under cold, stormy skies. Great. The alfalfa has grown a lot, new volleyball net up, three more goats kidded, barn cleanings out to the field, two new big cherry trees into the orchard, new bushes out front, new fence, and the chickens are up to twenty-one eggs. Had a nice welcome home from Sandy. No more fooling around for me.

I'm right back in it again. Rebel and I started plowing—ground pretty wet. Yes, we're plowing and it feels great. Goes pretty fast. Kemal, Larry, Raz, and I worked on the rig. Kemal also cooked a ham for our dinner.

April 14, 1975: The sky is clear this morning for the first time in a long while. I sold candles and Peggi got money from her mom, which was spent all on chicken feed. Peggi collected thirty-seven eggs. We found our problem; we weren't feeding them enough.

Kemal and Michael got $7.50 a day each for two days' work. Ron had $10 stashed that he put in for the plowshares. So we're making it. Kim, Michael, Reb, and Mike intend to sell some manure for $40 a load today. John is planning to sell milk this week to meet hay expenses. Our hay crop is growing now, plenty for the cows to eat. Feels great to earn a few bucks.

Kemal disced the two fields this morning, and Larry started dragging them. I fixed the kids' swing. Two guests are asleep in the circle, plus little Saafi.

The Chinese elms are showing life! What a pleasure it will be to watch them grow. And while we are enjoying getting our farm together here, the Liberation Army of Vietnam is ending the rule of the American puppet governments.

At long last, and after so many cruel deaths, the fighting is ending. War is bad enough; this was a long and so torturous war. Patriotism and virtue mixed up with money-hungry, powerful capitalists. The US spent $150 billion, I believe, on the Vietnam War. All the slick McNamaras, all the wealthy generals and captains of industry, could never conceive of spending such funds to build, to help. They love their extravagant modern weapons and munitions. And with all their intelligence and war colleges they could never see what I could see. They had created a myth. Our leaders reinvented history saying there was not a popular revolution because the VC [Viet Cong] had foreign help. Like didn't France help us win our revolution? They were blind to the size and power of the popular forces and the righteousness of their complaints. After fighting for so long, they became so immensely powerful that the end now is involving little fighting, actually.

It is amazing to me to read about the ending of a war that for ten years, I have wanted to see resolved. I wish we could have spent that money in a barrage of aid. Where is the dream to improve the lot of mankind? In World War II we did so well. I never questioned the greatness of the US. But here we stumbled. Can't get it right all the time.

Tomorrow we wake up to our farm. Everyone has tasks they are anxious to do. Kim is going to make pizzas for one thing, and we have acres and acres of ground to plant.

Mid-April—very pastoral. The alfalfa is getting lush, a picnic for Nelly after a long hard winter. John had the goats out, too, for most of the day. They go for that alfalfa. All the grass around keeps them from bloating, which is a worry with pure alfalfa.

Larry and I plowed some bare areas. Late in the afternoon, Michael and I started on another section that will bring our central alfalfa field to prairie dog hill. It will bring into alfalfa another acre of completely barren ground. Our plow is the brush with which we paint in the farm landscape.

All unused irrigation lands are now prepared. Actually rather momentous for Buffalo.

April 18: Courtyard is all set to go. One more bridge went in yesterday.

Our Kim changed the oil in the red truck, cleaned the pan and started to keep a record book of mechanical work—records for our three gas-driven machines. Peggi, too, is keeping a journal for the chickens.

Larry fixed the right-hand door of the red truck, so it really shuts— incredible! Pepe gave us $40. $35 went to tax fund, which is now complete!

From a hot tip, Kiva found a pasture for her two horses. This then is another first; after the four years I've been here, first time, no horses. The consciousness to use our little pastures to raise commune animals for our livelihood is on the ascent. Now to fill in the space with some milk cows.

Days are getting hot. I ran into Pepe when I went for a morning run and a look at the headlines. Americans are being evacuated from Saigon! Pepe and I had breakfast and came out to Buffalo on a mellow morning.

A girl Susan was here for a few days. A bit of a crazy rap, but pretty together. She washed dishes, baked bread and contributed $40. Bob from the nursery in town and some other volleyball players came over.

April 21: Kemal earned $30 and spent it on mower parts. Sandy got a whole bunch of phlox transplants from Señora Medina and some lilac transplants, too. Great. Carol made potato salad, Peggi Sue baked bread, and we had some of our own beets that are still excellent. There's plenty of milk to drink, too. Read about world poverty; it is incredible how well we can eat over here.

I worked cleaning Leo's ditch for pay. Ditches are supposed to be ready to run by Friday. Kim and Michael made rows in the lower garden and fertilized the strawberries.

Tuesday: Hot day. Quiet inside the house; two kids at school. Larry put in irrigation lines with the new invention while Mike and I took shovels and pruning shears and worked on our main ditch. We found a lot to do.

April 24: The weather has turned hot. Sandy planted more of the flower garden next to the outhouse. Al says water goes on Friday night! Lots of planting tomorrow and the next day until all the fields are in. This we have been waiting for.

Friday: I wheeled the spring wheat seed out to where Larry and Kemal were plowing in the west field. With Kiva too, we planted 200 pounds of spring wheat seed, thirty-five pounds of alfalfa and six pounds of brome. We each take a section and throw the seeds in the air to spread. Just like we learned in high school.

The water came on and we're right on the case. We'll get into serious irrigation tomorrow.

April 26: Water is on strong. I started out by finishing the planting and harrowing. Sandy drove the tractor and I plowed to put in a few lines.

Kemal and Larry got into cleaning ditches right away. About 12 noon, I switched over to irrigation. I replaced Larry who was out there alone. Kemal replaced me while I took a break. Later on, we got several people out there. Ron and Michael in the new western field. At one point I saw only a pair of boots out in the field; Kim got so stuck in the mud, he left the boots and came in barefoot.

Larry has the ditches very well set up; it took him over a full day to lay them out. It's challenging, watering such a slope. We're doing it.

Carol made fabulous cheese Danish for breakfast; then Peggi Sue helped with lunch and dinner. We ate our last ham with carrots. Sandy did a thorough cleaning of the back pantry.

Lots of company came to see us during the day.

April 28, 1975: Incredible change in weather Sunday with ferocious winds and snow on and off. We had to stop work pretty much, until the weather calmed down. Good day to get a rest. It is really a task watering bare ground. This is the last year we should have so much. Sandy slaved in the kitchen—casserole and chocolate cake.

Wednesday: Kachina's birthday, another great success. Adriana and the whole school of kids came and we had a clown and piñata, too. Michael made the cake, Larry got the ice, John concocted loads of delicious ice cream, cranking for hours with our ice cream maker. It's hard to feel better than this.

May 2: We had a guest today, a good fellow named Brice. The other day we had a different type hippie for company, who was so dirty he stank; kind of out of it, and with a big dog that he didn't feed. Brice, a bit of a mechanic, is more the type I enjoy to meet.

Rebel and Ron left on an adventure to Virginia.

JOURNAL SIXTEEN

May 6, 1975: Today was windy and cold. Kemal has been working with Leo. We adopted a newborn abandoned lamb; we'll bottle-feed it with the goat kids.

Kemal and I started plowing at the Learning Center. Sunday, Sandy and I will complete it. We're a common sight, driving around the dirt roads of Arroyo Hondo on our orange Alice Chalmers tractor.

Sandy, Kim, and Michael planted peas and spinach in the upper garden. Lots of guests here tonight: four religious students—nice people and brother Chris, an herbalist. Mom's staying for the night.

Thursday: I wore my heavy coat and two shirts, while Sandy and I plowed at TLC. The fields are sprouting. Trees are starting to show.

It certainly is dry out here. I can see the rye grows much faster than the spring wheat.

Today we got back into manure runs. The big field is germinating well. It took two weeks for the wheat and alfalfa to start showing. Onion sets and garlic are looking very good.

Most farms haven't irrigated their new fields yet, but our fields are started. And a good thing too, for the water has slowed to near nothing.

Carol said something about not working so much. She helps with the goats, washes a lot of dishes, and cooks. Sometimes she thinks she'd like to

Fig. 36. Peggi Sue with adopted lamb.
Photo by Clarice Kopecky.

do something else where she won't have to cook for twenty people every time.

We are getting some good working relationships. Kim and Michael work the garden. Kemal and I work well planting. Larry and I irrigated together. John is at least sharing some of "his" responsibilities with Carol. Sandy and I help each other. I think the scene is mellower than ever; fewer tensions as we start to have a real farm.

Our quiet guest John has left for Wyoming after about three weeks of finding shelter here. He didn't really fit too well, but we all let the situation run its course and thereby gave him a helping hand.

May 15: Finally into the upper garden we put lettuce, pumpkins, and sweet corn. Rebel and Ron are back—Ron with his son Jake.

ZOOM, ZOOM, ZOOM! Days seem to fly. Seems I'm always lying here, just about to get up and do another day. The trees are still just coming out.

Saturday evening: Fellow George here, who gave Reb and Ron a ride in Tennessee. Also Hap, a man from Massachusetts, who says he lives on a commune there on sixty-seven acres.

May 18: Many took the day off and went to a party in beautiful Cabristo Canyon—acid, volleyball, good acoustic music, loads of good food and pretty girls. As good as the party was, the ending was bad. A gang of local young men broke up the party. There was a little blood and a good 100 people were dispersed rudely and quickly. I saw boxer Eddie Gaudet take off with a bloody face. I heard some pistol shots and left with some of the crew and went to see the mayor of Questa, whom I knew.

I've written a letter to Daddy Dave to see if we can get an electric generator so we can move the party that descends on New Buffalo once a year, June 21. Michael can remember when they didn't have it. It has been getting bigger and bigger and all the booze and all the vehicles we don't want. Masses of people on all our planted areas, which are most everywhere now, we don't want. The possibility of having to leave our house and fields to the whims of a lot of drunks or get in a big scene of violence to remove them is not appealing. John definitely doesn't want it. Mike, Larry, and Kim don't care for the scene one bit. They leave—not their vibe. I agree it is too heavy. Hundreds of dollars spent on liquor in one day. All the tensions that we've seen often enough, right in our face, make us leery. Alfred has offered a five-acre site, and we've just got to get a generator.

So the word is now, the bash isn't here. A relief to the others and me too, I think. We just have to help organize it elsewhere.

I think of the party, and I think of Mike Pot's vibration. I like Mike's approach: beer, liquor, tobacco, even pot—he cares nothing for them. Fresh air, clean water, outdoors on foot, that's his high. Driving around in gasoline driven things—not for him, though he is learning to drive when it is necessary for business.

Larry, too, has a very gentle vibe. He likes the company of sober elders, and his music is the very precise music of the peyote circle, not the wild scene.

Sandy loves her plants so much and really will be happy not to have to spend a day pointing out plants to dozens if not hundreds of people who can't see them and some who could care less.

Fellow Hap is here. Hap was a Marine advisor in Vietnam for two years when we were making it hotter. Now he is a Bahá'í. We've sung for hours each night, and he is becoming a good friend. He has a stuttering affliction, but can sing like a pro. Hap is a real mechanic, listens to the engine and says the timing is just slightly too advanced. We'll fix it tomorrow. Great.

Kim had the Tarot cards laid before him this evening. They did not especially prophesize for the best (anger). He accepts it with a shrug and also a kind of fatalism, saying, "as though I didn't know"—a slightly gloomy view.

Kim told me a story I never really appreciated. He and Paul Rotman were doing a wood run to lonely Eagle's Nest in the dead of winter. The truck stalled. They could not start it and had to hitchhike back on a night that went to -30°. The only ride they got was in the back of a pickup. When they reached Taos they had to be helped out, they were so stiff. This is dedicated service to their friends back here. Going on wood runs fifty miles away from home with ax, truck and heavy logs, is no pleasant chore to look forward to, especially if your luck is warning you to skip it.

The heating trip is simply out of hand. Twenty full-fledged wood runs, $200 investment, wear on the truck, plus about 1000 man-hours away from home, bringing in 100 tons of wood. We've done it—lots. There's no future in it. The sooner we can find solutions, the better. Solar heat is the by-word.

Monday: Energy day—sometimes you meet some helpful people. Just now brother Hap compliments our house. Right away, he got me into showing him the Bird truck, and he was a bit shocked. I knew that we were falling badly behind on maintenance. Can't do too much without money.

Then our luck with our friends held out, and Chuck, Paul, and Joe Novocavich showed up—beers in hand—dogs at their heels. Joe has mentioned something about giving us a $1000, and he said let's do it! I cleaned up and we went to town. Joe handed me a $1000, and I gave him a kiss right in the bank and said, "Thanks." Then we came back to Buffalo. All very low key. That was awfully right on.

May 22: Very disturbing news: Our benefactor, Joe Novocavich was hospitalized along with some others, after another little party up at Questa. It was broken up by this same gang, I suppose, who got so mean at the party last weekend. Brass knuckles and pistols. But it's mellow down here.

Friday: Superb growing weather. Courtyard is starting to sprout, the new alfalfa in the fields all showing. Back to having more water in the ditch than we can use.

Larry started hooking up the new hot water tank to run off the wood cook stove. He worked all day on it. The thirty-gallon tank sits behind the firebox, the smoke goes where the insulation used to be, and a water pipe goes right in the fire and back out. If you were on a colony spaceship, you'd want this guy with you.

The weather remains cool. Kim and Michael went into the mountains at about 10,000 feet. The lakes were still frozen and the snow waist deep. Plenty of water stored.

May 26: We played some volleyball. Mike was out in the wilds along the river much of the day. He comes home with a least one trout each night.

Sandy is caring for the chickens when Peggi is away. Thirty eggs today. Big event—two new baby chicks alive. Peggi has a separate room set up for brooding, and we're starting to hatch some chicks. Nelly is going to drop soon, too.

Sandy cooked a very complete dinner—rice, beans, hot sauce and sautéed vegetables. John served cheese, and we still had some loaves of Carol's bread.

OK, WOMEN! We've got a nice home, an attractive farm, good work, simple way of life, a real cooperative effort and handsome men. So why the great imbalance? Who will break the impasse?

John has a weekly milk run. Sandy went along to sell eggs. This is great. Every week, we sell farm produce. This is the idea.

June 1, 1975: Good planting day. John and I went down to the pasture about 9 a.m. and sure enough, there was the calf, an all-brown bull. We picked him up and Nelly followed. John said we've got to milk her out right away. I already gave him his first bottle-fed meal. So we have the calf separated right away. Very smart.

Leo, across the Rio Hondo from us, is planting the field we are to irrigate for him.

June 4: Carol, Sandy, and Larry took apart the kitchen, washed it, and oiled the vigas. Spring-cleaning with tierra blanca painted on the walls and the washroom, too. Put all back together by dinner!

June 5: A very hot day. John and I are getting along quite well. It's Jason's birthday! Sandy was very good and made a most fabulous blueberry cake with white frosting. Presents came in and my mom and Carol's parents came.

Romance: Reb and Kim both have some nice girls staying with them.

Saturday: Hot day again. John went on a milk run. He has more customers than milk. Very nice. One day, he'll be able to bring home cash instead of hay. And we'll have to get something to deliver milk in besides the Bird truck.

Gaskin's Farm in Tennessee is into direct-to-humans food. But here we have to raise animals first and depend on them, because we're in dry mountains at 7000 feet. Mountain culture—milk, cheese, and meat. We have the start of a dairy, with fourteen gallons of milk a day from our one cow and eleven goats. Another hot water heater would make the dairy independent of the kitchen sink. The more things we do to make the dairy a permanent enterprise the better.

On Sunday we had a nice bunch of friends over for volleyball and dinner. Loads of kids were here, mostly investigating the holding pond.

A heavy frost last night. Kim covered the squash that were up and the pinto beans got hit rather hard. Peas, alfalfa, bushes and trees look good. Thirty-eight eggs from the chickens.

A faucet is now installed at the barn. A huge change. Hauling water gets old. Also momentous—IRS form 1120 Corporate Income Tax we filled out for 1973 and 1974, saying we earned $610 this year and $660 last year. We'd been hung up because the form was so complicated. The thing is to fill in something and send in the form. Done!

Monday: We must keep a better eye on the goats. Each day, they get in the wheat for about ten minutes or more. They are discovered quickly. Lost a plum tree to them and don't want to lose more.

The weather is very, very dry. Sandy is mudding the outside of her room. Larry is setting up the new water heater with some improvements. This morning, Reb got hurt by the tractor. It crushed him against Tito's wall after getting gas downtown. He crank-started it in gear by accident. Holy Cross Hospital found nothing broken. He seems to be recovering very well. Quite a scare. I brought the machine home with the rake that Rebel had fetched.

Day before the Solstice. David Henry and Daddy Dave showed up. We have Kemal's perfect guest room for tall David to stay in. Sandy and John went to town selling thirteen gallons of milk, eggs, cheese, and candles.

June 21, 1975: Very peaceful on our traditional birthday! Some went to a party down in Pilar, so we had only about ten people here instead of hundreds.

Ron had the goats out twice. Sandy gathered willows from the upper ditch for pole beans to climb on. Mike put two stones in the kitchen floor.

Monday: We finished the irrigation lines at Leo's. The three-percent ditches are a great innovation for the neighborhood. I took the wrong road up to Leo's field and almost turned over the tractor. The front wheels came off the ground. Instinctively I gave it full throttle, the tractor lurched forward, I changed direction a little and made it to the top, shaking a bit. That tractor doesn't steer worth a damn with the front wheels off the ground.

Rebel and John resurrected the summer outhouse and started fixing it up. Alfalfa is beginning to bloom.

Thursday: A great advance—the water heater works! A complete success. Gas has been off for three days.

Big clean-up around the barn. Wind blew off half the second-story roof; probably did as neat a job as we could. Sandy and I took mucho nails out of the fallen roof and stacked the lumber. The rest of that roof should come off.

The ditch is full to the brim. Sandy's off to bathe in the run-off, where it cascades into the Rio Hondo. Rebel and John cut the majority of our hay.

July 7: We picked up a lot of our cut hay yesterday, bringing in three-and-a-half truckloads with an expanded base on the red truck. Stacking the hay on the flatbed with pitchforks as we drive along the windrows is very gratifying.

We have a new friend it appears, and perfect she is. Name is Freedom! Quiet, young lady whom Ron attracted and I think she will stay. Excellent. She and Peggi cleaned the kitchen stove. Larry had to clean the smoke jacket around the water tank and take out some tin strips that were collecting soot. He also hung a heavy chain down from the top of the stovepipe. When you shake the hell out of it, it does an excellent job cleaning out the soot.

Sandy is feeling very good today; one big poppy is blooming. Ron and Freedom weeded the sweet corn.

July 9: Volleyball! Lama Beans played the Buffalos. We won two out of three games in some of the best action we've seen on the court. Forty people for dinner. Neil and Holly are here for a bit—Holly, four months pregnant. We've got a good thing with these folks. They feel more family each time they come.

The freezer is fixed and installed in the milk room. We can make ice to keep milk cold.

Saturday: Hap took apart a mower blade and put on the new teeth. He has to keep busy. Hap is short for Hapawa, a name meaning "tail held in the air," as when a deer or horse runs—a sign of freedom. Freedom is a new person for us. Wonderful, quiet young lady—clean and very helpful. And speaking of family, Louisa is here, my onetime love. We hold hands; Sandy is worried, but I remain true.

Monday: Young couple from San Francisco is staying with us. My mom is visiting for a few days and feeling quite at home.

We're getting carrots now to eat out of the garden. There is lettuce for 100 people at least. A few peas starting to come in.

We need to develop solar heat as soon as we can. The Chinese have burned up so much wood that they have no wood fences and burn straw to cook with. The old civilizations in North Africa and the Mid-East have created tremendous deserts, leaving hardly a bush or tree or blade of grass in vast areas. Another 100 years of us here and we might create a similar desolation. Best if we don't.

Buffalo is beautiful. I'm glad I stopped by.—Writer unknown.

We are yet very rudimentary in knowing about farming. Our hay is an obvious case in point. We haven't been able to agree on how to stack it.

John started taking the aircraft carrier-style stack apart today. The hay, especially in the bowl, in the center, is wrong; damp, gray, and it started to mold. It gets hot like compost.

The haystack he set up is modeled on a compost heap. It rained three times on that big four-foot-high hay collection before we got the big cover. It should be a lot taller, with a smaller base for less exposure.

Today there were big puddles of water on the plastic, because the stack is concave in the middle. Not right. Without a dome or bread loaf shape, water goes right into the stack. With an odd collection of a dozen covers, they drained most of the water toward the center. Now the stack has a lot of wet hay.

John still will not agree with me; he is so stubborn. He thinks the hay was put up too early, and the storage is not to blame. Perhaps we'll be able to tell when we get bright sun and start reworking it, separating the good and the damp. There are a few sharp tempers and other sensibilities involved. Very soon, though, I hope we can all agree on how to make a dry haystack.

Michael Glassman is back and very likely he will stay with us! Yeah, I told him we wouldn't let him go.

Thursday: I got into unstacking the haystack immediately. By evening, we had the old pile heavily broken into and a new pile with a much better design started. Michael and Kim in on the repairs. The hay is spread out all over to dry. Most of it is turned brown. Some comes off steaming. It is hot three or four feet from the top. Fortunately we have an abundance of fields, and the ones just cut already have remarkable re-growth.

New Buffalo, now with the wheat fields and alfalfa coming back thicker than ever, looks like real cropland from ditch to fence.

July 25: Rebel is gone—moved out and said goodbye. I didn't even see him. He's left the commune and making a new life with friend Shirley.

Events: Kemal bought a three-week-old Jersey heifer at Macalray's jersey dairy near Albuquerque for $100! Expensive, but now it is ours—small, thin, and very pretty.

Why cows? We have graze; it is our basic resource, and cows can range free with little care. They are the only ones, too, that can graze in the wet pastures and most people prefer cows' milk and a few cows can equal 100 goats in production.

Also a factor is John's complete monopoly of goat milking. We could easily have everyone who wants to learn the operations of milking doing it with cows. Too bad John doesn't feel like that. It is not a goal of John's it seems, to be a teacher. Hopefully this will change. One thing's for sure, without the goats we wouldn't have a dairy.

Walking Horse, Pepe, and wonderful Lenore were here for the late afternoon and dinner. Pepe and Walking Horse may team up for some international travel. Great. International, that's us; Indians, Africans, Chinese, Arabs, they're all part of my family.

Though now I am immersed in a parochial down-home venture, my brothers will keep the faith; poor people roaming our beautiful earth, seeing the fascinating sights and telling of our life—world peace envoys. Depend on the hospitality of our world friends.

August 3, 1975: Communal life—who's interested? We have received several letters lately, from some people out there, who ask how they can join. Rebel's back. He's interested for sure. Hap's interested but he's gravitating toward the Faracita farm.

A slightly heavy girl is here, asking how one gets in. People dropping in to see what the scene looks like, as always.

Debt to Lama Foundation is settled. Now John is settling the debt to his dad. Then, I guess, the money will be free to put into Buffalo—cement, milk buckets, whatever we need. A crew of Reb, Ron, Boston Beans, and Peggi Sue are mudding the chicken coop.

Our alfalfa looks great—thick, high, and bushy. Some green beans and loads of peas are coming in. We already sold $25 worth, a very good crop. Sandy bought a gadget that does a thorough job shelling them. I've always wanted to see whirled peas.

Tuesday: Mike brought home a big pot of apricots and cooked them up with honey after taking out the pits for us. Peggi cooked and cooked all day—custard, donuts, rice and vegetables, beans and sauce. Quite a gal.

Contrary to rumor, we did not get busted today.

August 8: Hap has returned from Colorado and seems to be settling into the middle south wing room. He, Kemal, and Ron went to Albuquerque with one pig, the last part of a cream separator deal. Rebel is in the pit house. Freedom's sister Ester has been in the hogan for a few days.

Sunday: John and Rebel cut hay. The tractor pulls the old horse-drawn mower and the operator raises and lowers the blade. It click-clacks along, neatly dropping the hay.

In exchange for fixing some conveyor belts, we have borrowed Manuel's ancient combine. It only cuts a four-foot swath and looks like a time machine off of a movie set. Larry got the thing running and we had to rebuild the wooden paddle wheel that pushes the grain in. It's ready to go tomorrow.

Carol cleaned the kitchen—says she's no. 1 candidate for the Gold Star for hours and hours of dishwashing. Then to show she's really got the spunk, she swept and cleaned the circle and took the kids away, camping! Peggi went too.

We had a big neighborhood gathering here, as usual for Sunday: volleyball, watermelons, swimming, and a little pot too.

The fields are lush, grain is ripening, peas and carrots for dinner. Kim started to harvest the garlic and small tasty turnips, and there is loads of lettuce.

Kemal cleaned the cow barn and then worked in his room. He's talking of connecting the two rooms and will have just one door to the outside. Kiva is thinking of getting an Ashley for their end room and a big $110 Shenandoah for the circle. Very good.

We should be conscious now of how to prepare for winter. Getting wood is only one thing; we can also fix windows and make doors close tight, add greenhouses and solariums for the entrances, make storm windows, get good stoves.

Wednesday: The first field is in: 2,160 pounds of wheat, we estimate. It's laying out in several rooms to dry thoroughly. That's a lot easier than trucking it to Julian's and back. The old machine worked well. Rattling along with belts turning and trays shaking, it looks like it could come apart in a thousand pieces at any moment. But it doesn't.

Our hay, field by field, is ready to harvest.

Following Wednesday: Straw was gathered off the first wheat field, and then it got plowed. Sandy picked lots of string beans and she, Michael, and Carol washed, cut, steamed, and froze them. John made some extremely thick whipped cream, solid like ice cream. He likes the new cream separator we got.

Saturday: We made an extra big set of candles and Sandy colored them. Mike put away the wheat that was dried in his room. He very carefully screened it and then winnowed it in the late afternoon wind.

Now we have perfect weather, but I don't think we are making the best hay we can. Sort of have a big stack of stems; it was out too long and got too dry. The leaves come off when brittle; picked up one day late.

This is how we learn, and it is difficult to get eight or so guys to agree on what is a delicate and precise operation; drying hay just right and picking it up at the elusive right time.

Fudge and Crystal are pastured down below the clothesline in the day.

Tuesday: Peggi Sue made fabulous deep-fried squash for lunch while Sandy froze lots of beans. Poor injured Michael had to help cut them up because he got a foot bone cracked playing volleyball.

We might have a new woman quietly slipping into our midst. Rather nice-looking English-Spanish girl, Nina is her name.

Wednesday: Sandy has put away all the wheat that got dried on her floor. A big job to do the final cleaning, winnowing. Very nice-looking wheat; I hope it is dry enough. Grains at the right dryness will keep for many years. I was told that some wheat grains from the pyramids, over 2,000 years old, were able to sprout!

August 30: Kim has the farmer's market trip ready to go. The Dodge is ready for take off.

Hap cooked Cossack borscht of all things. Carol working equally hard in the kitchen, as anyone does outside. Looking rather sexy too, in her short skirt.

September 1, 1975: Larry had a great birthday. Kemal cooked and my mom brought the cake. Lots of very nice guests. My friend Manuel, the fruit vendor, was out to see us—very impressed. Larry is a very communal person, and today he got a little return.

Kim, Ron, and Mike went to set us up to pick apples down in Embudo for a third of the harvest.

Friday night: County Fair tomorrow! Carol baked coffee cakes for the contest, and she's really got a chance to produce the best. Kim is bringing fresh carrots, beets, onions, yellow squash, and lettuce. He is already putting carrots away—colors so lush in the humid air—beautiful produce. John intends to enter cheese, butter and maybe some goats.

September 9: The cow's milk is going up. She's been given free range and maybe that's improving her milk.

Mike put in an alcove canale and he and Sandy mudded the entire alcove interior. Kim preparing holes for fall transplanting of apricot trees. Carol has been freezing sweet corn. We eat it everyday too—corn fritters—oh, the best!

Friday night: Big rain—no cut hay out on the fields for a change. Three acres of alfalfa and one-half acre of rye planted and now well watered.

Larry and I went to a solar energy meeting. They were talking about just what we've got in mind; greenhouses attached to the houses. It was very encouraging. The concept is becoming clearer, and I think we'll actually get a greenhouse structure together in the next few months. It shouldn't be so painful. First to do the goat barn roof with the beams and planks we have foraged.

September 14: Big volleyball tournament here on Sunday. The local downtown team defeated the Lama Beans. Then the Buffalo and Seco team tied one to one. Next the locals beat a pretty good-looking Dixon team twice. New Buffalo kept the trophy in the following three close games. Pepe, Ed Morgan, Dennis Hopper (who has given up drinking), and a whole crowd were here. Very nice day with good friends. Carol and Kiva cooked up a great big delicious meal for everyone, featuring chili with our own tender cabritos.

This particular young group of local fellows and a few sisters have been coming here a lot. We are getting to know them better. Seems to be a good friendship. Jojo, Killer, Alvin, Penny, Richard, and Edwin.

Late last night, singing songs by a flickering candlelight, enjoying a midnight toke, outside door swings open and in steps a burly, hunter-guide fellow announcing he's got bear meat! How could we refuse? Michael cooked some up for us—not too bad!

Thursday: Heavy frost—so pretty when the frost melts off and green fields are revealed. Kemal and Michael went hunting. Mike took the grinder apart to clean it. He's also spreading out the wheat in the sun to dry more. Tractor work is done. Now to finish irrigating, and then the land needs no work until spring. All it needs is to be grazed.

Harvest: John, Kim, and Peggi Sue harvested the squash and put it on the roof, 300 pounds or more. White corn taken in too. Ron and I watering two fields. A corral is going to have to go up around the haystack.

September 24: So what's happening? Michael and I got armed-robbed by an escaped convict, who once spent some time here. After visiting for a while, he held a big pistol to my head; said he was desperate for some money. Mellow for a robbery; fellow hugged us goodbye after taking $40 from me (my candle supply fund).

Freezer is ordered—$75 put down, $11 a month. Aren't we the all-American family buying a freezer on credit? (With a little help from my mom). Kim did an overhaul on some Mind Machine brakes.

Watering is done. Combine is back at Manuel's. We scored some pig grain; Kemal is cooking up a week's worth at a time, fifty pounds a week.

Lower garden all harvested and disced. Barn started to get cement-walled. Kiva resurfaced two kitchen counters. Kemal taking out the honey—full hives—our gift from Carl. Kitchen always busy with the harvests.

Nelly is loose for the night. It makes feeding her a lot easier—no hay out of the stack.

The resources are in our hands to do great works.

September 30, 1975: Kemal and Kiva have been very busy; all the potatoes are in—a good harvest. Kemal and Kiva also finished extracting the honey. Kemal got the bee suit together, and the smoker, gloves, and extractor. Kiva did a lot of the sticky work uncapping the combs and separating the wax.

Michael and Kim plowed the lower garden and are making a new drag. The old one is coming apart.

We should get through without buying any hay, especially with the bales coming in from Leo's, but we have already used maybe a fifth of our hay cut on the captive goats.

John figures his earnings from dairy were a little under a $1000, a pretty big effort.

Money: Greenhouse and skylights want fiberglass. Barn roof needs wood and tarpaper; that's three projects held up by lack of funds. I'm out of wax and the replacement fund is stolen. We're still so damn poor, and that fancy motorcycle of Hap's is just sitting in the workshop. I'd like to sell that machine. We could go on with all our business rather than being hung up for no money.

Jerry, one of our lost members from Bolinas days, showed up. He's another one that does not fit in any slot the normal society has to offer. Jerry and I finished using all the straight aspens on the barn's second-story wall.

Jerry reclaimed all the spikes we needed from the bridge wood I scored five weeks ago.

I hit the billy goat in the eye by accident when we tried to separate him from the does in heat yesterday. He'll probably be all right. John got bucked pretty badly and is walking very funny today.

We had our annual meeting to keep the corporation alive. We switched to having officers who live here—Larry, Carol, and now me.

The days really whiz by. Fall colors of yellow and gold are taking over. Kim plowed both gardens; bottom one is planted with a cover crop of rye. He is already talking about next year's production. Pepe brought us a box of excellent apples. Kemal and Mike off on potato and carrot run to Colorado.

Saturday: The big chest freezer arrived. We had to take the milk room door off, move the stove and honey extractor, and put the machine in level. This is a big advance for us. Then a little two-on-two volleyball.

October 6: Rick Klein was married yesterday at a wonderful celebration. Afterward Mike and I did a little mowing—alfalfa for the chickens.

Local young folks were over for volleyball, as usual. Tall Paul, Mei, baby, Jimmy, and Angela are staying for a few days. They joined us on a big two-day apple run. We were royally welcomed in that little piece of the world. The people there, about a dozen of them, are much like us—survivors, easygoing, food conscious. We ended up with fifty bushels. Our La Bolsa friends were pleased with their share and our quick work. Beautiful apples, all hard, but only a quarter in perfect condition.

Hap is returned from back East with a girl. Brought a bunch of books, paint, and a dresser, but no truck, sinks, trailer, electric fence, or a freezer that he was talking about. Hap is a certain amount of talk, but a good man. He did bring a bench grinder. We never replaced the one that Jade broke.

The circle is full of apples and squash. Kim picked up seventy-five bales of oat hay from Leo, as payment for work we did. Produce still coming in.

We sought some "professional advice." Steve Kenin and Chris West will come up here to help us precisely plan the greenhouses. Steve, from NY and Philadelphia, I have known much of my life. I stayed at his encampment in the fabulous desert of the Ajo years ago. He coincidentally gravitated to Taos. Ron stopped greenhouse construction until our friends come with some advice.

Monday: Real fall now—leaves turning and dropping off the trees. Grass, alfalfa, and winter grains look green and vibrant. I put six poles in to protect our rose, lilac, and forsythia at the front entrance, then made a bin from a refrigerator and started cleaning the spring wheat.

This is the first season that New Buffalo's cultivated land is all in some crop: pasture, alfalfa, and winter grain. It was a big chore. I love to cross the fields where I've spent so many hours and see all the life where a few years ago, we had a regular moonscape. (Do prairie dogs live on the moon?) Their 500 holes gave the crater effect.

October 14, 1975: Clear skies persist. Getting colder now though nobody's making fires. Sandy and I have been staying together, and now wouldn't you know it, she's pregnant. Sandy felt a little depressed today, but she's keeping herself busy. She moved her stove to a better heating location.

Carol helping John cement the barn. Kim still figuring out the greenhouse design. Kemal decided to butcher Bozo yesterday, and he did it with Jerry's assistance. The weather is getting cold and butchering outside is very unpleasant.

Peggi's sister and brother, Judy and Peter, are staying for several weeks. A few guests tonight, three gals and a guy. That's a switch.

October 16: Just before I sat down to sort apples, cousin Steve, wife Jean, and baby Noah arrived. We spent some time walking around seeing all the improvements of the last two years, enjoying the pastures and finally discussing greenhouse plans. In this Steve is an expert. In a few hours, we were able to make clear plans.

First, we were going to put the greenhouse extending ten feet away from the wall. Less air space will make for more heat, our prime objective—save on wood fuel. So seven or eight feet out is best. Second: One transmitting surface with a regular insulated roof. Third: very simple foundation can suffice; a piece of 2 x 6 laid on the ground and held in by spikes. And last, use cut lumber. We discussed how to attach to the building and a few other ideas. Two alternatives in plastic; Montesano 602—air pocket wall—uses blower ($8) and electrical conduit for frame, or Lascolite, greenhouse fiber glass, which comes in rolls.

Hap earned $10 working for Lucky and he bought no. 15 felt tarpaper for the barn roof.

Kemal, Sandy, and Kiva got more yellow delicious apples from Dixon and Embudo. These are the winner of the season.

I applied for a job; I start tomorrow.

Sunday: Kemal finished the butchering and all is wrapped, cut, and frozen. Done in very good time! Jerry set the skull out to dry. Such the life, surrounded by apples and friends. The circle has over twenty boxes in it. Pumpkins and squash grace the circular earth bench that lines the walls. The cider press is set right up in the new grass in the courtyard. Something very festive about squeezing apple cider!

Wednesday: Clear, clear days. Lots of neighborhood young folks up; quite a few ladies from the local teenage crowd coming over now.

I've started my new job being a carpenter. Sunday, Jerry and I got the tarpaper on the barn roof and trimmed the sides straight with the new skill saw. We heated up the tar, laid the rolls out in the sun to get warm, and put them on.

Hap had his turn for washing dishes today and not only bore up well under the strain, but cleaned and mopped the floor! He then took a shank and made a very good stew for dinner. He has quite a few auto jobs in mind, and we just had a truck towed here from Lama so he could fix it, but it's a wreck. Back to the old junkyard days, instead of the neat Buffalo equipment yard. It's going to take a big effort to clean it up. We have a heavy metal trailer and trencher that don't work, both abandoned here, and now a very abused four-wheel drive all belonging to the same guy Jeff.

Also here is a green Ford Pinto, belonging to Peggi's kin, the getaway car. Within the month they're planning on taking Michael and going to Florida!

October 23: Hap checked all the radiators for antifreeze. Still few fires and the adobe rooms are warm and comfortable. By second week in November, we should have all the skylights in. Hap proved himself today and got the Dodge truck door to work perfectly. It closes with ease and the window goes up. Only the best body men can do it; usually such deterioration never gets repaired. Our red truck is the real challenge; we need the tanks of oxy-acetylene for that.

October 25: I've worked six days this past week, and should have $72.70. Earned only $2.10 an hour doing carpentry. We want to buy fiberglass.

Among our house full of guests is a college class where the average age must be over thirty. There are five kids with a dozen adults. We made them feel very welcome. Hap and I entertained. Most are sleeping in the Circle with the fire burning. Outside the temperature is going down to 10°. The giant kiva

Fig. 37. Long time resident Jason Lopresti. Photo by Clarice Kopecky.

has an awesome quality. We have great discussions. These folk are from Denver and have good sleeping bags.

John does his usual thing: makes butter, cheese, and sells dairy products on Saturday. He's got regular constant work. Kim needs a cold-weather craft. He is up at Rebel's learning some methods of jewelry inlay work. He wants to raise money to travel south in the winter. Peggi and Michael too, are planning on leaving for three months or so. We'll miss them.

Hap has plenty of mechanics to keep him busy. Not having a good weatherproof shop will be a big problem, though. Four-wheel drive is fixed and out of here but not paid for. VW is out. The owner couldn't afford to pay for the necessary parts.

Sunday, I went on a wood run with Kemal, Mike, and Peter. We drove up five miles of logging roads still heavily wooded. There is a sign "no permit required"—free wood area. We got some thin poles for fences and some aspens for the barn also.

Cream separator broke down. John, of course, is in a rage—mostly silent—plenty of evil eye, though. That is a bit of an unfortunate thing about

John; he doesn't seem so close to a lot of us. Carol gives me a hug once in a while, and I always try to have a pleasant greeting for my friends, but John frequently is in a sort of nasty mood and doesn't seem to make the effort to either get help (he is such a loner in "his" chores), or see a brighter side of something.

Good man Larry, who has been very handy this year, put on the kitchen door and added a latch. Great advance again—almost no doors at Buffalo have latches, though they do help a lot to keep the doors closed on a blustery day.

Kemal came to work with me, and Hap did a thorough exam of Armando's dump truck. I'm just one of the boys, says Armando.

On arriving home, I see the circle is very fine and swept with four bright lamps lighting up our big room. Larry brought the cow in, and I milked her by lamplight.

Carol is getting a little pissed with John, too, for being in such a black mood. He feels over-worked, under-appreciated, somehow frustrated. I feel something is bound to happen to him in the way he handles his end of the trip.

Great opportunity here, but people are kept away instead of encouraged to learn. Not one single person besides John has milked even one goat once. He doesn't even like people going back there to see them.

Dairy is Buffalo's main economic enterprise. It isn't right for one person to exclude others from participation in "our" basic business. Time will tell.

November 1, 1975: We went to a great Halloween party last night. My wizard's cape that has the lightening bolts and moons on it is missing, so I got dressed up as a cowboy and we headed out to Taos for an evening of mischief. Kiva turned heads at the bar in her perfect nun outfit.

Mike and Michael filled the truck, bought five gallons of kerosene and put up $10 to kick off land tax fund. Jerry and Larry each added $20.

I put wheat away in the bin, changed the irrigation water, and helped Kemal castrate Fudge. Root cellar was at 50°, so I opened the doors last night to cool it down.

November 3: Ron, with Larry and I, poured the foundation for the first room-heating greenhouse. Next Monday the woodwork will go up. We will get some more growing space and Kim's room, on the south wing, will have an atrium. It will warm the southern wall and heat will enter the room through the access door.

Fig. 38. Halloween. From top left: Judy, Arty, John, Kiva,
Jerry, Hap. Bottom left, Peter, Carol, Peggi-Sue, and Ron.
From the personal collection of Kiva Harris.

The bull calf is doing well. He's penned up and getting some hay and grain. He also got blackleg shot. It wasn't difficult to handle him.

Couple of guests on the floor, a guy and a rather frightened-looking young lady. Also Arnie is here, honored guest from Faracita, one of the finest fellows in our hippie farmer's circle.

Kitchen wood needs cutting. Mike has given up his monopoly of it; he did a very thorough job for a year or so.

How about our equipment yard? I had a long talk with Hap about our backyard scene. He's very conscientious, and I like to discuss it with him. It is like molasses, getting it where we want it, though. And there is the "piece de resistance," the very fancy 750 cc Triumph motorcycle. It is Hap's bike, but the roads are too rough for it, and it is too noisy for around here, so he doesn't ride it. Yet it's here. It's worth money, which we need and don't have, but he is hung up on his biker image and can't get off of it. C'est la vie.

Larry's got a real craft going now with inlay woodwork. He's well on his way to his first finished piece.

Wednesday: Emergency! Sinks wouldn't drain. Larry stepped in right away and unclogged the drain with the snake; good thing we left that accessible point when we put in the drains. The other frequent emergency is the kitchen stove pipe getting clogged and creating smoke. Larry is the usual expert for cleaning that too.

Ron and Arnie laid the first course of cement bricks on the greenhouse foundation.

Kemal and Arnie squeezed more apple juice. Jerry and Kemal killed Homer, the bad rooster, and four hens. Jerry prepared dinner with them, and Hap made soup with the stock.

A new day: I am often pulled, as if by a magnet, to look and look at all the fields we've planted. Michael is cooking up homemade corned beef. Excellent. Peggi Sue is making banana nut bread, a last treat from our retiring zoo-zoo queen. Hap, our new cook, jumped in there and made vegetable noodle soup.

November 7: Clear days. Shirts off by 9 a.m. I did some asparagus planting with Sandy; also we planted chard in the greenhouse. Hap rebuilt the kid's bunk beds in Peggi Sue's old room, in-between Carol and Sandy's rooms.

It was Sandy's birthday, 27 years old. Kim made special lasagna, and Carol made two pineapple upside-down cakes. Sandy's the only gal for me. She takes good care of us. We get a lot of reading done, as the nights get colder, propped up in bed with the kerosene lamps glowing.

Saturday: We put a $140 deposit with Steve for Lascolite. We'll have it within two weeks. Hap, Ron, Sandy, and I bought lumber for the greenhouse frame. Broke again.

Monday: Yesterday our white cow Pamela was discovered missing. I felt pretty much like relaxing, but searched for our cow and got into putting in a fence post, which was completely down, admitting a wandering herd of seven cows every day. Took me an hour to dig a hole in very rocky ground.

Still no cow—very curious—smells of foul play. Kemal and Hap went out after her for hours; talked to Tieder and Leo, local ranchers. They haven't seen her and suggest the possibility of a very local job. We'll have to put our cows away at night—no feed—just corralled. A real bitch.

Ron and good friend Dick McKracken from next door put on the frame for the new greenhouse. Hap had the wood braces already painted. Dick is quite professional, and they made a very good-looking structure.

Last night, Wild Swiss Willy showed up, fresh in from Alaska—old friend, adventurer, and wandering worker. He has been working on the pipeline in -43° weather. He brought some little fellow who spent the night. I had to give him my bed because he had no bedroll. In the morning we exchanged him for a more resourceful and cleaner fellow, Cheyenne, who is camped out west after working with me all day.

Arnie went walking our southern mesa, above our end of the valley, out to Nambe hot springs, an old stagecoach stop. Larry went on a wood run across the gorge that went to Teles's. Neither saw our cow. Word is out and a very thorough search has been made. Our cow appears to be gone.

November 12: It has been about 0° at night. Still very pleasant by 9:30 in the morning. Before Carol's terrific breakfast of cheesecake was over, I was off running cross-country. Looked at Leo's herd, crossed to Tieder's and talked with him, then all the way down the Hondo to the Rio Grande. After that, up the west side and then up and way up the east side, climbed the gorge following old cow signs. Got back about 3:30. No luck. Arnie was out on horseback. No cow—a hell of a blow.

Thursday: Ron is digging out the greenhouse floor for insulation. I sealed up one circle door. Sandy took Jason to the public health center for free exam. Sandy gets a quart of cow milk every other day; special for sweet pregnant mothers who don't like goaty milk.

November 14: Clear blue skies. I hear Larry fixed the cream separator! This guy could make a telescope out of rocks. Hap and I got on the roof and worked on windows.

Kemal goes off to his new job and John is in very good spirits these days. Goats have been on their best behavior, not trying to get out. Sandy making a new dress and then jumped in there and made beans and rice for dinner.

Sunday morning: Kemal and Arnie branded two calves with NB) on their right hips. This is another important first for us. We applied for the brand a month ago, and now we are official.

John did his last milk run. True to his loner trip, I don't think he once took anyone along.

Kim left for Massachusetts and Mexico. He did say he intends to return and hopes that he will fit right back in as one of our master growers. We are developing trust, and it is a great thing to be able to depend on such an excellent man returning to our little enterprise.

Hap took the poor engine out of the red truck and then cooked beef stew for dinner.

November 17: Yesterday was actually hot—another clear one today. Ron went out looking for the cow. No luck.

A new dam has been built on the Rio Grande. A city of 50,000 is being promoted for the site, and they're looking at our water supply for this and other cities.

This is what we counter, unending development. The trend to get everyone into cities—abandoning small farms—getting people to buy all they need. We keep building cities, freeways, suburbs, and shopping centers. It's disturbing. Our culture is so addicted to building, as though the earth were expanding beneath our feet. Us, I see as an alternative, not dependent on having jobs building cities and roads, destroying the natural landscape. I would rather see us spread out in the country, oriented to the land and streams and plains; not oriented to the commute and pavement.

Then there's our new gal Annie. Can't take the cold; can't work because she thinks she's got lactic acid problems. Sounds psychological to me. Has with her not one tool, just perfumes and loads of clothes and knick-knacks.

I thought of Raz because Raz is so the opposite: pretty, but tough—likes physical work—a country girl. And here she arrives with Saafi for a visit!

November 19: Insto presto chango! By evening clouds covered the sky; then rain turning to snow. In the morning it's snowing strong. We've been looking for this and here it is, first big storm of the season.

Yesterday was John's birthday. I was still irrigating and cutting poles for trees. *Dumb Arty irrigated. It snowed shortly thereafter.*—Writer unknown.

Annie is away. Kim and Michael help us gather wood; then they leave. Very nice to help us out and then not burn the wood themselves.

Thursday: Beautiful winter scene all over. Raz here—very lively and energetic. She fixed dinner for us. With her flaming red hair and ready laugh, she seems to go around just on her tiptoes, like she's almost completely off the ground. The day we left California, she was in the Mind Machine with us.

This will be the coziest winter yet; new stove is working well in the circle; new Lascolite on skylights and windows. These adobes are really good. For the most part, we don't make fires in the morning.

Kemal made donuts for us.

November 22: Sky cleared completely this morning—real winter scene. Below zero and snow all over.

Ron and I were out cutting cedar wood when Kemal happened to catch a glance of some cows passing by the Buffalo gate, and he saw Pamela! I took off and sure enough, there was our heifer among three others. Rounded her up and got her back with our herd for a very affectionate reunion. She seems in good health. Sure gave me a good run; I'm the cowboy, but my two legs are my horse. This Charolais is a big animal, looking like a polar bear with those loose layers of white fur. I really like to see those animals out on our hills, foraging in the meadows.

Other momentous events: Annie showed up with a new boyfriend from Colorado, packed her things, rolled up her new rug and left for a less demanding situation. That resolved itself with no hassle.

And we have some new prospective ladies, much more our style. One is a young guitar player, Carolyn, who's been out a few times. She may be moving into Michael's room. She has a good sleeping bag and warm clothes. Baked us some bread. Her father runs a tree nursery in Maryland where she often worked.

And Ron has a new, rather good-looking girlfriend, Sylvie. Met her first at the hot springs. She has three kids and has been house-sitting in Taos Canyon, hauling water, cutting firewood. Ron is going to fix up the pit house. Now this sounds a lot more like it.

Mike is our undisputed physical education master. He has a trapeze set up in the circle room, and two big foam pads for spotting on the bar and tumbling—nightly entertainment and exercise—no just sitting around. When the day is warm enough, we open doors that face south and let in the sun.

Even a simple thing like opening the door to the air and sun has become a rare thing in the USA, the way people have come to live. With its locks, the door is a cut-off point rarely left open to the world.

Sandy slaved in the kitchen all day; made it very neat and clean. Also baked bread and fabulous soup. She used our own green beans, basil, garlic, onions, wheat, and honey. Hap and crew got the new engine in position to go in.

Wednesday: Kemal and I went to work. Then a snowstorm descended on us; I stayed out in it much of the time. Coming home I marvel at our little earth pueblo in the snow; brown buildings against a white low sky and white ground. It looks mystic and like a vision. Inside very quiet and swept; empty floor in the circle except for the four pillars of wood, the big cedar table, and fire platform in the center, and stove—simple, uncluttered, spacious, like a mosque.

Jerry is gone. Basically this is felt to be good. There are good things about my tough brother Jerry—also some drawbacks. He can weird people out with his nonsensical rap. He once kind of stunned the poet, Lawrence Ferlinghetti in Bolinas with odd conversation. It is like poetry, but what is he saying? In the winter, his lack of initiative would mean months of basically hanging out. So why not hang out where it's warm.

Wood: We may never see such a pile of piñon here again. Last time Larry was out to our piñon stash at Pot Mountain, he says it was unrecognizable, because a lot of people had descended on the area and left with dead and much green wood also. All the forests around us are threatened. We certainly aren't trying to get into solar heat too soon.

8° outside. Still, we basically don't make fires in the morning except in the kitchen—good sort of rugged way. Mike doesn't make any fires. Get up in the cold—not really bad in our adobes—go to work in the near dark like John or exercise some or go to the kitchen.

Thursday: It's Thanksgiving. Sylvie came over, hitchhiked with her three children. She is quiet and well-dressed for the season. The Duncans came over, and my mom, and lots of local friends for a fabulous dinner—very good celebration. A good harvest it was for us this year, and lots of good friends help create that holiday feeling. Mother earth, Father sky, thank you for our many blessings. In our neo-ancient dwelling, built with mud and beams and labor of love, we join hands.

Saturday: A foot of snow fell in the night storm. It is continuing through the day. We cleared some pathways and cleaned snow off skylights. Young Jim, Sylvie's oldest son, did a lot of shoveling on the kitchen, washroom and circle roofs. The fresh snow is light and fluffy.

Carol made posole last night with fry bread, and Sandy cooked the beans. Our onions are going into everything except the cookies.

It feels so good to be close to the storm and yet snug inside our earthen buildings. Our stashes—food, wood, and hay—still not appreciatively diminished. It was winter of 1972, I think, that we had hepatitis here. No more of that; going to town to buy the sick people a little piece of meat; going out in the dead of winter to get wood.

December 4, 1975: Sylvie has taken over care of the chickens. I took her up to the barn to show her our supplies. Good ol' John gave us the evil eye and some strictly sour words on what he thought of our touching the hay. I just can't believe it. John has got such a lovely attitude. Where is the joy? I give him so much slack, and he gives me so much shit. The other morning in the snow, I went up to clear snow off the stacks. It was so beautiful out and I felt so good. He's ranting and raving, cursing and swearing.

The Lascolite arrived. We put on two sheets.

Friday: I was over to Pepe's mansion, the Mabel Dodge Luhan House, which is rented from Dennis Hopper. Very impressive. It is a great place for the jeweler's commune with its history as an artist's center. There are lots of bedrooms and windy stairs to studios. Off the main courtyard is the great country kitchen. Like me, this fellow is not living alone. There are a dozen people living there at least: Sherry, Sequoia, Pat, Sonya, Jeff, Nancy, plus many others. It's a perfect house—clean—a real piece of art, carvings, paintings, fine woodwork all over. They have one of the finest jewelry shops and meet all expenses together.

Workshop there has hundreds of small tools, files, punches, vises, lapidary, and stone-polishing machines. There are lots of workbenches, with spaces for six or seven artists. Silver, turquoise, some gold, and lots of works in progress scattered around. And I am treated as the honored guest.

And there's my partner Pepe, right in the middle. Great. Always extremely welcoming to me. Always excited about a dozen things, and who is he with now? Jennifer.

Monday: Back at the ranch, Kemal and I started off with building a fire at the corral and roping and branding Pamela, who must weigh near 800 pounds We did it without much trouble; got the brand a little low, but it's on.

Kemal, Ron, Larry, and I put two more sheets of Lascolite on the greenhouse. Then we put three-eight-inch plywood on the roof.

John did a very thorough cleaning in the kitchen in addition to washing dishes. Sandy made incredible chocolate cake and soup for us. She was a bit tired and a tiny bit peeved by the time it was over.

December 11: Very warm tonight—road muddy. I'm very anxious to get some good producing milk cows. At the same time, we should upgrade the dairy trip with deep sinks, hot water, and good drainage for the milk room.

Hap went to town because he's getting involved in a university trip, taking four courses. Larry is installing electric lights in both the pantries. No more journeys to the back pantry with the kerosene lamp.

A few weeks ago, Sylvie and her kids just met us and now four complete strangers have been accepted into the heart of our lives, into our home, and to share in our work. This traveling musician Carolyn has taken advantage of our hospitality and stays here frequently—has her own room. The other night, a stranger passing through was referred to us by Taos Social Services as a place to stay overnight.

Pepe here for dinner, feeling very high. He helped cook a great combination Mexican dinner: posole, refried beans, chile relleno, and hot sauce. He whizzed around cleaning dishes and counters, my good partner. We smoked a couple of joints and sat around the stove and spoke a few words. Now this man is really dynamic.

The circle seemed very warm tonight. That new Shenandoah stove is saving a lot of wood and with the skylights all sealed and double doors, we have a big space well-heated. And thanks to Kiva for coming through with that beautiful stove.

I ran around our place in the moonlight. The coyotes think I am one of them.

December 15: Into our panoramic snow vision, Larry went out with the kids, Jonesy, Jason, Monica, and Tony and cut a Christmas tree right off of our own place; actually cut just the top so he's not killing a tree at all. They dragged it through the snow and carried it down the earthen stairs into the kiva.

We made ninety pairs of short tapers. Sandy colored—good Christmas presents. Rebel is back with us. Says he can see how we have to make the conscious effort to keep mellow. He's gotten fairly skillful doing some stone-cutting and channel work inlay and has some pieces to sell. Gave me $20.

We're working all right and it feels good. The engine is in the red truck and the chickens are up to twenty eggs a day.

Another Day: Mike and I went to work today, as yesterday. We almost have the job done. Sandy and Jason are off to California for a visit.

Larry is putting a door into the adjoining milk room, so he no longer has to open his front door to the cold. He neatly took out the bricks, exactly in the shape of the heavy-duty frame he built out of "junk" lumber in our pile.

On December 21, at 12:15 noon, Kiva had a baby boy. Perfect. Tish and Liz were here and then the doctor too—very nice in her and Kemal's room. Looks like a fine new son. The baby couldn't be more welcomed into the world. Kemal's toothy grin is even wider than usual.

I put another window on. There are eighteen skylights on that roof that have been worked on.

Hap's been quite busy with mechanics. He got Leo's truck out of here. Greenhouse only lacks some mud to be pretty well sealed.

Kemal and Jim gave Fudge, Crystal, and a visiting calf blackleg, pasteurosis, and some other shots. These are below-the-skin shots, not muscle shots as is penicillin. Also separated two pigs for slaughter.

We did have a visitor for a few hours. He slept for a while, had a crazy rap about the CIA and what a bad thing he'd done. I gave him some food and he left.

Big Dolores Yellow Eagle showed up—bear-like Indian friend from Oklahoma who spent a month with us two years ago. If he could get off the drinking and cigarettes and get into a little serious craft, he'd make a real valuable compatriot. He's mellow and wise, but the alcohol has a strong hold.

Thirty-four eggs yesterday. Still going up.

December 22: Finally we're in real winter. The new greenhouse got nice and cozy, but heat doesn't move into the room so well.

Event: Last Lascolite skylight went on today. We had a party for Jonesy, Kiva's son. He is now two years old. Another big party here tonight.

December 23: Mike and Jim getting the circle back together. It was a good party. I was asleep before the band stopped playing.

Al, Judy, Dick, Kathy, and some friends and kids came over for eggnog, Christmas carols, and fruitcake. Nice evening after a simple carrot salad and rice dinner.

Candlemaking is all right, but I need something else. Carpentry is appealing and I've had some experience. I have some projects in mind that would be useful.

Christmas 1975: I took the day off to rest, but I did go get the bull for Pamela who was acting in heat—nice present for her. Max is back in town. Merry Christmas.

Friday: Forty-five eggs from the chickens. Kemal was making sausage all day with young Tony's help, while Larry installed electricity in the washroom. Mike roofing the new pig house and new goat house.

Hap went into town twice today, accomplishing very little; forgot the errands for me and got the wrong muffler for his job. Then he went to Santa Fe the other day, but couldn't get a fuel pump for our truck—didn't try. Job for Rebel he never made any money on. Worked on Chuck's girlfriend's car and those bucks went toward his rifle. Fixed two vehicles for Leo and was too shy to charge him. His heart is in the right place, but it is still only a potential business. He does have a lot of skill.

There is a rumor that John is going to split the herd and move to Mike Duncan's. It could be just him alone with Carol and goats and no partners that he doesn't really want. That would be good for him and would open a burst of energy here.

I guess I'm feeling a bit lonesome for my long-legged girlfriend.

Sunday: Last night Kemal took the kids to the movies, *Planet of the Apes,* so we could all go to the dance.

Tomas and Phil are visiting from Colorado. We had good sausages and eggs to feed them. Tomas, an honored guest, is real hardcore and an Ortiviz veteran. It was his refrigerator like bus that I stayed in last spring when I was up there.

This Morningstar business is really in the air. Duncan wants to see Morningstar live. Great. He's talked to John and Rebel about moving up there. I think they're going to look it over tomorrow.

Max Finstein is in town; I saw him at the dance. He was very happy and proud to see me. I've picked up the dream, so to speak, and stuck with it, and I know it helps make all the good things Max has believed in seem like they still have a chance. He was dancing very gracefully, and his hug is real strong. He looked just a bit older, people thought, with his short gray beard and barrel chest.

That's a magic moment when you haven't seen someone like that in some time, but with whom you are mystically tied. Because of fate, we've come to do a big thing together.

When I first met Max four years ago, he was a bit discouraged, living in a shack ten miles from New Buffalo. Max couldn't tell me, and my wild-eyed friend Pepe, from all the other people, though we tried to show him our enthusiasm and faith, that we could help carry this commune further.

Now, four short years later, he beams the biggest smile at me, and hugs the biggest hug.

He hears tales and rumors of Buffalo when he's away, and they're saying good things about his baby—big family taking care of people, real farm, still pray together, eat together, work together. And he knows I'm his man working in there for him and for ideas that are so essential to us that we don't even ever really talk about them.

His baby that was sort of near death. Reality and Morningstar communes went under, but Buffalo came through. Now the energy has grown so that some life just might be breathed back into Morningstar.

Hap chose the worst words when talking to Max, suggesting what we really need is an auto repair shop. Max was just so happy to see all the animals, great haystack, and the food room; he didn't have a vision of an auto repair business. I believe it is our karma to have a lot of success with different types of work. A decent mechanic shop here would be terrific.

I also introduced Max to Mike Pots, a very quiet man, but not to be forgotten. He provides a great balance. I went to get him for dinner. He was laying on his bed reading, at about 40° F. He has not yet had a fire in his room this year, yet he is one of the staunchest wood runners we have.

In a year Mike won't spend a dime on potato chips or candy, to say nothing of beer. Not a cent wasted, and he works hard for any money he can get, and he saves it for pet projects for improvement for the commune. He also has good outdoor clothing and camping equipment. His close-cropped brown hair, army cap, and warm clean army jacket, make him our Boy Scout, U.S. Marine, *par excellence.*

His eating is ideal; very strict, no added sugar, no going to town for the "delights" of the city. He eats three meals, lots of apples, brushes his teeth and no other eating after. Electricity he sees the use of, and he wants to help install more. He has learned to drive in the past year. He is not any kind of purist; survival is the word: every day close to the earth, close to the cold. And to him as to me, the commune is a basic ingredient for our survival in this world.

The outdoors—the wilds—this is our home, our freedom. Some may dream of big houses to own; we want mother earth as she has always been—a challenge—a joy to be in. Where is a bird's home? Where do fish live? Where do bears reside? Like us on our mother earth.

But we can't just live in the brush. We must be part of civilization too, and the commune is our connection, not exclusively ours, but ours. We can help build and maintain cooking, washing, growing facilities, shelter; a place for kids to be healthy.

This has been a long rap, and I am feeling excited. We're not at the bottom of the ladder anymore. We can add to what we already have and come out with a great farm and warm home. I have energy, ideas, and good friends. But where's that cute girlfriend of mine?

December 31, 1975: Cold. This morning we got the tractor started, then dragged the Mind Machine down the road. Hap applied ether-spray, and it started before we reached the tree, snowing heavily all the while.

Our friend Eric is going to trade us two yearling Hereford heifers for our Wonder Bread truck. We're jumping at the chance. The poor thing has taken us around so many curves, up so many hills, with goats and pigs and sometimes twenty people. Pepe and I have slept in it beneath the stars in Washington. Nancy and I shared some blissful moments parked in Manhattan. We were in it at Granny's Turkey Farm in Kansas, at Johnson's Pastures in Vermont. She's made a thousand trips for the family here in New Mexico, and now she serves us one more time. Good old Mind Machine. We had a lot of adventures with our palace on wheels.

John and Carol are now quite sure that they want to move. It certainly makes sense to my mind. It makes sense for John, because Duncan will give him a very free hand to set up a goat farm.

John has talked to Mike about taking over the goats down here. Sounds good. Mike will immediately make a partnership out of the chores. Mike said John intends to leave us six milkers. This will create a communal herd, because no one else here is of the mind to put a claim on any of the animals.

Of course Carol is going, too. I first met her when I was a student with a briefcase at Berkeley. I looked through the looking glass and she was there, and I wondered, "How do I get over there?" It seems I found out. She'll be sorely missed. Of course, we'll see her a lot. And she has returned many times. We'll miss little Kachina too; she's been a bright light, always.

John wants to be lord and master over a goatherd. This sounds like a good opportunity. He didn't come here because he wanted to live on a commune. He desperately needed a place to live, and we certainly have supported his goat trip, wanting to see Buffalo have a good dairy scene. He made a big contribution.

Monday I get my pregnant girlfriend back, and I get to go shopping for lumber.

January 2, 1976: New Year's Eve was quiet. Local teenagers had a party here. Circle was all theirs. I got up at midnight to wish everyone a good new year. I was the only Buffalo up.

And my companion the Bird truck, the Mind Machine, is gone; I drove it to town. Years ago, I never would have believed I'd be driver and part owner of such a hippie relic, and now that chapter is over. Now it lives on with a new man at the wheel. Good luck. Eric is an old friend from Frisco, so it is still quite close to the family. Few people ever get such use out of one vehicle as we've gotten. Of course, Wonder Bread got near twenty years of service out of it, too.

Back at Hondo, we showed Leo our new heifers. He said they looked very good; should cut the horns off the one in March and should not breed for another year. Now we've got something resembling a herd.

Lots of people. Kids, Larry, and Sylvie making a picture calendar in the kitchen.

January 4: This morning Kemal, teenage Jim, and I put our brand lightly on the two heifers, gave them each shots, and a big worm pill. Tomorrow they go out to graze. Goats, too, are going to go on a grazing program—save the hay.

Tuesday: Snow today, mostly in the mountains. Picked up Sandy and Jason yesterday and delivered Carol to the train: a happy reunion in Lamy at the depot. Hap came along for the ride and drove. We went to three lumber places.

Sandy worked her very first day back; fixed her room, did loads of wash, cleaned the washroom very thoroughly, cooked a dish for dinner, too. She looks very nice.

Larry worked on his solar project in front of his room.

January 11: Very pleasant day—mellow, quiet and quite warm. Sandy, Kemal, and I walked around and looked at our fields and meadows, and fed the two calves some oats.

Carolyn has vacated Kim's room and now where is Kim?

Swiss Rudi is staying with us for a bit. Sandy has known him about four years. She was the first person he met in Taos. A hardy, robust, outdoor type, he's a good mechanic, knows leather and woodcraft. He and Mike cut up all the last of the cedar and some big piñon logs with Rudi's chainsaw.

Larry has his solar heater near completed. Kemal has a new job south of Taos in Embudo. I made a sink stand for the milk room.

Thursday morning: Mike and I cleaned out the dairy room; bagged all the wheat, took out the broken freezer; we are going to cement that floor for better cleaning. Mike is jumping in, making the project whiz right on.

Constant flow of guests. Two crashed in my room last night. I was pleasant to them, but I'm not crazy about them—dirty and too assuming. The fellow's on tour, but hasn't changed his shirt in two months. I can see where hippies get a bad rap. The gal is from the old Hog Farm commune that had a lot of rough times.

Monday: Really getting warm with no storm. Alfalfa is growing a bit; so is the winter grain. These are the right crops.

We were approached by a young, attractive, dark-skinned lady about using Buffalo as a place for her to collect welfare, something I'm quite clear in not wanting. She however is moved into the hogan with some boxes and two kids. She is welcome to take a breather here and see what happens. She was evicted, just up from Mexico. Why Taos, I don't know. No place to go— no money.

Kemal came home and was unhappy to see Buffalo filling up with people he didn't know; a constant racket in the kitchen, not the life he wants, nor I either. Commune is a place for a family group to live together and work together, not a catch-all for an unrelated bunch of hard luck cases. There is the ebb and flow. It is important to have guests and friends visit and to be able to teach.

Tuesday: Kemal cooked dinner for a good-sized crowd. Jonathon and Tish were over for dinner, too. Plus there is new Sasha, baby Juan, and six-year-old daughter Olahlay, who came yesterday. She is a hardy, humble gal, happy to see a little dirt hogan. Wouldn't take any wood. Kids seem healthy and happy. She'll have to have a warm fire, though. The hogan is a small round building a little to the east. It and the larger pit house are the only residences not connected to the pueblo.

Continually we discuss the commune; what we are doing. I spoke to Ron about a rather rough vibe he puts out sometimes. He is aware of it. It is tough being conscious of all the political problems, all the work problems and still keeping a constant mellow outlook in the day-to-day confrontation with the family. We had a good hug and are none the worse for putting the issue right out front. Anyhow, wood run tomorrow.

Kim sent us a letter. He'll be back soon catching a ride with Hickory and

Marianne. He sounds very anxious now to get back, thinking of us often. He sent me $50. All are eagerly anticipating his return. His room is ready; Kemal saw to that.

Walking Horse also sent us a letter; he's keeping in close touch. He's with us too— radical, unconventional—very free spirit. I wish I heard from other old friends, and that they felt the same brotherly spirit and could feel the wonderful hope coming out of the commune.

Just at sundown, our man Mike heads for the toboggan slope with the kids. Larry and Ron have tried it out, too. They've got one spectacular and slightly dangerous run that has given Mike a few hard knocks. Our land rises to the mesa, facing north providing many places for sled runs.

January 25: Light storm. The coldest and longest part of winter has passed. We are over the hump.

I spoke to Hap calmly several times to make it clear I've changed my mind about partnership with him. Rather than being close, I feel he's more ready to turn on me, and say we've taken him for a ride—used him—taken his money. He's got that rap deeply ingrained. After seven months or so, he's more obstinate than ever in his views. Thinks I'm wild-eyed to see Buffalo as I do. He still thinks it's shoddy. He'd be better off, I suggest, starting his own business and wouldn't see his money absorbed in a scene he is not completely in sympathy with. Poor Hap. He doesn't have my ear anymore to hear his complaints. We humans make life so difficult, so complicated for no apparent reason. Tough for me because I really like the man.

Mr. Ron, meanwhile, is really going through it, but more quietly. He's fasting in his tower, not talking either. Except he broke the silence with me, trying to get me to end a party a bunch of local teenagers were having here; I did not intervene, though.

The fast is making him look very haggard—more distraught. Some people carry so much emotional baggage. His project, Sylvie's floor, lies in pieces on the floor, not worked on. He talks about revolutionary consciousness, can force himself to not eat, not talk; why can't he force himself to finish a job he's assigned himself? Well, good luck Ron and happy meditations, brother.

Wednesday: We answered a few questions for NBC: Hap, Larry, and I. The three men took some motion picture footage and some sound recording. They were here for about an hour, just at sundown. Lots of kids running around.

Friday: Went to our good friends at the Tortoise Foundation to get our sow bred. Very nice at their place, just about all families. They've got pigs, goats, and are thinking of getting a milk cow. They have twenty-six acres of farming land, but only eight hours a week of irrigation. They have been very selective about who lives in the "commune."

The melt is on! I went down the driveway with shovel diverting water off the road. Much of the alfalfa fields are clear.

Sylvie had the goats out. Excellent. Sasha is going to take a turn and then Ron. Once John's dominant hand is out, we can cut the barnyard feed more and they'll really start getting a significant part of their diet from the abundant graze.

Mike started digging the trench for the milk room drain. We poured the concrete on the last half of the milk room floor. This is the stuff of legends.

Ron has moved to the hogan, and Sasha is in the tower, a better place for a woman and child. She likes it, and Ron likes other people to feel that deep joy of really digging some of the rooms here.

January 31, 1976: No end of clear days it seems. There's an edge to the weather, but it doesn't want to change.

At 4:30 a few of us went to the Learning Center to see the news and sure enough, there was a report on communes with a few shots of New Buffalo, our cows and a few words from me. They had footage of a big suburban commune. There's so much room in those big houses for communal living. Glad to see that, and I'm sure some were glad to see us, the country cousins making it.

Learn to cooperate, live together on a small scale to help achieve world cooperation and peace. Share responsibilities of making a farm function.

Hap went to town three times. He's moving his big tool collection.

Tuesday: The thaw is on—water running all over. It's hard to run across the land now because of the mud. I pick my way. The fields are very soggy.

Two young fellows came by, and I went on a gravel run with them. These fellows, Willy and Rick, were camped out in a local cave. They saw Pepe at the hot springs and he gave them some mushrooms. I saw him while I was running around and he gave me a few mushrooms too—quite psychedelic. So I went out and shoveled gravel. Did I just meet the caterpillar from *Alice in Wonderland?*

Mike, Ron, and crew made an elaborate deep-fried dinner; Kiva, Sandy, and Jason got sick. I didn't eat. I was too psychedelic. Good timing.

Guests, two from Oregon, and also Lance and Jill from the Huerfano Valley are visiting. Lance, a good brother and a doctor, lives in a school bus parked at Ortiviz's. Susie is soon to have a baby; my sweet buddy from travels in the Northwest.

Hap showed up after all day away. I'm feeling better toward him again. I am grateful for the use we have of his vehicles. He needs a good workshop. Sounds like he's got a crazy thing happening in town—found just the wrong place. He doesn't discuss with me what it is he's doing there.

Kemal is wonderful.— Who wrote this?

February 4, 1976: Finally clouds in the morning—a real heavy sky. Mike painted the milk room, and then he and I dumped the gravel that was on the truck. We went to look for more, but it was too frozen. Kemal sold sausages that he made.

Besides our other guests, three additional ones showed, fellow David and two young gals. John and Carol are back from their trip. They got married and have a very nice Chevy pickup for a present. How about that!

With a storm blowing outside Hap washed dishes and the washroom floor. Then he did a quick buzz to town not to miss a day.

Today I drove Sasha to the hospital, where her baby son was admitted for pneumonia and a hernia operation. Poor little fella. He didn't appear especially sick.

February 12: Progress. Last year electric lights and outlets were added to the kitchen, washroom, and pantries. Record wheat stored—record potatoes stored. We ate our first good-sized steer this winter, and there's still some left. First winter our own hay fed the animals and first winter with water at the barn.

We also added solar projects to two rooms this winter, a new and good stove in the circle.

Today almost the whole troop went for streptococci test at the Public Health Center; throat smears from everyone and then back home. All the kids have a little cough or don't feel good for a day or two, and then they feel much better.

Ron the mystic. With Ron ideologically, I am the closest, I guess. He believes commune members should be politically conscious—conscious of helping create a better world—see the commune as important part of our society. But ideology means what? "Words are turds on the backs of birds," says Pepe.

For all the ideas, what motivation does it give my man Ron? One day drifts into another. He's troubled. He goes to town fairly often, took a long midnight hike the other night, talks about being moved by God.

What disturbs me, though, is a very rough side he shows me. He accused me of being inhospitable to Sasha, when actually I helped move her in and then he said yesterday, "I hear you are trying to get rid of all the vegetarians," a fine hello, how are you. I never came close to saying anything like that.

He's loud in the kitchen, not gentle. He's got a very harsh word for the kids fairly often. Then he suggested Peggi Sue and Michael left because of me. Where does he get this stuff? I am very close with them. They're young and went off to have more experience in the world than just Arroyo Hondo. And they're coming back, I'm sure.

This hostility I feel is something new. I hope it goes away. Sylvie too, says she has been feeling it from Ron lately.

Wednesday: Early this morning I looked in my room and there was Marianne, Hickory, and the fellow sleeping in the circle—Kim! A great day. Hugs and kisses and falling all over Kim, showing him the new cows, new milk room, the not-so-big haystacks, the new baby, new furniture, new road in the making.

Looking very handsome, Kim is sort of like a new man. Michael has decided to not come back to Buffalo for some time, and is earning money for Mexico or maybe college. Sounds like he has a good job at a butcher's.

But Kim has decided to come back here! A very good move for us. Very soon spring will spring and Kim's just in time to get in the rhythm. And there will be some rewards for him too, I'm sure.

Hap is going and John and Carol, too. But to offset that loss, we've got Kim who really knows how to do a lot and wants to know the farm. He's strong but gentle and never a bad word. Kim is a great fan of the commune and this is important. To him what we have is a dream coming true. So it is for me too.

This is a new era opening for us. It is the first year when we'll see near our full hay crop, near maximum graze, and a communal dairy also for the first time. Those who want a share will be able to develop their interest and ability. And for me, it will be a great relief to have the heavy prejudice against cows gone.

So we've got a better commune than ever: barn, fields, house, and good stock. And through it all, despite the ripples, we have a lot of love, and a lot of good people.

Fig. 39. Kim milking Nelly. From the personal collection of the author.

The machinery, the ditches, are all ready and the fields, after four years of building, are ready to produce. This is the essential step, to put all our land in production. Now to develop the commune's stock to use our graze and hay.

And we've got the personnel. Kim really tips the scales. As much as ever, a group of people very commune oriented: Mike, Larry, myself, Kim, Kemal, Kiva, Sylvie, Sandra, Ron, and young Jim (doing just as much work as any of us now).

Tish, midwife, hospital nurse and a special friend of the family, was over and discussed home delivery with Sandy and medicine with several people and me. She also suggests a little Clorox in the wash water for dishes. She says home delivery is the best and will help.

February 21: Absolutely clear day. Cold. Shockingly clear view of the just snowed-on mountains—awe-inspiring. We walk past the woodpile and look in amazement at the view to the east—call each other's attention to the panorama.

Kim, Mike, and I just started replacing the shelves in the new pantry. Larry wants to take on the kitchen cabinet task, replacing the crusty ones. Feels good to be able to take on jobs, do them well and get on to the next. We have been struggling and floundering for years, but have stuck right with it, and it is going to feel better now. Working is going to be very pleasant, and we will be able (God willing) to take care of a lot. Right with us too is Kemal. In our major enterprise of animal husbandry, he will take on major responsibilities. He's a good man with animals; knows how to milk, and he wants to work as part of a group.

Hap has changed his scene. I am pleased I got to know and live with the man and he helped us quite a lot. I'm glad to have him as a friend, and I'm glad he's trying to put something else together. Sylvie cleaned up the remains of his room. He's gone and we're not liable to see much of him. A good soul.

Monday: There's a few wispy clouds in the blue sky. The crocuses are flowering and the grasses growing after thawing. I'm right back in the swing feeling good. Kemal feeling pretty good, too. Rudi and girl Elizabeth here for a few days. Rudi and Kemal are working together at the barn making a tight body stall for cattle handling.

Sandy cleaned up the terraces overlooking our drive. There's phlox, irises, spinach, chives, hollyhocks, and some badly damaged but alive lilacs.

Kim and I did a gravel run. From our own place we gathered rocks of good size, to make a solid foundation in the ruts.

Larry has a lot of the pieces for the kitchen cabinet cut out and grooved. He's the master carpenter around here. Little Juan is home and feeling fairly well. He had a major operation last week. His brave Mom found a home and got that taken care of.

February 26: With another gravel run we finished the worst section of road. Kemal worked at his new job at the gun shop. The pantry shelves got another coat of urethane; Jim a great help.

The winter wheat looks very good in the moist soft earth. It definitely has come back to life.

Friday: Event! I picked up a twenty-gallon LP gas water heater at Wards for the milk room, got a propane tank and a regulator at Washam Gas. Kemal and I also picked up our sow from Felipe that was getting bred. We used Hap's truck. Thanks.

Kemal and I looked at Felipe's milking cows. He's suggesting we buy a Guernsey from him, which is already a mature cow. Five gallons did he say? Not much. The cow looks good, but hard to say about the udder, since she isn't due until June. Our goats are dropping kids.

In the news, Jacques Cousteau says the ocean is changing. There is an oil slick on the entire surface. There are less fish. The major source of oxygen for the earth could be killed off. All the microscopic plants are threatened. Ozone layer is threatened.

Can the people slow down the pollution, even reverse it? Can we achieve real disarmament, less world tensions, and apply our resources to the accumulating problems of mankind? Will we further brotherhood and one day not have such a divided world? I certainly still believe we will get there.

March 1, 1976: February is out of the way now. For good luck, there is a big storm blowing in. The grass in the courtyard is all starting to show; the green is so deep and clean.

This is a prosperous time for us. Goats' bags are swelling up with milk, new stock being born. Baby goats are very cute—frisky—beautiful colors. So far it's Toltec, Blanca, Marigold, and Sundance that have kidded, all ones John has arranged to keep.

Milk in the refrigerator again. I started to get some plumbing together in the milk room. Mike worked on the grinder, Larry advising. Kim made tongue-and-groove jointed shelves for the second pantry.

Wednesday we woke up to a real winter's scene with an inch of snow covering everything. Tomas and Michael Pair are here with the Ortiviz truck, moving Mike to the Huerfano Valley. They have a few pieces of farm machinery and hay. We're supposed to join the caravan. It's a regular hippie stunt, but we will probably make this 400-mile round trip over several passes with a $100 cargo in return for $15 worth of hay. Kemal said we'd help. And we will. Michael is a very good man for working with horse teams doing farm chores. Both make their lives in the countryside helping to raise crops and animals. Tomas helped buy a combine, $500 investment for a 1958 model. They'll build a trailer for it. He also told me they feed twelve pounds of grain mix a day, plus lots of alfalfa, to get seven gallons from their Brown Swiss.

Thursday: Winter has returned. There are three or four inches of snow, blizzard winds and drifts. The kids' room door blew open in the night and a snowdrift formed part way into the room. Jason and Kachina, asleep deep in their blankets, never noticed. That won't be able to happen once we get a green-house in front of these three rooms.

Had to crank up the tractor to start the big trucks. Ice and snow all over, the mountains white. Very good weather for us—keep that moisture around until real spring.

I took a short run on the mesa, cut some wood, hooked up the gas end of the hot water heater.

Rebel appeared, in from New Orleans. He's going to help put the new farm scene together at Morningstar. Big challenge—big piece of work.

To be noted: Winter wheat crop just east of our mountains has suffered greatly. Some 400,000 acres in Oklahoma, Kansas, Colorado, and Texas are parts affected—too little snow. Wheat blew away, got buried or frost-killed. The storms are making us look good here.

March 8: Kim and I returned from the Huerfano Valley, a western winter scene in the Rocky Mountains. Snow covers the ground throughout Colorado.

We delivered the hay and the wagon wheels for Michael and unloaded the Ortiviz truck and then went to the farm. Everything is fairly snowed in. We were quite comfortable on the schoolhouse floor with the snow falling out-side. Enchanting to be so at home in the middle of many mountain peaks, everything covered in snow, among friends.

It's a great location for organic farming and a cooperative community. All who live there six months or more are members. Three-fourths of mem-bers can expel anyone for gross behavior if need arises. The group has juris-diction over all animals on the land and over building. They're just writing up some by-laws, getting more commune-conscious.

Heightens consciousness to face these issues. We're looking at it too, down here where John is pulling out half of the goats. We want a commune with commune animals.

We're growing; small groups actually, but with a lot of experience now and many of the communards have a fairly clear and common vision of what we want—what a commune is. The group should be able to identify itself; they want people who can work together with the group. If someone wants an aloof or non-involved part, chances are they could do it privately as they want on some private land.

Sky is often feeling the private realm is being invaded. He doesn't see the need for people of like minds to join and organize and plan to turn these hangout communes into productive farms that have top production for their acreage. Great visit.

March 9: Lots of work now: manure out to the fields, trees to be transplanted, post holes to be dug, gravel runs. Kemal says Lama Foundation wants to buy cows' milk products from us. Larry heard of a cow for sale in town. Rebel and Carol were up cleaning Morningstar.

Pepe came over with Jeff to show us the Bicentennial belt. Pepe is very excited about it—fame and recognition. It will be displayed at the bank in town; lots of people will see it. Jeff says they just stand with mouths hanging open and eyes bulging when Pepe gives his rap. They say someone appraised it at $60,000 but no offers yet. It is definitely a masterpiece. And it's going to get a lot of publicity and get around. Ed Morgan had a major part in the creation along with Pepe and Jeff.

Each of the eight conchas is designed around an historic American flag. The inlaying, engraving, and design are exquisite. Pepe loves the symbolism—the images and legends—the Eagle's eye and the pyramid.

Whoever is going to clean the goat pens, I want the straw to use for mudding the pueblo this year. We won't have any straw of our own until July, and I would like to have a good deal of mudding done by then. The whole pueblo needs mud, and I can't see buying straw.—Mike

Wednesday: I helped Kim put a tree into the big hole out in front of the pueblo. Then Kim put up posts and chicken wire. Still plenty of room for parking and maneuvering vehicles, but one day there will be some beautiful trees, too. This is the place the eye surveys the most, which should reflect our love of being close to nature.

Mike had dishes today and cooked dinner of pea soup and bread. He is apprenticing with John; He milks the two goats twice a day and helps feed the kids. He'll really know John's routines.

Michael Pair and his partner Babe are our guests tonight. Mike is off tomorrow with his four stunning horses.

March 11: Wind blew up a lot of clouds today. I was out running, watching a storm high in the mountains. The cows are concentrating on the far new alfalfa and grass fields.

Sylvie made candles and Sandy dipped them beautiful colors. Kim put the new shelves into the back pantry. They look very good and are 100 percent washable. John and Mike trimmed hoofs. So many aspects that are being related to Mike, only at the last moment.

Saturday: Clear beautiful day. Nights are cold, 15° or so. Ground is solid in the morning, and water freezes an inch. Crested wheat is growing and the cows and horse are enjoying it. I painted the milk room floor this morning. Soon it will go into operation.

Good friends Paul and Mei are here. Genie is visiting Ron. A girl Pam came with her with boyfriend. Then there's a couple with a kid from Massachusetts just passing through.

Pepe and Jennifer were out for dinner and a little visit. Glad to see them. Pepe's feeling good. I think they go to see the Governor on Monday with the belt. My good partner Pepe. I had to give him a buck to buy some gas. Next week he may have $5000, and the week after he'll need another dollar. I hope I've always got it. He is really going good now, riding this new wave. We'll see how his rap develops. From the start I knew he had great powers of communication, talking about freedom, love, and peace and revolution; that's the word now: revolution, in the bi-centennial year. The whole country is celebrating our old revolution. So how about digging some of the new revolution! Pepe took a copy of my earliest journal to pass on to someone.

And spring is coming up and this will be the first year of the commune-run dairy. Gardens, field planting, irrigation, fencing, milking, landscaping—things we like.

Wood runs: This is getting to be a very sour note. We don't want to go; but we have to go so far, so often. So more solar heat and collectors are needed.

Sasha says she's selling some jewelry. She gave Mike money for a grinding stone, a pick, and gas for manure runs. This is a very stand-up lady; she wants to do her part. I can see she didn't like to ask for help, but she did what was needed for her children. This, in part, is what New Buffalo is for.

Thursday: Second hot day in a row. Grass is growing faster. These have been the first hot days since last year. Watching spring come in. Kim planted peppers and tomatoes in flats in the greenhouse. There are cabbages coming up, and cold set tomatoes. He has a great feel for planting those seeds.

I set up the milk room: lit the gas fire and washed all the pails, bottles, and strainer. Today it went into operation.

Friday: Rather big young lad showed up with backpack. I'd been wondering where our good quality visitors and searchers for the good way were, and here is this fellow Jon. Immediately we had him doing a manure run with us. We also gathered some flat stones. Came home, Carol cooking another exceptional meal for us. Mike is very happy with the new milk room.

March 21: New fellow Jon is very willing to lend a working hand. He is a muscular, quiet-spoken fellow with a good pack and bag—clean. I put him up in Kemal's guest room. He's turned over soil out back for grass and alfalfa, and moved dirt on the roof and worked with Ron, Mike, and me.

Greta dropped two does; then Chandra dropped two bucks. Kim is gathering bones to process into bone meal for phosphorous for plants.

Monday: Another fabulous clear day. Ron and new Jon, Larry, and I went after wood. We got a full load and headed home. We ran around so much though, that I lost my ax. Ron gathered fence posts on the run. He's back in his element with spring and that's good.

Kim really fancied up the little terraces by the root cellar and mixed in lots of manure. Like me, he has traveled through the Pennsylvania Amish country and wants to emulate their beautiful farming. Sandy's flower terraces already greet people coming up the road.

Sylvie and Sasha making candles. The wood run was sponsored by money from candle sales. Sylvie and son Jim dipped, Sandy colored, and Ron sold.

I got word from Al that there was a joint Desmontes-Hondo meeting about the ditch, an excellent thing to get the people together. Desmontes community pushing for an equal priority agreement; Hondo rather distrustful. Many points were discussed: 2.5-acre water duty, meters, state authorities, Valdez and Cañoncito water systems.

Tuesday: Nice warm day. Wind with some clouds came up in the evening. The house looks great. The circle table is newly polished, floor and benches clear. I like that openness, like a mosque—uncluttered. The new kitchen cabinet now has doors on it, and it looks terrific.

Carol says she's so happy; her prince has come. They're going to go off to make their own life, a bit more private—dream cottage. She and Rebel say to me, on parting, that they think there should be more organization; some system as to how people are accepted.

Perhaps we'll do this. Define us all as members, and then make some rules. Also could institutionalize a spring planting meeting annually so everyone has an idea of what the plan is for the growing season.

I, myself, have no objection to formalizing these things; probably they'll help the place be stable and long-lasting. Then again, things have been working well as is, I think.

March 26: Clear days with windy afternoons—typical weather—drying out. We need a storm.

In *Time* magazine it says seventy percent of Colorado winter wheat crop was killed; also parts of Oklahoma hit. Our own fields that have good cover are still moist.

There were six high school girls in a course studying communes up here for a few hours. Then a bearded fellow from South Dakota just up to visit.

Sandy has daffodils, bright yellow, on both sides of her door and a big ultra velvet red tulip.

Saturday: On the Morningstar mesa, Reb says water is already running; parts of our ditch, though, are still frozen. Hondo never runs it this early. Master Duncan is away in Hawaii. John and Reb want to plant twelve new acres.

The sky is baby blue and clear; the wind blows from the west. We are an oasis in the desert. The ground is safe under the carpet of plants and cannot blow away. The moisture is shaded from the incessant sun. To me, farming out here is preparation for this type of weather; this is normal. If you can live with it, it is to be loved.

Our mud houses are solid in the wind. In our cloistered rooms, the oiled vigas shine in contrast with the whitewashed walls. Kids are running around. Overall, a deep quiet pervades: just the on-and-off gusts of wind and the stillness of intense sun.

Sunday: Finally, the sky clouded up. We got a little snow during the night, and we hope the mountains are in a heavy storm. Mike came to the door and said, "There's a young lady here to see you." I jumped up; it was only Crystal the heifer. Mike has been catching her every day and teaching her to lead. It's good that she gets handled. Her dark eyes on the tan face are so expressive. The kids love to give her something to eat.

Pepe came out to see us. His Bicentennial belt is in Albuquerque on display under armed guard. They might sell it for $150,000.

Ron not-so pleasant: Reb says, "Why do you antagonize me?" They got in a heated argument. Ron clean forgets, sometimes, how to behave. Rebel's been very mellow, but Ron has got a heavy weight on him and is uptight. He doesn't seem to realize this side of him exists, but it is very unpleasant. He talks a lot but . . . Anyhow, no major thing. We remember these incidents, though.

Young Jon went on. He was here about a week. Ron got uptight at him, too. We should take on some people to see our life close up—share our scene. Didn't need to vibe him out. I think we will see this young man again.

We hope to inspire people to live this way. We want people to feel good knowing that there are mellow, down-to-earth places where they can find friendship; a place to feel at home with the earth, where people respect you as a traveler and a seeker.

The big storm continues, just what we need. We are coming now into a period where we hope to establish a record of quality farm produce. We are bright, tough, and have a good attitude, and we are on the case. We are the Cultural Revolution, a lifestyle of sharing and learning crafts and participating in agriculture. I am sure it has its saving graces, for we are on a good path.

So closes another chapter in our lives. Here is hope that the next will bring greater strength, accomplishment, and perhaps, a compliment of spice and adventure.

Power to the people. The resources are in our hands to do great works. More will come if we do well with what we have. May peace continue and grow as we persevere toward the fulfillment of our dreams.

EPILOGUE

February 13, 2003

In Volume II we will part the mists of time again. Without giving away the rest of the story, suffice it to say my family left New Buffalo under rather dramatic circumstances in 1979.

It has been noted that this scene attracted "the best and the worst." The paranoid, anti-social attitude of some worked against creating a group in harmony with the larger community. In time, fewer conscientious people joined and the lack of a unifying idea, and an income, made the upsurge recede.

In our contemporary world, students and poor people continue to create numerous group-living arrangements for survival. Centered around the magazine *Communities*, a host of groups find various ways to share and enjoy.

The American dream of nice house and enough income to own A through Z has been achieved by millions. But the concept that the best result is achieved by everyone pursuing their own selfish interest, is proving deeply flawed. For all our advances almost everything in society seems in crisis.

The idea that an expanding population and expanding economy can go on exponentially is fast becoming even a more ridiculous proposition than the idea that people can learn to live together.

Today, to purchase the individual dream of house, cars, college, eleven kinds of insurance, etc., costs several million dollars. For each couple to be that productive we have to keep adding cities upon cities. Each, individually, can hope to achieve the secure life, but for the big group, no. We need a concept of a mature economy leveling off, and a way for all people to have a happy life.

First and foremost we have to mature beyond blaming someone or some group for society's ills. These are just problems intrinsic to being human; they are not anyone's fault. It is going to take all our intellect and civility to find harmony and a sustainable future. We can do it joyously. There is no fate but what we make. We have a huge opportunity. Our forbears have bequeathed us great freedom and the still blossoming creed of democracy.

I believe we have to honor those who are willing to pursue a simple life. Prosperous farms and craft and learning centers that embrace the people, teach harmony, and supply the basics, are going to be a part of our future. And some of you are going to create it. What did John Lennon say? "You may say that I'm the dreamer. But I'm not the only one."

ABOUT THE AUTHOR

My father, Joe Kopecky, was born in New York City in 1895. His father rolled cigars in a sweatshop. They spoke Czech at home and made their own shoes. Joe picked up a love for classical music, but his piano kept getting repossessed so—the next best thing—he went to work at the Steinway piano factory on Long Island.

At age fifty he went to tune the piano of a young woman, Clarice. They fell instantly in love and in a few weeks were married. I was born in 1944 and my sister Anne in 1948. The bliss of their marriage lasted their entire lives. The apartments were ordinary, the income ordinary, but the love was extraordinary. My caring for people, my belief in the potential goodness of humans, comes from my parents in those formative years.

The family would take marvelous trips to the countryside and we spent summers at a little chicken farm in Connecticut. The huge honeysuckle bush by the clothesline, the fireflies, the colorful gardens—all confirmed in me a love of country life. Later summers were spent near Woodstock, New York,. at camp Hurley, an idyllic, integrated, summer camp where Pete Seeger would occasionally come and sing. In the flatbed truck the work campers took a trip to the Pennsylvania Amish country. Though I logged much time on the subways of New York, it is those hours traveling among the farms that left an indelible impression.

Clarice and I went on the civil rights marches to Washington. At seventeen I was organizing Bayside Students for Peace. As the Vietnam War heated up I wrote papers and organized. However, I never was strident; I was always very impressed with the U.S., which had sheltered my parents, helped win WWII, and provided such a good life. Marxists tended to see democracy as capitalist propaganda. I saw the reality that the founding fathers set the country on the right path with an emphasis on human rights.

A modest but conscientious student, I went to the City College of New York. My girlfriend Bobbi and I got married, traveled in Europe and rented an apartment for $35 a month in Manhattan. I studied history and politics believing we could avoid a massive war. The humanistic tendencies in the U.S. and communist countries would eventually resolve differences amicably if we could keep from blowing ourselves up.

My studies required a foreign language and I chose Chinese, traveling to Columbia University for classes. Accepted to several graduate schools I switched coasts and went to Berkeley. Bobbi and I were separated shortly before I left New York. I came West very much as one person alone. (However Bobbi does reappear as Kiva in the story. We are still close.) In the background the counterculture was developing.

I saw myself turning into a dull bookworm, while around me something marvelous was occurring. I dropped out and soon met Carol, then Pepe, and Dennis McHone and lots of other people. Before long I was headed out cross-country in a Wonder Bread truck with Persian carpets. The notion occurred to me of "we declare peace"; we could promote the better world we wanted by living it; lots of people were doing it.

The journals kick in here. I was twenty-four years old. Skip now to 1979 when I was thirty-five. I always knew that the effort was experimental. Even though I gave 100 percent to the cause, I was able to quickly change gears. Unlike some radicals, I have great respect for the American scene. If I couldn't create a country life one way, I'd achieve it the more regular way.

If you are looking to do farm work, Nebraska is a good choice. With $500 borrowed from my mother, Sandy, our two boys, and I headed out and I found work on a modern 100-cow milking dairy near Fairbury. After thirteen months we returned to California to be near Sandy's family. We again found dairy work; this time in the beautiful countryside north of the Golden Gate. By making furniture on the side I was able to start a new career in cabinetry and construction, which I have pursued for twenty years. In time we bought a one-and-a-half-acre homestead site. Sandy, the boys, and I built our house and shop and we were back on the land, surrounded by gardens.